For Dean

CW00342713

The Bible,
The Qur'an
and Science

The Bible, The Qur'an and Science

"La Bible, Le Coran et la Science"

THE HOLY SCRIPTURES EXAMINED IN
THE LIGHT OF MODERN KNOWLEDGE

Maurice Bucaille

Translated from the French
By
Alastair D. Pannell and The Author

Islamic Book Service

The Bible, The Qur'an and Science
By Maurice Bucaille

ISBN 81-7231-009-9

First Edition 1989
Reprint Edition 2010

Published by

Islamic Book Service
2872-74, Kucha Chelan, Darya Ganj
New Delhi-110 002 **(India)**
Ph.: 011-23253514, 23286551, 23244556
Fax: 011-23277913, 23247899
E-mail: islamic@eth.net / ibsdelhi@del2.vsnl.net.in
Website: www.islamicindia.co.in / www.islamicindia.in

Our Associates

- Al-Munna Book Shop Ltd., **(U.A.E.)**
  (Sharjah) *Tel.:* 06-561-5483, 06-561-4650
  (Dubai) *Tel.:* 04-352-9294
- Azhar Academy Ltd., **London (United Kingdom)**
  Tel.: 020-8911-9797
- Lautan Lestari (Lestari Books), **Jakarta (Indonesia)**
  Tel.: 0062-21-35-23456
- Husami Book Depot, **Hyderabad (India)**
  Tel.: 040-6680-6285

Printed in India

Foreword

In his objective study of the texts, Maurice Bucaille clears way many preconceived ideas about the Old Testament, the Gospels and the Qur'an. He tries, in this collection of Writings, to separate what belongs to Revelation from what is the product of error or human interpretation. His study sheds new light on the Holy Scriptures. At the end of a gripping account, he places the believer before a point of cardinal importance: the continuity of Revelation emanating from the same God, with modes of expression that differ in the course of time. It leads us to meditate upon those factors which, in our day, should spiritually unite—rather than divide—Jews, Christians and Muslims.

As a surgeon, Maurice Bucaille has often been in a situation where he was able to examine not only people's bodies, but their souls. This is how he was struck by the existence of Muslim piety and by aspects of Islam which remain unknown to the vast majority of non-Muslims. In his search for explanations which are otherwise difficult to obtain, he learnt Arabic and studied the Qur'an. In it, he was surprised to find statements on natural phenomena whose meaning can only be understood through modern scientifc knowledge.

He then turned to the question of the authenticity of the writings that constitute the Holy Scriptures of the monotheistic religions. Finally, in the case of the Bible, he proceeded to a confrontation between these writings and scientific data.

The results of his research into the Judeo-Christian Revelation and the Qur'an are set out in this book.

CONTENTS

Introduction

Each of the three monotheistic religions possess its own collection of Scriptures. For the faithful—be they Jews, Christians or Muslims—these documents constitute the foundation of their belief. For them they are the material transcription of a divine Revelation; directly, as in the case of Abraham and Moses, who received the commandments from God Himself, or indirectly, as in the case of Jesus and Muhammad, the first of whom stated that he was speaking in the name of the Father, and the second of whom transmitted to men the Revelation imparted to him by Archangel Gabriel.

If we take into consideration the objective facts of religious history, we must place the Old Testament, the Gospels and the Qur'an on the same level as being collections of written Revelation. Although this attitude is in principle held by Muslims, the faithful in the West under the predominantly Judeo-Christian influence refuse to ascribe to the Qur'an the character of a book of Revelation.

Such an attitude may be explained by the position each religious community adopts towards the other two with regard to the Scriptures.

Judaism has as its holy book the Hebraic Bible. This differs from the Old Testament of the Christians in that the latter have included several books which did not exist in Hebrew. In practice, this divergence hardly makes any difference to the doctrine. Judaism does not however admit any revelation subsequent to its own.

Christianity has taken the Hebraic Bible for itself and added a few supplements to it. It has not however accepted all the published writings destined to make known to men the Mission of Jesus. The Church has made incisive cuts in the profusion of books relating the life and teachings of Jesus. It has only preserved a limited number of writings in the New Testament, the most important of which are the four Canonic Gospels. Christianity takes no account of any revelation subsequent to Jesus and his Apostles. It therefore rules out the Qur'an.

The Qur'anic Revelation appeared six centuries after Jesus. It resumes numerous data found in the Hebraic Bible and the Gospels since it quotes very frequently from the 'Torah'[1] and the 'Gospels.' The Qur'an directs all Muslims to believe in the Scriptures that precede it (sura 4, verse 136). It stresses the important position occupied in the Revelation by God's emissaries, such as Noah, Abraham, Moses, the Prophets and Jesus, to whom they allocate a special position. His birth is described in the Qur'an, and likewise in the Gospels, as a supernatural event. Mary is also given a special place, as indicated by the fact that sura 19 bears her name.

The above facts concerning Islam are not generally known in the West. This is hardly surprising, when we consider the way so many generations in the West were instructed in the religious problems facing humanity and the ignorance in which they were kept about anything related to Islam. The use of such terms as 'Mohammedan religion' and 'Mohammedans' has been instrumental—even to the present day—in maintaining the false notion that beliefs were involved that were spread by the work of man among which God (in the Christian sense) had no place. Many cultivated people today are interested in the philosophical, social and political aspects of Islam, but they do not pause to inquire about the Islamic Revelation itself, as indeed they should.

In what contempt the Muslims are held by certain Christian circles! I experienced this when I tried to start an exchange of ideas arising from a comparative analysis of Biblical and Qur'anic stories on the same theme. I noted a systematic refusal, even for the purposes of simple reflection, to take any account of what the Qur'an had to say on the subject in hand. It is as if a quote from the Qur'an were a reference to the Devil!

A noticeable change seems however to be under way these days at the highest levels of the Christian world. The Office for Non-Christian Affairs at the Vatican has produced a document resulting from the Second Vatican Council under the French title *Orientations pour un dialogue entre Chrétiens et Musulmans*[2]

---

1. What is meant by Torah are the first five books of the Bible, in other words the Pentateuch of Moses (Genesis, Exodus, Leviticus, Numbers and Deuteronomy).

2. Pub. Ancora, Rome.

(Orientations for a Dialogue between Christians and Muslims), third French edition dated 1970, which bears witness to the profound change in official attitude. Once the document has invited the reader to clear away the "out-dated image, inherited from the past, or distorted by prejudice and slander" that Christians have of Islam, the Vatican document proceeds to "recognize the past injustice towards the Muslims for which the West, with its Christian education, is to blame". It also criticizes the misconceptions Christians have been under concerning Muslim fatalism, Islamic legalism, fanaticism, etc. It stresses belief in unity of God and reminds us how surprised the audience was at the Muslim University of Al Azhar, Cairo, when Cardinal Koenig proclaimed this unity at the Great Mosque during an official conference in March, 1969. It reminds us also that the Vatican Office in 1967 invited Christians to offer their best wishes to Muslims at the end of the Fast of Ramadan with "genuine religious worth".

Such preliminary steps towards a closer relationship between the Roman Catholic Curia and Islam have been followed by various manifestations and consolidated by encounters between the two. There has been, however, little publicity accorded to events of such great importance in the western world, where they took place and where there are ample means of communication in the form of press, radio and television.

The newspapers gave little coverage to the official visit of Cardinal Pignedoli, the President of the Vatican Office of Non-Christian Affairs, on 24th April, 1974, to King Faisal of Saudi Arabia. The French newspaper *Le Monde* on 25th April, 1974, dealt with it in a few lines. What momentous news they contain, however, when we read how the Cardinal conveyed to the Sovereign a message from Pope Paul VI expressing "the regards of His Holiness, moved by a profound belief in the unification of Islamic and Christian worlds in the worship of a single God, to His Majesty King Faisal as supreme head of the Islamic world".

Six months later, in October 1974, the Pope received the official visit to the Vatican of the Grand Ulema of Saudi Arabia. It occasioned a dialogue between Christians and Muslims on the "Cultural Rights of Man in Islam". The Vatican newspaper, *Observatore Romano*, on 26th October, 1974, reported this historic event in a front page story that took up more space than the report on the closing day of the meeting held by the Synod of Bishops in Rome.

The Grand Ulema of Saudi Arabia were afterwards received by the Ecumenical Council of Churches of Geneva and by the Lord Bishop of Strasbourg, His Grace Elchinger. The Bishop invited them to join in midday prayer before him in his cathedral. The fact that the event was reported seems to be more on account of its unusual nature than because of its considerable religious significance. At all events, among those whom I questioned about this religious manifestation, there were very few who replied that they were aware of it.

The open-minded attitude Pope Paul VI has towards Islam will certainly become a milestone in the relations between the two religions. He himself said that he was "moved by a profound belief in the unification of the Islamic and Christian worlds in the worship of a single God". This reminder of the sentiments of the head of the Catholic Church concerning Muslims is indeed necessary. Far too many Christians, brought up in a spirit of open hostility, are against any reflection about Islam on principle. The Vatican document notes this with regret. It is on account of this that they remain totally ignorant of what Islam is in reality, and retain notions about the Islamic Revelation which are entirely mistaken.

Nevertheless, when studying an aspect of the Revelation of a monotheistic religion, it seems quite in order to compare what the other two have to say on the same subject. A comprehensive study of a problem is more interesting than a compartmentalized one. The confrontation between certain subjects dealt with in the Scriptures and the facts of 20th century science will therefore, in this work, include all three religions. In addition it will be useful to realize that the three religions should form a tighter block by virtue of their closer relationship at a time when they are all threatened by the onslaught of materialism. The notion that science and religion are incompatible is as equally prevalent in countries under the Judeo-Christian influence as in the world of Islam—especially in scientific circles. If this question were to be dealt with comprehensively, a series of lengthy exposés would be necessary. In this work, I intend to tackle only one aspect of it:

the examination of the Scriptures themselves in the light of modern scientific knowledge.

Before proceeding with our task, we must ask a fundamental question: How authentic are today's texts? It is a question which entails an examination of the circumstances surrounding their composition and the way in which they have come down to us.

In the West the critical study of the Scriptures is something quite recent. For hundreds of years people were content to accept the Bible—both Old and New Testaments—as it was. A reading produced nothing more than remarks vindicating it. It would have been a sin to level the slightest criticism at it. The clergy were priviledged in that they were easily able to have a comprehensive knowledge of the Bible, while the majority of laymen heard only selected readings as part of a sermon or the liturgy.

Raised to the level of a specialized study, textual criticism has been valuable in uncovering and disseminating problems which are often very serious. How disappointing it is therefore to read works of a so-called critical nature which, when faced with very real problems of interpretation, merely provide passages of an apologetical nature by means of which the author contrives to hide his dilemma. Whoever retains his objective judgment and power of thought at such a moment will not find the improbabilities and contradictions any the less persistent. One can only regret an attitude which, in the face of all logical reason, upholds certain passages in the Biblical Scriptures even though they are riddled with errors. It can exercise an extremely damaging influence upon the cultivated mind with regard to belief in God. Experience shows however that even if the few are able to distinguish fallacies of this kind, the vast majority of Christians have never taken any account of such incompatibilities with their secular knowledge, even though they are often very elementary.

Islam has something relatively comparable to the Gospels in some of the Hadiths. These are the collected sayings of Muhammad and stories of his deeds. The Gospels are nothing other than this for Jesus. Some of the collections of Hadiths were written decades after the death of Muhammad, just as the Gospels were written decades after Jesus. In both cases they bear human witness to events in the past. We shall see how, contrary to what many people think, the authors of the four Canonic Gospels were not the witnesses of the events they relate. The same is true of the Hadiths referred to at the end of this book.

Here the comparison must end because even if the authenticity of such-and-such a Hadith has been discussed and is still under discussion, in the early centuries of the Church the problem of the vast number of Gospels was definitively decided. Only four of them were proclaimed official, or canonic, in spite of the many points on which they do not agree, and order was given for the rest to be concealed; hence the term 'Apocrypha'.

Another fundamental difference in the Scriptures of Christianity and Islam is the fact that Christianity does not have a text which is both revealed and written down. Islam, however, has the Qur'an which fits this description.

The Qur'an is the expression of the Revelation made to Muhammad by the Archangel Gabriel, which was immediately taken down, and was memorized and recited by the faithful in their prayers, especially during the month of Ramadan. Muhammad himself arranged it into suras, and these were collected soon after the death of the Prophet, to form, under the rule of Caliph Uthman (12 to 24 years after the Prophet's death), the text we know today.

In contrast to this, the Christian Revelation is based on numerous indirect human accounts. We do not in fact have an eyewitness account from the life of Jesus, contrary to what many Christians imagine. The question of the authenticity of the Christian and Islamic texts has thus now been formulated.

The confrontation between the texts of the Scriptures and scientific data has always provided man with food for thought.

It was at first held that corroboration between the scriptures and science was a necessary element to the authenticity of the sacred text. Saint Augustine, in letter No. 82, which we shall quote later on, formally established this principle. As science progressed however it became clear that there were discrepancies between Biblical Scripture and science. It was therefore decided that comparison would no longer be made. Thus a situation arose which today, we are forced to admit, puts Biblical exegetes and scientists in opposition to one another. We cannot, after all, accept a divine Revelation making statements which are totally inaccurate. There was only one way of logically reconciling the two; it lay in not considering a passage containing unacceptable scientific data to be genuine. This solution was not adopted. Instead, the integrity of the text was stubbornly maintained and experts were obliged to adopt a position on the truth of the Biblical Scriptures which, for the scientist, is hardly tenable.

Like Saint Augustine for the Bible, Islam has always assumed that the data contained in the Holy Scriptures were in agreement with scientific fact. A modern examination of the Islamic Revelation has not caused a change in this position. As we shall see later on, the Qur'an deals with many subjects of interest to science, far more in fact than the Bible. There is no comparison between the limited number of Biblical statements which lead to a confrontation with science, and the profusion of subjects mentioned in the Qur'an that are of a scientific nature. None of the latter can be contested from a scientific point of view; this is the basic fact that emerges from our study. We shall see at the end of this work that such is not the case for the Hadiths. These are collections of the Prophet's sayings, set aside from the Qur'anic Revelation, certain of which are scientifically unacceptable. The Hadiths in question have been under study in accordance with the strict principles of the Qur'an which dictate that science and reason should always be referred to, if necessary to deprive them of any authenticity.

These reflections on the scientifically acceptable or unacceptable nature of a certain Scripture need some explanation. It must be stressed that when scientific data are discussed here, what is meant is data definitely established. This consideration rules out any explanatory theories, once useful in illuminating a phenomenon and easily dispensed with to make way for further explanations more in keeping with scientific progress. What I intend to consider here are incontrovertible facts and even if science can only provide incomplete data, they will nevertheless be sufficiently well established to be used without fear of error.

Scientists do not, for example, have even an approximate date for man's appearance on Earth. They have however discovered remains of human works which we can situate beyond a shadow of a doubt at before the tenth millenium B.C. Hence we cannot consider the Biblical reality on this subject to be compatible with science. In the Biblical text of Genesis, the dates and genealogies

given would place man's origins (i.e. the creation of Adam) at
roughly thirty-seven centuries B.C. In the future, science may be
able to provide us with data that are more precise than our
present calculations, but we may rest assured that it will never
tell us that man first appeared on Earth 5,736 years ago, as does
the Hebraic calendar for 1975. The Biblical data concerning the
antiquity of man are therefore inaccurate.

This confrontation with science excludes all religious problems in the true sense of the word. Science does not, for example,
have any explanation of the process whereby God manifested
Himself to Moses. The same may be said for the mystery surrounding the manner in which Jesus was born in the absence of
a biological father. The Scriptures moreover give no material
explanation of such data. This present study is concerned with
what the Scriptures tell us about extremely varied natural phenomena, which they surround to a lesser or greater extent with
commentaries and explanations. With this in mind, we must note
the contrast between the rich abundance of information on a
given subject in the Qur'anic Revelation and the modesty of the
other two revelations on the same subject.

It was in a totally objective spirit, and without any preconceived ideas that I first examined the Qur'anic Revelation. I was
looking for the degree of compatibility between the Qur'anic
text and the data of modern science. I knew from translations
that the Qur'an often made allusion to all sorts of natural phenomena, but I had only a summary knowledge of it. It was only
when I examined the text very closely in Arabic that I kept a list
of them at the end of which I had to acknowledge the evidence
in front of me: the Qur'an did not contain a single statement
that was assailable from a modern scientific point of view.

I repeated the same test for the Old Testament and the Gospels, always preserving the same objective outlook. In the former
I did not even have to go beyond the first book, Genesis, to find
statements totally out of keeping with the cast-iron facts of
modern science.

On opening the Gospels, one is immediately confronted with a
serious problem. On the first page we find the genealogy of Jesus,
but Matthew's text is in evident contradiction to Luke's on the
same question. There is a further problem in that the latter's

data on the antiquity of man on Earth are incompatible with modern knowledge.

The existence of these contradictions, improbabilities and incompatibilities does not seem to me to detract from the belief in God. They involve only man's responsibility. No one can say what the original texts might have been, or identify imaginative editing, deliberate manipulations of them by men, or unintentional modification of the Scriptures. What strikes us today, when we realize Biblical contradictions and incompatibilities with well-established scientific data, is how specialists studying the texts either pretend to be unaware of them, or else draw attention to these defects then try to camouflage them with dialectic acrobatics. When we come to the Gospels according to Matthew and John, I shall provide examples of this brilliant use of apologetical turns of phrase by eminent experts in exegesis. Often the attempt to camouflage an improbability or a contradiction, prudishly called a 'difficulty', is successful. This explains why so many Christians are unaware of the serious defects contained in the Old Testament and the Gospels. The reader will find precise examples of these in the first and second parts of this work.

In the third part, there is the illustration of an unusual application of science to a holy Scripture, the contribution of modern secular knowledge to a better understanding of certain verses in the Qur'an which until now have remained enigmatic, if no' incomprehensible. Why should we be surprised at this when we know that, for Islam, religion and science have always been considered twin sisters? From the very beginning, Islam directed people to cultivate science; the application of this precept brought with it the prodigious strides in science taken during the great era of Islamic civilization, from which, before the Renaissance, the West itself benefited. In the confrontation between the Scriptures and science a high point of understanding has been reached owing to the light thrown on Qur'anic passages by modern scientific knowledge. Previously these passages were obscure owning to the non-availability of knowledge which could help interpret them.

The Old Testament

General Outlines

Who is the author of the Old Testament?

One wonders how many readers of the Old Testament, if asked the above question, would reply by repeating what they had read in the introduction to their Bible. They might answer that, even though it was written by men inspired by the Holy Ghost, the author was God.

Sometimes, the author of the Bible's presentation confines himself to informing his reader of this succinct observation which puts an end to all further questions. Sometimes he corrects it by warning him that details may subsequently have been added to the primitive text by men, but that nonetheless, the litigious character of a passage does not alter the general 'truth' that proceeds from it. This 'truth' is stressed very heavily. The Church Authorities answer for it, being the only body, with the assistance of the Holy Ghost, able to enlighten the faithful on such points. Since the Councils held in the Fourth century, it was the Church that issued the list of Holy Books, ratified by the Councils of Florence (1441), Trent (1546), and the First Vatican Council (1870), to form what today is known as the Canon. Just recently, after so many encyclicals, the Second Vatican Council published a text concerning the Revelation which is extremely important. It took three years (1962-1965) of strenuous effort to produce. The vast majority of the Bible's readers who find this highly reassuring information at the head of a modern edition have been quite satisfied with the guarantees of authenticity made over past centuries and have hardly thought it possible to debate them.

When one refers however to works written by clergymen, not meant for mass publication, one realizes that the question concerning the authenticity of the books in the Bible is much more complex than one might suppose *a priori*. For example, when one consults the modern publication in separate installments of the Bible in French translated under the guidance of the Biblical School of Jerusalem[1], the tone appears to be very different. One realizes that the Old Testament, like the New Testament, raises problems with controversial elements that, for the most part, the authors of commentaries have not concealed.

We also find highly precise data in more condensed studies of a very objective nature, such as Professor Edmond Jacob's study: *The Old Testament* (L'Ancien Testament)[2]. This book gives an excellent general view.

Many people are unaware, and Edmond Jacob points this out, that there were originally a number of texts and not just one. Around the Third century B.C., there were at least three forms of the Hebrew text: the text which was to become the Masoretic text, the text which was used, in part at least, for the Greek translation, and the Samaritan Pentateuch. In the First century B.C., there was a tendency towards the establishment of a single text, but it was not until a century after Christ that the Biblical text was definitely established.

If we had had the three forms of the text, comparison would have been possible, and we could have reached an opinion concerning what the original might have been. Unfortunately, we do not have the slightest idea. Apart from the Dead Sea Scrolls (Cave of Qumran) dating from a pre-Christian era near the time of Jesus, a papyrus of the Ten Commandments of the Second century A.D. presenting variations from the classical text, and a few fragments from the Fifth century A.D. (Geniza of

1. Pub. Cerf, Paris

2. Pub. Presses Universitaires de France, Paris "Que sais-je?" collection

Cairo), the oldest Hebrew text of the Bible dates from the Ninth century A.D.

The Septuagint was probably the first translation in Greek. It dates from the Third century B.C. and was written by Jews in Alexandria. It was on this text that the New Testament was based. It remained authoritative until the Seventh century A.D. The basic Greek texts in general use in the Christian world are from the manuscripts catalogued under the title *Codex Vaticanus* in the Vatican City and *Codex Sinaiticus* at the British Museum, London. They date from the Fourth century A.D.

At the beginning of the Fifth century A.D., Saint Jerome was able to produce a text in latin using Hebrew documents. It was later to be called the *Vulgate* on account of its universal distribution after the Seventh century A.D.

For the record, we shall mention the Aramaic version and the Syriac (Peshitta) version, but these are incomplete.

All of these versions have enabled specialists to piece together so-called 'middle-of-the-road' texts, a sort of compromise between the different versions. Multi-lingual collections have also been produced which juxtapose the Hebrew, Greek, Latin, Syriac, Aramaic and even Arabic versions. This is the case of the famous Walton Bible (London, 1657). For the sake of completeness, let us mention that diverging Biblical conceptions are responsible for the fact that the various Christian churches do not all accept exactly the same books and have not until now had identical ideas on translation into the same language. *The Ecumenical Translation of the Old Testament* is a work of unification written by numerous Catholic and Protestant experts now nearing completion[1] and should result in a work of synthesis.

Thus the human element in the Old Testament is seen to be quite considerable. It is not difficult to understand why from version to version, and translation to translation, with all the corrections inevitably resulting, it was possible for the original text to have been transformed during the course of more than two thousand years.

---

1. Translator's Note: Published December 1975 by Les Editions du Cerf and Les Bergers et les Mages, Paris

ORIGINS OF THE BIBLE

Before it became a collection of books, it was a folk tradition that relied entirely upon human memory, originally the only means of passing on ideas. This tradition was sung.

"At an elementary stage, writes E. Jacob, every people sings; in Israel, as elsewhere, poetry preceded prose. Israel sang long and well; led by circumstances of his history to the heights of joy and the depths of despair, taking part with intense feeling in all that happened to it, for everything in their eyes had a sense, Israel gave its song a wide variety of expression". They sang for the most diverse reasons and E. Jacob mentions a number of them to which we find the accompanying songs in the Bible: eating songs, harvest songs, songs connected with work, like the famous Well Song (Numbers 21, 17), wedding songs, as in the Song of Songs, and mourning songs. In the Bible there are numerous songs of war and among these we find the Song of Deborah (Judges 5, 1-32) exalting Israel's victory desired and led by Yahweh Himself, (Numbers 10, 35); "And whenever the ark (of alliance) set out, Moses said, 'Arise, oh Yahweh, and let thy enemies be scattered; and let them that hate thee flee before thee' ".

There are also the Maxims and Proverbs (Book of Proverbs, Proverbs and Maxims of the Historic Books), words of blessing and curse, and the laws decreed to man by the Prophets on re- ception of their Divine mandate.

E. Jacobs notes that these words were either passed down from family to family or channelled through the sanctuaries in the form of an account of the history of God's chosen people. History quickly turned into fable, as in the Fable of Jotham (Judges 9, 7-21), where "the trees went forth to anoint a king over them; and they asked in turn the olive tree, the fig tree, the vine and the bramble", which allows E. Jacob to note "ani- mated by the need to tell a good story, the narration was not perturbed by subjects or times whose history was not well known", from which he concludes:

"It is probable that what the Old Testament narrates about Moses and the patriarchs only roughly corresponds to the suc- cession of historic facts. The narrators however, even at the stage of oral transmission, were able to bring into play such

grace and imagination to blend between them highly varied episodes, that when all is said and done, they were able to present
as a history that was fairly credible to critical thinkers what
happened at the beginning of humanity and the world".

There is good reason to believe that after the Jewish people
settled in Canaan, at the end of the Thirteenth century B.C.,
writing was used to preserve and hand down the tradition. There
was not however complete accuracy, even in what to men seems
to demand the greatest durability, i.e. the laws. Among these,
the laws which are supposed to have been written by God's own
hand, the Ten Commandments, were transmitted in the Old
Testament in two versions; Exodus (20, 1-21) and Deuteronomy
(5, 1-30). They are the same in spirit, but the variations are
obvious. There is also a concern to keep a large written record
of contracts, letters, lists of personalities (Judges, high city
officials, genealogical tables), lists of offerings and plunder. In
this way, archives were created which provided documentation
for the later editing of definitive works resulting in the books
we have today. Thus in each book there is a mixture of different
literary genres: it can be left to the specialists to find the reasons for this odd assortment of documents.

The Old Testament is a disparate whole based upon an initially
oral tradition. It is interesting therefore to compare the process
by which it was constituted with what could happen in another
period and another place at the time when a primitive literature
was born.

Let us take, for example, the birth of French literature at the
time of the Frankish Royalty. The same oral tradition presided
over the preservation of important deeds: wars, often in the
defense of Christianity, various sensational events, where heroes
distinguished themselves, that were destined centuries later to
inspire court poets, chroniclers and authors of various 'cycles'.
In this way, from the Eleventh century A.D. onwards, these
narrative poems, in which reality is mixed with legend, were
to appear and constitute the first monument in epic poetry.
The most famous of all is *the Song of Roland* (La Chanson de
Roland) a biographical chant about a feat of arms in which
Roland was the commander of Emperor Charlemagne's rear-
guard on its way home from an expedition in Spain. The sacri-

fice of Roland is not just an episode invented to meet the needs of the story. It took place on 15th August, 778. In actual fact it was an attack by Basques living in the mountains. This literary work is not just legend; it has a historical basis, but no historian would take it literally.

This parallel between the birth of the Bible and a secular literature seems to correspond exactly with reality. It is in no way meant to relegate the whole Biblical text as we know it today to the store of mythological collections, as do so many of those who systematically negate the idea of God. It is perfectly possible to believe in the reality of the Creation, God's transmission to Moses of the Ten Commandments, Divine intercession in human affairs, e.g. at the time of Solomon. This does not stop us, at the same time, from considering that what has been conveyed to us is the gist of these facts, and that the detail in the description should be subjected to rigorous criticism, the reason for this being that the element of human participation in the transcription of originally oral traditions is so great.

II

The Books of the Old Testament

The Old Testament is a collection of works of greatly differing length and many different genres. They were written in several languages over a period of more than nine hundred years, based on oral traditions. Many of these works were corrected and completed in accordance with events or special requirements, often at periods that were very distant from one another

This copious literature probably flowered at the beginning of the Israelite Monarchy, around the Eleventh century B.C. It was at this period that a body of scribes appeared among the members of the royal household. They were cultivated men whose rôle was not limited to writing. The first incomplete writings, mentioned in the preceding chapter, may date from this period. There was a special reason for writing these works down; there were a certain number of songs (mentioned earlier), the prophetic oracles of Jacob and Moses, the Ten Commandments and, on a more general level, the legislative texts which established a religious tradition before the formation of the law. All these texts constitute fragments scattered here and there throughout the various collections of the Old Testament.

It was not until a little later, possibly during the Tenth century B.C., that the so-called 'Yahvist'[1] text of the Pentateuch was written. This text was to form the backbone of the first five books ascribed to Moses. Later, the so-called 'Elohist'[2] text was to be added, and also the so-called 'Sacerdotal'[3] version. The

---

1. So called because God is named Yahweh in this text.
2. So called because God is named Elohim in this text.
3. From the preachers in the Temple at Jerusalem.

initial Yahvist text deals with the origins of the world up to the
death of Jacob. This text comes from the southern kingdom,
Judah.

At the end of the Ninth century and in the middle of the
Eighth century B.C., the prophetic influence of Elias and Elisha
took shape and spread. We have their books today. This is also
the time of the Elohist text of the Pentateuch which covers a
much smaller period than the Yahvist text because it limits itself
to facts relating to Abraham, Jacob and Joseph. The books of
Joshua and Judges date from this time.

The Eighth century B.C. saw the appearance of the writer-
prophets: Amos and Hosea in Israel, and Michah in Judah.

In 721 B.C., the fall of Samaria put an end to the Kingdom of
Israel. The Kingdom of Judah took over its religious heritage.
The collection of Proverbs dates from this period, distinguished
in particular by the fusion into a single book of the Yahvist and
Elohist texts of the Pentateuch; in this way the Torah was con-
stituted. Deuteronomy was written at this time.

In the second half of the Seventh century B.C., the reign of
Josiah coincided with the appearance of the prophet Jeremiah,
but his work did not take definitive shape until a century later.

Before the first deportation to Babylon in 598 B.C., there
appeared the Books of Zephaniah, Nahum and Habakkuk.
Ezekiel was already prophesying during this first deportation.
The fall of Jerusalem in 587 B.C. marked the beginning of the
second deportation which lasted until 538 B.C.

The Book of Ezekiel, the last great prophet and the prophet of
exile, was not arranged into its present form until after his death
by the scribes that were to become his spiritual inheritors. These
same scribes were to resume Genesis in a third version, the so-
called 'Sacerdotal' version, for the section going from the Creation to the death of Jacob. In this way a third text was to be
inserted into the central fabric of the Yahvist and Elohist texts
of the Torah. We shall see later on, in the books written roughly
two and four centuries earlier, an aspect of the intricacies of
this third text. It was at this time that the Lamentations
appeared.

On the order of Cyrus, the deportation to Babylon came to an
end in 538 B.C. The Jews returned to Palestine and the Temple

at Jerusalem was rebuilt. The prophets' activities began again, resulting in the books of Haggai, Zechariah, the third book of Isaiah, Malachi, Daniel and Baruch (the last being in Greek).

The period following the deportation is also the period of the Books of Wisdom: Proverbs was written definitively around 480 B.C., Job in the middle of the Fifth century B.C., Ecclesiastes or Koheleth dates from the Third century B.C., as do the Song of Songs, Chronicles I & II, Ezra and Nehemiah; Ecclesiasticus or Sirah appeared in the Second century B.C.; the Book of Wisdom and the Book of Maccabees I & II were written one century before Christ. The Books of Ruth, Esther and Jonah are not easily datable. The same is true for Tobit and Judith. All these dates are given on the understanding that there may have been subsequent adaptations, since it was only circa one century before Christ that form was first given to the writings of the Old Testament. For many this did not become definitive until one century after Christ.

Thus the Old Testament appears as a literary monument to the Jewish people, from its origins to the coming of Christianity. The books it consists of were written, completed and revised between the Tenth and the First centuries B.C. This is in no way a personal point of view on the history of its composition. The essential data for this historical survey were taken from the entry *The Bible* in the Encyclopedia Universalis[1] by J. P. Sandroz, a professor at the Dominican Faculties, Saulchoir. To understand what the Old Testament represents, it is important to retain this information, correctly established today by highly qualified specialists.

A Revelation is mingled in all these writings, but all we possess today is what men have seen fit to leave us. These men manipulated the texts to please themselves, according to the circumstances they were in and the necessities they had to meet.

When these objective data are compared with those found in various prefaces to Bibles destined today for mass publication, one realizes that facts are presented in them in quite a different way. Fundamental facts concerning the writing of the books are passed over in silence, ambiguities which mislead the reader are maintained, facts are minimalised to such an extent

1. Paris, 1974 edition, Vol. 3, pp. 246-253.

that a false idea of reality is conveyed. A large number of pre
faces or introductions to the Bible misrepresent reality in thi
way. In the case of books that were adapted several times (lik
the Pentateuch), it is said that certain details may have beer
added later on. A discussion of an unimportant passage of :
book is introduced, but crucial facts warranting lengthy expo
sitions are passed over in silence. It is distressing to see such
inaccurate information on the Bible maintained for mass publi
cation.

THE TORAH OR PENTATEUCH

Torah is the Semitic name.

The Greek expression, which in English gives us 'Pentateuch'
designates a work in five parts; Genesis, Exodus, Leviticus
Numbers and Deuteronomy. These were to form the five primary
elements of the collection of thirty-nine volumes that makes up
the Old Testament.

This group of texts deals with the origins of the world up to
the entry of the Jewish people into Canaan, the land promised
to them after their exile in Egypt, more precisely until the death
of Moses. The narration of these facts serves however as a gen
eral framework for a description of the provisions made for the
religious and social life of the Jewish people, hence the name
Law or Torah.

Judaism and Christianity for many centuries considered that
the author was Moses himself. Perhaps this affirmation was
based on the fact that God said to Moses (Exodus 17, 14) : "Write
this (the defeat of Amalek) as a memorial in a book", or again,
talking of the Exodus from Egypt, "Moses wrote down their
starting places" (Numbers 33, 2), and finally "And Moses wrote
this law" (Deuteronomy 31, 9). From the First century B.C.
onwards, the theory that Moses wrote the Pentateuch was up-
held; Flavius Josephus and Philo of Alexandria maintain it.

Today, this theory has been completely abandoned; everybody
is in agreement on this point. The New Testament nevertheless
ascribes the authorship to Moses. Paul, in his Letter to the
Romans (10, 5) quoting from Leviticus, affirms that "Moses
writes that the man who practices righteousness which is based
on the law . . ." etc. John, in his Gospel (5, 46-47), makes Jesus

say the following: "If you believed Moses, you would believe me, for he wrote of me. But if you do not believe his writings, how will you believe my words?" We have here an example of editing, because the Greek word that corresponds to the original (written in Greek) is *episteuete,* so that the Evangelist is putting an affirmation into Jesus's mouth that is totally wrong: the following demonstrates this.

I am borrowing the elements of this demonstration from Father de Vaux, Head of the Biblical School of Jerusalem. He prefaced his French translation of Genesis in 1962 with a General Introduction to the Pentateuch which contained valuable arguments. These ran contrary to the affirmations of the Evangelists on the authorship of the work in question. Father de Vaux reminds us that the "Jewish tradition which was followed by Christ and his Apostles" was accepted up to the end of the Middle Ages. The only person to contest this theory was Abenezra in the Twelfth century. It was in the Sixteenth century that Calstadt noted that Moses could not have written the account of his own death in Deuteronomy (34, 5-12). The author then quotes other critics who refuse to ascribe to Moses a part, at least, of the Pentateuch. It was above all the work of Richard Simon, father of the Oratory, *Critical History of the Old Testament* (Histoire critique du Vieux Testament) 1678, that underlined the chronological difficulties, the repetitions, the confusion of the stories and stylistic differences in the Pentateuch. The book caused a scandal. R. Simon's line of argument was barely followed in history books at the beginning of the Eighteenth century. At this time, the references to antiquity very often proceeded from what "Moses had written".

One can easily imagine how difficult it was to combat a legend strengthened by Jesus himself who, as we have seen, supported it in the New Testament. It is to Jean Astruc, Louis XV's doctor, that we owe the decisive argument.

By publishing, in 1753, his *Conjectures on the original writings which it appears Moses used to compose the Book of Genesis* (Conjectures sur les Mèmoires originaux dont il parait que Moyse s'est servi pour composer le livre de la Genèse), he placed the accent on the plurality of sources. He was probably not the first to have noticed it, but he did however have the courage to make public an observation of prime importance: two texts, each denoted by the way in which God was named either Yahweh or Elohim, were present side by side in Genesis. The latter therefore contained two juxtaposed texts. Eichorn (1780-1783) made the same discovery for the other four books; then Ilgen (1798) noticed that one of the texts isolated by Astruc, the one where God is named Elohim, was itself divided into two. The Pentateuch literally fell apart.

The Nineteenth century saw an even more minute search into the sources. In 1854, four sources were recognised. They were called the Yahvist version, the Elohist version, Deuteronomy, and the Sacerdotal version. It was even possible to date them:

1) The Yahvist version was placed in the Ninth century B.C. (written in Judah)

2) The Elohist version was probably a little more recent (written in Israel)

3) Deuteronomy was from the Eighth century B.C. for some (E. Jacob), and from the time of Josiah for others (Father de Vaux)

4) The Sacerdotal version came from the period of exile or after the exile: Sixth century B.C.

It can be seen that the arrangement of the text of the Pentateuch spans at least three centuries.

The problem is, however, even more complex. In 1941, A. Lods singled out three sources in the Yahvist version, four in the Elohist version, six in Deuteronomy, nine in the Sacerdotal version, "not including the additions spread out among eight different authors" writes Father de Vaux. More recently, it has been thought that "many of the constitutions or laws contained in the Pentateuch had parallels outside the Bible going back much further than the dates ascribed to the documents themselves" and that "many of the stories of the Pentateuch presupposed a background that was different from—and older than—the one from which these documents were supposed to have come". This leads on to "an interest in the formation of traditions". The problem then appears so complicated that nobody knows where he is anymore.

The multiplicity of sources brings with it numerous disagreements and repetitions. Father de Vaux gives examples of this

/erlapping of traditions in the case of the Flood, the kidnap-
ing of Joseph, his adventures in Egypt, disagreement of names
elating to the same character, differing descriptions of impor-
.nt events.

Thus the Pentateuch is shown to be formed from various tra-
itions brought together more or less skillfully by its authors.
he latter sometimes juxtaposed their compilations and some-
mes adapted the stories for the sake of synthesis. They allowed
nprobabilities and disagreements to appear in the texts, how-
/er, which have led modern man to the objective study of the
ources.

As far as textual criticism is concerned, the Pentateuch pro-
ides what is probably the most obvious example of adaptations
iade by the hand of man. These were made at different times in
he history of the Jewish people, taken from oral traditions and
exts handed down from preceding generations. It was begun
n the Tenth or Ninth century B.C. with the Yahvist tradition
/hich took the story from its very beginnings. The latter
ketches Israel's own particular destiny to "fit it back into God's
rand Design for humanity" (Father de Vaux). It was con-
luded in the Sixth century B.C. with the Sacerdotal tradition that
s meticulous in its precise mention of dates and genealogies.[1]

Father de Vaux writes that "The few stories this tradition
as of its own bear witness to legal preoccupations: Sabbatical
est at the completion of the Creation, the alliance with Noah,
he alliance with Abraham and the circumcision, the purchase
f the Cave of Makpela that gave the Patriarchs land in Canaan".
Ve must bear in mind that the Sacerdotal tradition dates from
he time of the deportation to Babylon and the return to Pales-
ine starting in 538 B.C. There is therefore a mixture of religious
nd purely political problems.

For Genesis alone, the division of the Book into three sources
as been firmly established: Father de Vaux in the commentary
o his translation lists for each source the passages in the present

---

1. We shall see in the next chapter, when confronted with modern scientific data, the extent of the narrative errors committed by authors of
the Sacerdotal version on the subject of the antiquity of man on Earth,
his situation in time and the course of the Creation. They are obviously
errors arising from manipulation of the texts.

text of Genesis that rely on them. On the evidence of these data
it is possible to pinpoint the contribution made by the various
sources to any one of the chapters. For example, in the case of
the Creation, the Flood and the period that goes from the Flood
to Abraham, occupying as it does the first eleven chapters of
Genesis, we can see alternating in the Biblical text a section of
the Yahvist and a section of the Sacerdotal texts. The Elohist
text is not present in the first eleven chapters. The overlapping
of Yahvist and Sacerdotal contributions is here quite clear. For
the Creation and up to Noah (first five chapters), the arrangement is simple: a Yahvist passage alternates with a Sacerdotal
passage from beginning to end of the narration. For the Flood
and especially chapters 7 and 8 moreover, the cutting of the text
according to its source is narrowed down to very short passages
and even to a single sentence. In the space of little more than
a hundred lines of English text, the text changes seventeen times.
It is from this that the improbabilities and contradictions arise
when we read the present-day text. (see Table on page 15 for
schematic distribution of sources)

THE HISTORICAL BOOKS

In these books we enter into the history of the Jewish people,
from the time they came to the Promised Land (which is most
likely to have been at the end of the Thirteenth century B.C.)
to the deportation to Babylon in the Sixth century B.C.

Here stress is laid upon what one might call the 'national
event' which is presented as the fulfilment of Divine word. In
the narration however, historical accuracy has rather been
brushed aside · a work such as the Book of Joshua complies first
and foremost with theological intentions. With this in mind, E.
Jacob underlines the obvious contradiction between archaeology
and the texts in the case of the supposed destruction of Jericho
and Ay.

The Book of Judges is centered on the defense of the chosen
people against surrounding enemies and on the support given to
them by God. The Book was adapted several times, as Father A.
Lefèvre notes with great objectivity in his Preamble to the
Crampon Bible: the various prefaces in the text and the appen-

TABLE OF THE DISTRIBUTION OF THE YAHVIST AND SACERDOTAL TEXTS IN CHAPTERS 1 TO 11 in GENESIS)
The first figure indicates the chapter.
The second figure in brackets indicates the number of phrases, sometimes divided into two parts indicated by the letters a and b.
Letters: Y indicates Yahvist text
             S indicates Sacerdotal text
Example: The first line of the table indicates: from Chapter 1, phrase 1 to Chapter 2, phrase 4a, the text published in present-day Bibles is the Sacerdotal text.

Chapter	phrase	to	Chapter	phrase	text
1	(1)		2	(4a)	S
2	(4b)		4	(26)	Y
5	(1)		5	(32)	S
6	(1)		6	(8)	Y
6	(9)		6	(22)	S
7	(1)		7	(5)	Y
7	(6)				S
7	(7)		7	(10)	Y adapted
7	(11)				S
7	(12)				Y
7	(13)		7	(16a)	S
7	(16b)		7	(17)	Y
7	(18)		7	(21)	S
7	(22)		7	(23)	Y
7	(24)		8	(2a)	S
8	(2b)				Y
8	(3)		8	(5)	S
8	(6)		8	(12)	Y
8	(13a)				S
8	(13b)				Y
8	(14)		8	(19)	S
8	(20)		8	(22)	Y
9	(1)		9	(17)	S
9	(18)		9	(27)	Y
9	(28)		10	(7)	S
10	(8)		10	(19)	Y
10	(20)		10	(23)	S
10	(24)		10	(30)	Y
10	(31)		10	(32)	S
11	(1)		11	(9)	Y
11	(10)		11	(32)	S

What simpler illustration can there be of the way men have manipulated the Biblical Scriptures?

dices bear witness to this. The story of Ruth is attached to the narrations contained in Judges.

The Book of Samuel and the two Books of Kings are above all biographical collections concerning Samuel, Saul, David, and Solomon. Their historic worth is the subject of debate. From this point of view E. Jacob finds numerous errors in it, because there are sometimes two and even three versions of the same event. The prophets Elias, Elisha and Isaiah also figure here, mixing elements of history and legend. For other commentators, such as Father A. Lefèvre, "the historical value of these books is fundamental."

Chronicles I & II, the Book of Ezra and the Book of Nehemiah have a single author, called 'the Chronicler', writing in the Fourth century B.C. He resumes the whole history of the Creation up to this period, although his genealogical tables only go up to David. In actual fact, he is using above all the Book of Samuel and the Book of Kings, "mechanically copying them out without regard to the inconsistencies" (E. Jacob), but he nevertheless adds precise facts that have been confirmed by archaeology. In these works care is taken to adapt history to the needs of theology. E. Jacob notes that the author "sometimes writes history according to theology". "To explain the fact that King Manasseh, who was a sacrilegious persecutor, had a long and prosperous reign, he postulates a conversion of the King during a stay in Assyria (Chronicles II, 33/11) although there is no mention of this in any Biblical or non-Biblical source". The Book of Ezra and the Book of Nehemiah have been severely criticised because they are full of obscure points, and because the period they deal with (the Fourth century B.C.) is itself not very well known, there being few non-Biblical documents from it.

The Books of Tobit, Judith and Esther are classed among the Historical Books. In them very big liberties are taken with history: proper names are changed, characters and events are invented, all for the best of religious reasons. They are in fact stories designed to serve a moral end, peppered with historical improbabilities and inaccuracies.

The Books of Maccabees are of quite a different order. They provide a version of events that took place in the Second century B.C. which is as exact a record of the history of this period as may be found. It is for this reason that they constitute accounts of great value.

The collection of books under the heading 'historical' is therefore highly disparate. History is treated in both a scientific and a whimsical fashion.

THE PROPHETIC BOOKS

Under this heading we find the preachings of various prophets who in the Old Testament have been classed separately from the first great prophets such as Moses, Samuel, Elias and Elisha, whose teachings are referred to in other books.

The prophetic books cover the period from the Eighth to the Second century B.C.

In the Eighth century B.C., there were the books of Amos, Hosea, Isaiah and Michah. The first of these is famous for his condemnation of social injustice, the second for his religious corruption which leads him to bodily suffering (for being forced to marry a sacred harlot of a pagan cult), like God suffering for the degradation of His people but still granting them His love. Isaiah is a figure of political history: he is consulted by kings and dominates events; he is the prophet of grandeur. In addition to his personal works, his oracles are published by his disciples right up until the Third century B.C.: protests against iniquities, fear of God's judgement, proclamations of liberation at the time of exile and later on the return of the Jews to Palestine. It is certain that in the case of the second and third Isaiah, the prophetic intention is paralleled by political considerations that are as clear as daylight. The preaching of Michah, a contemporary of Isaiah, follows the same general ideas.

In the Seventh century B.C., Zephaniah, Jeremiah, Nahum and Habakkuk distinguished themselves by their preachings. Jeremiah became a martyr. His oracles were collected by Baruch who is also perhaps the author of Lamentations.

The period of exile in Babylon at the beginning of the Sixth century B.C. gave birth to intense prophetic activity. Ezekiel figures importantly as the consoler of his brothers, inspiring hope among them. His visions are famous. The Book of Obadiah deals with the misery of a conquered Jerusalem.

After the exile, which came to an end in 538 B.C., prophetic activity resumed with Haggai and Zechariah who urged the reconstruction of the Temple. When it was completed, writings going under the name of Malachi appeared. They contain various oracles of a spiritual nature.

One wonders why the Book of Jonah is included in the prophetic books when the Old Testament does not give it any real text to speak of. Jonah is a story from which one principle fact emerges: the necessary submission to Divine Will.

Daniel was written in three languages (Hebrew, Aramaic and Greek). According to Christian commentators, it is a 'disconcerting' Apocalypse from an historical point of view. It is probably a work from the Maccabaean period, Second century B.C. Its author wished to maintain the faith of his countrymen, at the time of the 'abomination of desolation', by convincing them that the moment of deliverance was at hand. (E. Jacob)

THE BOOKS OF POETRY AND WISDOM

These form collections of unquestionable literary unity.

Foremost among them are the Psalms, the greatest monument to Hebrew poetry. A large number were composed by David and the others by priests and levites. Their themes are praises, supplications and meditations, and they served a liturgical function.

The book of Job, the book of wisdom and piety *par excellence*, probably dates from 400-500 B.C.

The author of 'Lamentations' on the fall of Jerusalem at the beginning of the Sixth century B.C. may well be Jeremiah.

We must once again mention the Song of Songs, allegorical chants mostly about Divine love, the Book of Proverbs, a collection of the words of Solomon and other wise men of the court, and Ecclesiastes or Koheleth, where earthly happiness and wisdom are debated.

We have, therefore, a collection of works with highly disparate contents written over at least seven centuries, using extremely varied sources before being amalgamated inside a single work. How was this collection able, over the centuries, to constitute an inseparable whole and—with a few variations according to community—become the book containing the Judeo-Christian Revelation? This book was called in Greek the 'canon' because of the idea of intangibility it conveys.

The amalgam does not date from the Christian period, but from Judaism itself, probably with a primary stage in the Seventh century B.C. before later books were added to those already accepted. It is to be noted however that the first five books, forming the Torah or Pentateuch, have always been given pride of place. Once the proclamations of the prophets (the prediction of a chastisement commensurate with misdemeanour) had been fulfilled, there was no difficulty in adding their texts to the books that had already been admitted. The same was true for the assurances of hope given by these prophets. By the Second century B.C., the 'Canon' of the prophets had been formed.

Other books, e.g. Psalms, on account of their liturgical function, were integrated along with further writings, such as Lamentations, the Book of Wisdom and the Book of Job.

Christianity, which was initially Judeo-Christianity, has been carefully studied—as we shall see later on—by modern authors, such as Cardinal Daniélou. Before it was transformed under Paul's influence, Christianity accepted the heritage of the Old Testament without difficulty. The authors of the Gospels adhered very strictly to the latter, but whereas a 'purge' has been made of the Gospels by ruling out the 'Apocrypha', the same selection has not been deemed necessary for the Old Testament. Everything, or nearly everything, has been accepted.

Who would have dared dispute any aspects of this disparate amalgam before the end of the Middle Ages—in the West at least? The answer is nobody, or almost nobody. From the end of the Middle Ages up to the beginning of modern times, one or two critics began to appear; but, as we have already seen, the Church Authorities have always succeeded in having their own way. Nowadays, there is without doubt a genuine body of textual criticism, but even if ecclesiastic specialists have devoted many of their efforts to examining a multitude of detailed points, they have preferred not to go too deeply into what they euphemistically call 'difficulties'. They hardly seem disposed to study them in the light of modern knowledge. They may well establish paral-

lels with history—principally when history and Biblical narra
tion appear to be in agreement—but so far they have not com
mitted themselves to be a frank and thorough comparison wit
scientific ideas. They realize that this would lead people to co
test notions about the truth of Judeo-Christian Scriptures, whic
have so far remained undisputed.

III

The Old Testament and Science. Findings

Few of the subjects dealt within the Old Testament, and likewise the Gospels, give rise to a confrontation with the data of modern knowledge. When an incompatibility does occur between the Biblical text and science, however, it is on extremely important points.

As we have already seen in the preceding chapter, historical errors were found in the Bible and we have quoted several of these pinpointed by Jewish and Christian experts in exegesis. The latter have naturally had a tendency to minimize the importance of such errors. They find it quite natural for a sacred author to present historical fact in accordance with theology and to write history to suit certain needs. We shall see further on, in the case of the Gospel according to Matthew, the same liberties taken with reality and the same commentaries aimed at making admissible as reality what is in contradiction to it. A logical and objective mind cannot be content with this procedure.

From a logical angle, it is possible to single out a large number of contradictions and improbabilities. The existence of different sources that might have been used in the writing of a description may be at the origin of two different presentations of the same fact. This is not all; different adaptations, later additions to the text itself, like the commentaries added *a posteriori*, then included in the text later on when a new copy was made—these are perfectly recognized by specialists in textual criticism and very frankly underlined by some of them. In the case of the Pentateuch alone, for example, Father de Vaux in the General Introduction preceding his translation of Genesis (pages 13 and 14), has drawn attention to numerous disagreements. We shall not quote them here since we shall be quoting several of them later on in this study. The general impression one gains is that one must not follow the text to the letter.

Here is a very typical example:

In Genesis (6, 3), God decides just before the Flood henceforth to limit man's lifespan to one hundred and twenty years, ". . . his days shall be a hundred and twenty years". Further on however, we note in Genesis (11, 10-32) that the ten descendants of Noah had lifespans that range from 148 to 600 years (see table in this chapter showing Noah's descendants down to Abraham). The contradiction between these two passages is quite obvious. The explanation is elementary. The first passage (Genesis 6, 3) is a Yahvist text, probably dating as we have already seen from the Tenth century B.C. The second passage in Genesis (11, 10-32) is a much more recent text (Sixth century B.C.) from the Sacerdotal version. This version is at the origin of these genealogies, which are as precise in their information on lifespans as they are improbable when taken *en masse*.

It is in Genesis that we find the most evident incompatibilities with modern science. These concern three essential points:

1) the Creation of the world and its stages;
2) the date of the Creation of the world and the date of man's appearance on earth;
3) the description of the Flood.

THE CREATION OF THE WORLD

As Father de Vaux points out, Genesis "starts with two juxtaposed descriptions of the Creation". When examining them from the point of view of their compatibility with modern scientific data, we must look at each one separately.

First Description of the Creation

The first description occupies the first chapter and the very first verses of the second chapter. It is a masterpiece of inaccuracy from a scientific point of view. It must be examined one paragraph at a time. The text reproduced here is from the Revised Standard Version of the Bible.[1]

Chapter 1, verses 1 & 2:

"In the beginning God created the heavens and the earth. The earth was without form and void, and darkness was upon the face of the deep; and the Spirit of God was moving over the face of the waters."

It is quite possible to admit that before the Creation of the Earth, what was to become the Universe as we know it was covered in darkness. To mention the existence of water at this period is however quite simply pure imagination. We shall see in the third part of this book how there is every indication that at the initial stage of the formation of the universe a gaseous mass existed. It is an error to place water in it.

Verses 3 to 5:

"And God said, 'Let there be light', and there was light. And God saw that the light was good; and God separated the light from the darkness. God called the light Day, and the darkness he called Night. And there was evening and there was morning, one day."

The light circulating in the Universe is the result of complex reactions in the stars. We shall come back to them in ·the third part of this work. At this stage in the Creation, however, according to the Bible, the stars were not yet formed. The 'lights' of the firmament are not mentioned in Genesis until verse 14, when they were created on the Fourth day, "to separate the day from the night", "to give light upon earth"; all of which is accurate. It is illogical, however, to mention the result (light) on the first day, when the cause of this light was created three days later. The fact that the existence of evening and morning is placed on the first day is moreover, purely imaginary; the existence of evening and morning as elements of a single day is only conceivable after the creation of the earth and its rotation under the light of its own star, the Sun!

—verses 6 to 8

"And God said, 'Let there be a firmament in the midst of the waters, and let it separate the waters from the waters.' And God

---

1. Pub. W. M. Collins & Sons for the British and Foreign Bible Society, 1952.

made the firmament and separated the waters which were under the firmament from the waters which were above the firmament. And it was so. And God called the firmament Heaven. And there was evening and there was morning, a second day."

The myth of the waters is continued here with their separation into two layers by a firmament that in the description of the Flood allows the waters above to pass through and flow onto the earth. This image of the division of the waters into two masses is scientifically unacceptable.

—verses 9 to 13

"And God said, 'Let the waters under the heavens be gathered together into one place, and let the dry land appear.' And it was so. God called the dry land Earth, and the waters that were gathered together he called Seas. And God saw that it was good. And God said, 'Let the earth put forth vegetation, plants yielding seed, and fruit trees bearing fruit in which is their seed, each according to its kind upon the earth.' And it was so. The earth brought forth vegetation, plants yielding seed according to their own kinds, and trees bearing fruit in which is their seed, each according to its kind. And God saw that it was good. And there was evening and there was morning, a third day."

The fact that continents emerged at the period in the earth's history, when it was still covered with water, is quite acceptable scientifically. What is totally untenable is that a highly organized vegetable kingdom with reproduction by seed could have appeared before the existence of the sun (in Genesis it does not appear until the fourth day), and likewise the establishment of alternating nights and days.

—verses 14 to 19

"And God said, 'Let there be lights in the firmaments of the heavens to separate the day from night; and let them be for signs and for seasons and for days and years, and let them be lights in the firmament of the heavens to give light upon the earth.' And it was so. And God made the two great lights, the greater light to rule the day, and the lesser light to rule the night; he made the stars also. And God set them in the firmament of the heavens to give light upon earth, to rule over the day and over the night, and to separate the light from the darkness. And

God saw that it was good. And there was evening and there was morning, a fourth day."

Here the Biblical author's description is acceptable. The only criticism one could level at this passage is the position it occupies in the description as a whole. Earth and Moon emanated, as we know, from their original star, the Sun. To place the creation of the Sun and Moon after the creation of the Earth is contrary to the most firmly established ideas on the formation of the elements of the Solar System.

—verses 20 to 30

"And God said, 'Let the waters bring forth swarms of living creatures, and let birds fly above the earth across the firmament of the heavens.' So God created the great sea monsters and every living creature that moves, with which the waters swarm, according to their kinds, and every winged bird according to its kind. And God saw that it was good. And God blessed them saying, 'Be fruitful and multiply and fill the waters in the seas, and let birds multiply on the earth.' And there was evening and there was morning, a fifth day."

This passage contains assertions which are unacceptable.

According to Genesis, the animal kingdom began with the appearance of creatures of the sea and winged birds. The Biblical description informs us that it was not until the next day—as we shall see in the following verses—that the earth itself was populated by animals.

It is certain that the origins of life came from the sea, but this question will not be dealt with until the third part of this book. From the sea, the earth was colonized, as it were, by the animal kingdom. It is from animals living on the surface of the earth, and in particular from one species of reptile which lived in the Second era, that it is thought the birds originated. Numerous biological characteristics common to both species make this deduction possible. The beasts of the earth are not however mentioned until the sixth day in Genesis; after the appearance of the birds. This order of appearance, beasts of the earth after birds, is not therefore acceptable.

—verses 24 to 31

"And God said, 'Let the earth bring forth living creatures according to their kinds: cattle and creeping things and beasts of the earth according to their kinds.' And it was so. And God made the beasts of the earth according to their kinds and the cattle according to their kinds, and everything that creeps upon the ground according to its kind. And God saw that it was good."

"Then God said, 'Let us make man in our image, after our likeness; and let them have dominion (sic) over the fish of the sea, and over the birds of the air, and over the cattle, and over all the earth and over every creeping thing that creeps upon the earth".

"So God created man in his own image, in the image of God he created him; male and female he created them."

"And God blessed them, and God said to them, 'Be fruitful and multiply, and fill the earth and subdue it; and have dominion over the fish of the sea and over the birds of the air and over every living thing that moves upon the earth.' And God said, 'Behold, I have given you every plant yielding seed which is upon the face of the earth, and every tree with seed in its fruit; you shall have them for food. And to every beast of the earth, and to every bird of the air, and to everything that creeps on the earth, everything that has the breath of life, I have given every green plant for food." And it was so. And God saw everything that he had made, and behold, it was very good. And there was evening and there was morning, a sixth day."

This is the description of the culmination of the Creation. The author lists all the living creatures not mentioned before and describes the various kinds of food for man and beast.

As we have seen, the error was to place the appearance of beasts of the earth after that of the birds. Man's appearance is however correctly situated after the other species of living things.

The description of the Creation finishes in the first three verses of Chapter 2:

"Thus the heavens and the earth were finished, and all the host (sic) of them. And on the seventh day God finished his work which he had done, and he rested on the seventh day from all his work which he had done. So God blessed the seventh day and hallowed it, because on it God rested from all his work which he had done in creation;

These are the generations of the heavens and the earth when they were created."

This description of the seventh day calls for some comment.

Firstly the meaning of certain words. The text is taken from the Revised Standard Version of the Bible mentioned above. The word 'host' signifies here, in all probability, the multitude of beings created. As for the expression 'he rested', it is à manner of translating the Hebrew word 'shabbath', from which the Jewish day for rest is derived, hence the expression in English 'sabbath'.

It is quite clear that the 'rest' that God is said to have taken after his six days' work is a legend. There is nevertheless an explanation for this. We must bear in mind that the description of the creation examined here is taken from the so-called Sacerdotal version, written by priests and scribes who were the spiritual successors of Ezekiel, the prophet of the exile to Babylon writing in the Sixth century B.C. We have already seen how the priests took the Yahvist and Elohist versions of Genesis and remodelled them after their own fashion in accordance with their own preoccupations. Father de Vaux has written that the 'legalist' character of these writings was very essential. An outline of this has already been given above.

Whereas the Yahvist text of the Creation, written several centuries before the Sacerdotal text, makes no mention of God's sabbath, taken after the fatigue of a week's labor, the authors of the Sacerdotal text bring it into their description. They divide the latter into separate days, with the very precise indication of the days of the week. They build it around the sabbatic day of rest which they have to justify to the faithful by pointing out that God was the first to respect it. Subsequent to this practical necessity, the description that follows has an apparently logical religious order, but in fact scientific data permit us to qualify the latter as being of a whimsical nature.

The idea that successive phases of the Creation, as seen by the Sacerdotal authors in their desire to incite people to. religious observation, could have been compressed into the space of one week is one that cannot be defended from a scientific point of view. Today we are perfectly aware that the formation of the Universe and the Earth took place in stages that lasted for very long periods. (In the third part of the present work, we shall examine this question when we come to look at the Qur'anic data concerning the Creation). Even if the description came to a close on the evening of the sixth day, without mentioning the seventh day, the 'sabbath' when God is said to have rested, and even if, as in the Qur'anic description, we were permitted to think that they were in fact undefined periods rather than actual days, the Sacerdotal description would still not be any more acceptable. The succession of episodes it contains is an absolute contradiction with elementary scientific knowledge.

It may be seen therefore that the Sacerdotal description of the Creation stands out as an imaginative and ingenious fabrication. Its purpose was quite different from that of making the truth known.

Second Description

The second description of the Creation in Genesis follows immediately upon the first without comment or transitional passage. It does not provoke the same objections.

We must remember that this description is roughly three centuries older and is very short. It allows more space to the creation of man and earthly paradise than to the creation of the Earth and Heavens. It mentions this very briefly (Chapter 2, 4b-7): "In the day that Yahweh God made the earth and the heavens, when no plant of the field was yet in the earth and no herb of the field had yet sprung up—for Yahweh God had not caused it to rain upon the earth, and there was no man to till the ground; but a flood went up from earth and watered the whole face of the ground—then Yahweh God formed man of dust from the ground, and breathed into his nostrils the breath of life; and man became a living being."

This is the Yahvist text that appears in the text of present-day Bibles. The Sacerdotal text was added to it later on, but one may ask if it was originally so brief. Nobody is in a position to say whether the Yahvist text has not, in the course of time, been pared down. We do not know if the few lines we possess represent all that the oldest Biblical text of the Creation had to say.

The Yahvist description does not mention the actual formation of the Earth or the Heavens. It makes it clear that when God created man, there was no vegetation on Earth (it had not yet rained), even though the waters of the Earth had covered its surface. The sequel to the text confirms this: God planted a garden at the same time as man was created. The vegetable kingdom

therefore appears on Earth at the same time as man. This is
scientifically inaccurate; man did not appear on Earth until a
long time after vegetation had been growing on it. We do not
know how many hundreds of millions of years separate the two
events.

This is the only criticism that one can level at the Yahvist text.
The fact that it does not place the creation of man in time in relation to the formation of the world and the earth, unlike the
Sacerdotal text, which places them in the same week, frees it
from the serious objections raised against the latter.

THE DATE OF THE WORLD'S CREATION AND THE DATE OF MAN'S APPEARANCE ON EARTH.

The Jewish calendar, which follows the data contained in the
Old Testament, places the dates of the above very precisely. The
second half of the Christian year 1975 corresponds to the beginning of the 5,736th year of the creation of the world. The
creation of man followed several days later, so that he has the
same numerical age, counted in years, as in the Jewish calendar.

There is probably a correction to be made on account of the fact
that time was originally calculated in lunar years, while the calendar used in the West is based on solar years. This correction
would have to be made if one wanted to be absolutely exact, but
as it represents only 3%, it is of very little consequence. To sim-
plify our calculations, it is easier to disregard it. What matters
here is the order of magnitude. It is therefore of little importance
if, over a thousand years, our calculations are thirty years out.
We are nearer the truth in following this Hebraic estimate of
the creation of the world if we say that it happened roughly
thirty-seven centuries before Christ.

What does modern science tell us? It would be difficult to reply
to the question concerning the formation of the Universe. All we
can provide figures for is the era in time when the solar system
was formed. It is possible to arrive at a reasonable approxima-
tion of this. The time between it and the present is estimated at
four and a half billion years. We can therefore measure the margin separating the firmly established reality we know today and
the data taken from the Old Testament. We shall expand on this

in the third part of the present work. These facts emerge from a close scrutiny of the Biblical text. Genesis provides very precise information on the time that elapsed between Adam and Abraham. For the period from the time of Abraham to the beginnings of Christianity, the information provided is insufficient. It must be supported by other sources.

1. From Adam to Abraham

Genesis provides extremely precise genealogical data in Chapters 4, 5, 11, 21 and 25. They concern all of Abraham's ancestors in direct line back to Adam. They give the length of time each person lived, the father's age at the birth of the son and thus make it easily possible to ascertain the dates of birth and death of each ancestor in relation to the creation of Adam, as the table indicates.

All the data used in this table come from the Sacerdotal text of Genesis, the only Biblical text that provides information of this kind. It may be deduced, according to the Bible, that Abraham was born 1,948 years after Adam.

ABRAHAM's GENEALOGY

		date of birth after creation of Adam	length of life	date of death after creation of Adam
1.	Adam		930	930
	Seth	130	912	1042
	Enosch	235	905	1140
	Kenan	325	910	1235
	Mahalaleel	395	895	1290
	Jared	460	962	1422
	Enoch	622	365	987
	Methuselah	687	969	1656
	Lamech	874	777	1651
10.	Noah	1056	950	2006
	Shem	1556	600	2156
	Arpachshad	1658	438	2096
	Shelah	1693	433	2122
	Eber	1723	464	2187
	Peleg	1757	239	1996

Reu	1787	239	2026
Serug	1819	230	2049
Nahor	1849	148	1997
Terah	1878	205	2083
20. Abraham	1948	175	2123

From Abraham to The Beginnings Of Christianity

The Bible does not provide any numerical information on this
eriod that might lead to such precise estimates as those found
a Genesis on Abraham's ancestors. We must look to other
ources to estimate the time separating Abraham from Jesus. At
resent, allowing for a slight margin of error, the time of Abra-
am is situated at roughly eighteen centuries before Jesus. Com-
ined with information in Genesis on the interval separating
braham and Adam, this would place Adam at roughly thirty-
ght centuries before Jesus. This estimate is undeniably wrong:
e origins of this inaccuracy arise from the mistakes in the
ible on the Adam-Abraham period. The Jewish tradition still
ounds its calendar on this. Nowadays, we can challenge the
aditional defenders of Biblical truth with the incompatibility
etween the whimsical estimates of Jewish priests living in the
ixth century B.C. and modern data. For centuries, the events
f antiquity relating to Jesus were situated in time according to
formation based on these estimates.

Before modern times, editions of the Bible frequently provided
e reader with a preamble explaining the historical sequence
f events that had come to pass between the creation of the world
nd the time when the books were edited. The figures vary
ightly according to the time. For example, the Clementine Vul-
ate, 1621, gave this information, although it did place Abraham
little earlier and the Creation at roughly the 40th century B.C.
alton's polyglot Bible, produced in the 17th century, in addi-
on to Biblical texts in several languages, gave the reader tables
milar to the one shown here for Abraham's ancestors. Almost
l the estimates coincide with the figures given here. With the
rrival of modern times, editors were no longer able to maintain
ach whimsical chronologies without going against scientific dis-
overy that placed the Creation at a much earlier date. They were
ontent to abolish these tables and preambles, but they avoided

warning the reader that the Biblical texts on which these chr-
nologies were based had become obsolete and could no longer k
considered to express the truth. They preferred to draw a mode
veil over them, and invent set-phrases of cunning dialectics tha
would make acceptable the text as it had formerly been, withou
any subtractions from it.

This is why the genealogies contained in the Sacerdotal text
the Bible are still honoured, even though in the Twentieth cel
tury one cannot reasonably continue to count time on the bas
of such fiction.

Modern scientific data do not allow us to establish the date
man's appearance on earth beyond a certain limit. We may k
certain that man, with the capacity for action and intelliger
thought that distinguishes him from beings that appear to k
anatomically similar to him, existed on Earth after a certain est
mable date. Nobody however can say at what exact date he a
peared. What we can say today is that remains have been foun
of a humanity capable of human thought and action whose ag
may be calculated in tens of thousands of years.

This approximate dating refers to the prehistoric huma
species, the most recently discovered being the Cro-Magnon Ma
There have of course been many other discoveries all over th
world of remains that appear to be human. These relate to les
highly evolved species, and their age could be somewhere in th
hundreds of thousands of years. But were they genuine men?

Whatever the answer may be, scientific data are sufficient!
precise concerning the prehistoric species like the Cro-Magno
Man, to be able to place them much further back than the epoc
in which Genesis places the first men. There is therefore a
obvious incompatibility between what we can derive from th
numerical data in Genesis about the date of man's appearanc
on Earth and the firmly established facts of modern scientif
knowledge.

THE FLOOD

Chapters 6, 7 and 8 are devoted to the description of the Floo
In actual fact, there are two descriptions; they have not bee
placed side by side, but are distributed all the way through. Pa

ages are interwoven to give the appearance of a coherent suc-
ession of varying episodes. In these three chapters there are, in
eality, blatant contradictions; here again the explanation lies in
he existence of two quite distinct sources: the Yahvist and Sac-
rdotal versions.

It has been shown earlier that they formed a disparate amal-
am; each original text has been broken down into paragraphs
r phrases, elements of one source alternating with the other,
o that in the course of the complete description, we go from
ne to another seventeen times in roughly one hundred lines of
nglish text.

Taken as a whole, the story goes as follows:

Man's corruption had become widespread, so God decided to
nnihilate him along with all the other living creatures. He
arned Noah and told him to construct the Ark into which he
as to take his wife, his three sons and their wives, along with
ther living creatures. The two sources differ for the latter: one
assage (Sacerdotal) says that Noah was to take one pair of each
ecies; then in the passage that follows (Yahvist) it is stated
at God ordered him to take seven males and seven females
om each of the so-called 'pure' animal species, and a single pair
om the 'impure' species. Further on, however, it is stated that
oah actually took one pair of each animal. Specialists, such as
ather de Vaux, state that the passage in question is from an
daptation of the Yahvist description.

Rainwater is given as the agent of the Flood in one (Yahvist)
assage, but in another (Sacerdotal), the Flood is given a double
ause: rainwater and the waters of the Earth.

The Earth was submerged right up to and above the mountain
eaks. All life perished. After one year, when the waters had
eceded, Noah emerged from the Ark that had come to rest on
ount Ararat.

One might add that the Flood lasted differing lengths of time
ccording to the source used: forty days for the Yahvist version
nd one hundred and fifty in the Sacerdotal text.

The Yahvist version does not tell us when the event took place
n Noah's life, but the Sacerdotal text tells us that he was six
undred years old. The latter also provides information in its
enealogies that situates him in relation to Adam and Abraham.

If we calculate according to the information contained in Genesi
Noah was born 1,056 years after Adam (see table of Abraham
Genealogy) and the Flood therefore took place 1,656 years aft
the creation of Adam. In relation to Abraham, Genesis plac
the Flood 292 years before the birth of this Patriarch.

According to Genesis, the Flood affected the whole of tl
human race and all living creatures created by God on the fa
of the Earth were destroyed. Humanity was then reconstitut
by Noah's three sons and their wives so that when Abraham w
born roughly three centuries later, he found a humanity that w
already re-formed into separate communities. How could this r
construction have taken place in such a short time? This simp
observation deprives the narration of all verisimilitude.

Furthermore, historical data show its incompatibility wit
modern knowledge. Abraham is placed in the period 1800-185
B.C., and if the Flood took place, as Genesis suggests in its gen
alogies, roughly three centuries before Abraham, we would hav
to place him somewhere in the Twenty-first to Twenty-secon
century B.C. Modern historical knowledge confirms that at th
period, civilizations had sprung up in several parts of the worlc
for their remains have been left to posterity.

In the case of Egypt for example, the remains correspond t
the period preceding the Middle Kingdom (2,100 B.C.) at rough
the date of the First Intermediate Period before the Elevent
Dynasty. In Babylonia it is the Third Dynasty at Ur. We kno
for certain that there was no break in these civilizations, so tha
there could have been no destruction affecting the whole of h
manity, as it appears in the Bible.

We cannot therefore consider that these three Biblical narra
tions provide man with an account of facts that correspond t
the truth. We are obliged to admit that, objectively speaking, th
texts which have come down to us do not represent the expresio
of reality. We may ask ourselves whether it is possible for Go
to have revealed anything other than the truth. It is difficult t
entertain the idea that God taught to man ideas that were no
only fictitious, but contradictory. We naturally arrive therefor
at the hypothesis that distortions occurred that were made b
man or that arose from traditions passed down from one genera
tion to another by word of mouth, or from the texts of these tra

ditions once they were written down. When one knows that a work such as Genesis was adapted at least twice over a period of not less than three centuries, it is hardly surprising to find improbabilities or descriptions that are incompatible with reality. This is because the progress made in human knowledge has enabled us to know, if not everything, enough at least about certain events to be able to judge the degree of compatibility between our knowledge and the ancient descriptions of them. There is nothing more logical than to maintain this interpretation of Biblical errors which only implicates man himself. It is a great pity that the majority of commentators, both Jewish and Christian, do not hold with it. The arguments they use nevertheless deserve careful attention.

IV

Position Of Christian Authors With Regard To Scientific Error In The Biblical Texts.
A Critical Examination.

One is struck by the diverse nature of Christian commentators' reactions to the existence of these accumulated errors, improbabilities and contradictions. Certain commentators acknowledge some of them and do not hesitate in their work to tackle thorny problems. Others pass lightly over unacceptable statements and insist on defending the text word for word. The latter try to convince people by apologetic declarations, heavily reinforced by arguments which are often unexpected, in the hope that what is logically unacceptable will be forgotten.

In the Introduction to his translation of Genesis, Father de Vaux acknowledges the existence of critical arguments and even expands upon their cogency. Nevertheless, for him the objective reconstitution of past events has little interest. As he writes in his notes, the fact that the Bible resumes "the memory of one or two disastrous floods of the valleys of the Tigris and Euphrates, enlarged by tradition until they took on the dimensions of a universal cataclysm" is neither here nor there; "the essential thing is, however, that the sacred author has infused into this memory eternal teachings on the justice and mercy of God toward the malice of man and the salvation of the righteous."

In this way justification is found for the transformation of a popular legend into an event of divine proportions—and it is as such that it is thought fit to present the legend to men's faith—following the principle that an author has made use of it to illustrate religious teachings. An apologetic position of this kind justifies all the liberties taken in the composition of writings which are supposed to be sacred and to contain the word of God. If one acknowledges such human interference in what is divine, all the human manipulations of the Biblical texts will be accounted for. If there are theological intentions, all manipulations become legitimate; so that those of the 'Sacerdotal' authors of the Sixth century are justified, including their legalist preoccupations that turned into the whimsical descriptions we have already seen.

A large number of Christian commentators have found it more ingenious to explain errors, improbabilities and contradictions in Biblical descriptions by using the excuse that the Biblical authors were expressing ideas in accordance with the social factors of a different culture or mentality. From this arose the definition of respective 'literary genres' which was introduced into the subtle dialectics of commentators, so that it accounts for all difficulties. Any contradictions there are between two texts are then explained by the difference in the way each author expressed ideas in his own particular 'literary genre'. This argument is not, of course, acknowledged by everybody because it lacks gravity. It has not entirely fallen into disuse today however, and we shall see in the New Testament its extravagant use as an attempt to explain blatant contradictions in the Gospels.

Another way of making acceptable what would be rejected by logic when applied to a litigious text, is to surround the text in question with apologetical considerations. The reader's attention is distracted from the crucial problem of the truth of the text itself and deflected towards other problems.

Cardinal Daniélou's reflections on the Flood follow this mode of expression. They appear in the review *Living God* (Dieu Vivant)[1] under the title: 'Flood, Baptism, Judgment', (*Déluge, Baptême, Jugement*') where he writes "The oldest tradition of the Church has seen in the theology of the Flood an image of Christ and the Church". It is "an episode of great significance"

---

1. No. 38, 1974, pp. 95-112)

... "a judgment striking the whole human race." Having quoted from Origen in his *Homilies on Ezekiel,* he talks of "the shipwreck of the entire universe saved in the Ark", Cardinal Daniélou dwells upon the value of the number eight "expressing the number of people that were saved in the Ark (Noah and his wife, his three sons and their wives)". He turns to his own use Justin's writings in his *Dialogue:* "They represent the symbol of the eighth day when Christ rose from the dead" and "Noah, the first born of a new creation, is an image of Christ who was to do in reality what Noah had prefigured." He continues the comparison between Noah on the one hand, who was saved by the ark made of wood and the water that made it float ("water of the Flood from which a new humanity was born"), and on the other, the cross made of wood. He stresses the value of this symbolism and concludes by underlining the "spiritual and doctrinal wealth of the sacrament of the Flood" (sic).

There is much that one could say about such apologetical comparisons. We should always remember that they are commentaries on an event that it is not possible to defend as reality, either on a universal scale or in terms of the time in which the Bible places it. With a commentary such as Cardinal Daniélou's we are back in the Middle Ages, where the text had to be accepted as it was and any discussion, other than conformist, was off the point.

It is nevertheless reassuring to find that prior to that age of imposed obscurantism, highly logical attitudes were adopted. One might mention those of Saint Augustine which proceed from his thought, that was singularly advanced for the age he lived in.

At the time of the Fathers of the Church, there must have been problems of textual criticism because Saint Augustine raises them in his letter No. 82. The most typical of them is the following passage:

"It is solely to those books of Scripture which are called 'canonic' that I have learned to grant such attention and respect that I firmly believe that their authors have made no errors in writing them. When I encounter in these books a statement which seems to contradict reality, I am in no doubt that either the text (of my copy) is faulty, or that the translator has not been faithful to the original, or that my understanding is deficient."

It was inconceivable to Saint Augustine that a sacred text might contain an error. Saint Augustine defined very clearly the dogma of infallibility when, confronted with a passage that seemed to contradict the truth, he thought of looking for its cause, without excluding the hypothesis of a human fault. This is the attitude of a believer with a critical outlook. In Saint Augustine's day, there was no possibility of a confrontation between the Biblical text and science. An open-mindedness akin to his would today eliminate a lot of the difficulties raised by the confrontation of certain Biblical texts with scientific knowledge.

Present-day specialists, on the contrary, go to great trouble to defend the Biblical text from any accusation of error. In his introduction to Genesis, Father de Vaux explains the reasons compelling him to defend the text at all costs, even if, quite obviously, it is historically or scientifically unacceptable. He asks us not to view Biblical history "according to the rules of historical study observed by people today", as if the existence of several different ways of writing history was possible. History, when it is told in an inaccurate fashion, (as anyone will admit), becomes a historical novel. Here however, it does not have to comply with the standards established by our conceptions. The Biblical commentator rejects any verification of Biblical descriptions through geology, paleontology or prehistorical data. "The Bible is not answerable to any of these disciplines, and were one to confront it with the data obtained from these sciences, it would only lead to an unreal opposition or an artificial concordance."[1] One might point out that these reflections are made on what, in Genesis, is in no way in harmony with modern scientific data—in this case the first eleven chapters. When however, in the present day, a few descriptions have been perfectly verified, in this case certain episodes from the time of the patriarchs, the author does not fail to support the truth of the Bible with modern knowledge. "The doubt cast upon these descriptions should yield to the favorable witness that history and eastern archaeology bear them."[2] In other words: if science is useful in confirming the Biblical description, it is invoked, but if it invalidates the latter, reference to it is not permitted.

1. Introduction to Genesis, page 35.
2. Ibid., page 34

To reconcile the irreconcilable, i.e. the theory of the truth of the Bible with the inaccurate nature of certain facts reported in the descriptions in the Old Testament, modern theologians have applied their efforts to a revision of the classical concepts of truth. It lies outside the scope of this book to give a detailed exposé of the subtle ideas that are developed at length in works dealing with the truth of the Bible; such as O. Loretz's work (1972) *What is the Truth of the Bible?* (Quelle est la Vérité de la Bible?)[1]. This judgment concerning science will have to suffice:

The author remarks that the Second Vatican Council "has avoided providing rules to distinguish between error and truth in the Bible. Basic considerations show that this is impossible, because the Church cannot determine the truth or otherwise of scientific methods in such a way as to decide in principle and on a general level the question of the truth of the Scriptures".

It is obvious that the Church is not in a position to make a pronouncement on the value of scientific 'method' as a means of access to knowledge. The point here is quite different. It is not a question of theories, but of firmly established facts. In our day and age, it is not necessary to be highly learned to know that the world was not created thirty-seven or thirty-eight centuries ago. We know that man did not appear then and that the Biblical genealogies on which this estimate is based have been proven wrong beyond any shadow of a doubt. The author quoted here must be aware of this. His statements on science are only aimed at side-stepping the issue so that he does not have to deal with it the way he ought to.

The reminder of all these different attitudes adopted by Christian authors when confronted with the scientific errors of Biblical texts is a good illustration of the uneasiness they engender. It recalls the impossibility of defining a logical position other than by recognizing their human origins and the impossibility of acknowledging that they form part of a Revelation.

The uneasiness prevalent in Christian circles concerning the Revelation became clear at the Second Vatican Council (1962-1965) where it took no less than five drafts before there was any agreement on the final text, after three years of discussions. It

---

1. Pub. Le Centurion, Paris

was only then that "this painful situation threatening to engulf the Council" came to an end, to use His Grace Weber's expression in his introduction to the Conciliar Document No. 4 on the Revelation[1].

Two sentences in this document concerning the Old Testament (chap IV, page 53) describe the imperfections and obsolescence of certain texts in a way that cannot be contested:

"In view of the human situation prevailing before Christ's foundation of salvation, the *Books of the Old Testament* enable everybody to know who is God and who is man, and also the way in which God, in his justice and mercy, behaves towards men. These books, *even though they contain material which is imperfect and obsolete,* nevertheless bear witness to truly divine teachings."

There is no better statement than the use of the adjectives 'imperfect' and 'obsolete' applied to certain texts, to indicate that the latter are open to criticism and might even be abandoned; the principle is very clearly acknowledged.

This text forms part of a general declaration which was definitively ratified by 2,344 votes to 6; nevertheless, one might question this almost total unanimity. In actual fact, in the commentaries of the official document signed by His Grace Weber, there is one phrase in particular which obviously corrects the solemn affirmation of the council on the obsolescence of certain texts: "Certain books of the Jewish Bible have a temporary application and have something imperfect in them."

'Obsolete', the expression used in the official declaration, is hardly a synonym for 'temporary application', to use the commentator's phrase. As for the epithet 'jewish' which the latter curiously adds, it suggests that the conciliar text only criticized the version in Hebrew. This is not at all the case. It is indeed the Christian Old Testament alone that, at the Council, was the object of a judgment concerning the imperfection and obsolescence of certain parts.

---

1. Pub. Le Centurion, 1966, Paris.

V

Conclusions

The Biblical Scriptures must be examined without being embellished artificially with qualities one would like them to have. They must be seen objectively as they are. This implies not only a knowledge of the texts, but also of their history. The latter makes it possible to form an idea of the circumstances which brought about textual adaptations over the centuries, the slow formation of the collection that we have today, with its numerous substractions and additions.

The above makes it quite possible to believe that different versions of the same description can be found in the Old Testament, as well as contradictions, historical errors, improbabilities and incompatibilities with firmly established scientific data. They are quite natural in human works of a very great age. How could one fail to find them in the books written in the same conditions in which the Biblical text was composed?

At a time when it was not yet possible to ask scientific questions, and one could only decide on improbabilities or contradictions, a man of good sense, such as Saint Augustine, considered that God could not teach man things that did not correspond to reality. He therefore put forward the principle that it was not possible for an affirmation contrary to the truth to be of divine origin, and was prepared to exclude from all the sacred texts anything that appeared to him to merit exclusion on these grounds.

Later, at a time when the incompatibility of certain passages of the Bible with modern knowledge has been realized, the same attitude has not been followed. This refusal has been so insistent that a whole literature has sprung up, aimed at justifying the fact that, in the face of all opposition, texts have been retained in the Bible that have no reason to be there.

The Second Vatican Council (1962-1965) has greatly reduced this uncompromising attitude by introducing reservations about the "Books of the Old Testament" which "contain material that is imperfect and obsolete". One wonders if this will remain a pious wish or if it will be followed by a change in attitue towards material which, in the Twentieth century, is no longer acceptable in the books of the Bible. In actual fact, save for any human manipulation, the latter were destined to be the "witness of true teachings coming from God".

I

The Gospels

Introduction

Many readers of the Gospels are embarrassed and even abashed when they stop to think about the meaning of certain descriptions. The same is true when they make comparisons between different versions of the same event found in several Gospels. This observation is made by Father Roguet in his book *Initiation to the Gospels* (Initiation à l'Evangile) [1]. With the wide experience he has gained in his many years of answering perturbed readers' letters in a Catholic weekly, he has been able to assess just how greatly they have been worried by what they have read. His questioners come from widely varying social and cultural backgrounds. He notes that their requests for explanations concern texts that are 'considered abstruse, incomprehensible, if, not contradictory, absurd or scandalous'. There can be no doubt that a complete reading of the Gospels is likely to disturb Christians profoundly.

This observation is very recent: Father Roguet's book was published in 1973. Not so very long ago, the majority of Christians knew only selected sections of the Gospels that were read during services or commented upon during sermons. With the exception of the Protestants, it was not customary for Christians to read the Gospels in their entirety. Books of religious instruction only contained extracts; the *in extenso* text hardly circulated at

---

1. Pub. Editions du Seuil, Paris, 1973

44

all. At a Roman Catholic school I had copies of the works of Virgil and Plato, but I did not have the New Testament. The Greek text of this would nevertheless have been very instructive: it was only much later on that I realized why they had not set us translations of the holy writings of Christianity. The latter could have led us to ask our teachers questions they would have found it difficult to answer.

These discoveries, made if one has a critical outlook during a reading *in extenso* of the Gospels, have led the Church to come to the aid of readers by helping them overcome their perplexity. "Many Christians need to learn how to read the Gospels", notes Father Roguet. Whether or not one agrees with the explanations he gives, it is greatly to the author's credit that he actually tackles these delicate problems. Unfortunately, it is not always like this in many writings on the Christian Revelation.

In editions of the Bible produced for widespread publication, introductory notes more often than not set out a collection of ideas that would tend to persuade the reader that the Gospels hardly raise any problems concerning the personalities of the authors of the various books, the authenticity of the texts and the truth of the descriptions. In spite of the fact that there are so many unknowns concerning authors of whose identity we are not at all sure, we find a wealth of precise information in this kind of introductory note. Often they present as a certainty what is pure hypothesis, or they state that such-and-such an evangelist was an eye-witness of the events, while specialist works claim the opposite. The time that elapsed between the end of Jesus' ministry and the appearance of the texts is drastically reduced. They would have one believe that these were written by one man taken from an oral tradition, when in fact specialists have pointed out adaptations to the texts. Of course, certain difficulties of interpretation are mentioned here and there, but they ride rough shod over glaring contradictions that must strike anyone who thinks about them. In the little glossaries one finds among the appendices complementing a reassuring preface, one observes how improbabilities, contradictions or blatant errors have been hidden or stifled under clever arguments of an apologetic nature. This disturbing state of affairs shows up the misleading nature of such commentaries.

The ideas to be developed in the coming pages will witho
doubt leave any readers still unaware of these problems qui
amazed. Before going into detail however, I will provide an in
mediate illustration of my ideas with an example that seems
me quite conclusive.

Neither Matthew nor John speaks of Jesus's Ascension. Lu
in his Gospel places it on the day of the Resurrection and for
days later in the Acts of the Apostles of which he is said to
the author. Mark mentions it (without giving a date) in a co
clusion considered unauthentic today. The Ascension therefo
has no solid scriptural basis. Commentators nevertheless a
proach this important question with incredible lightness.

A. Tricot, in his *Little Dictionary of the New Testament* (Pe
Dictionnaire du Nouveau Testament) in the Crampon Bib
(1960 edition) [1], a work produced for mass publication, does n
devote an entry to the Ascension. *The Synopsis of the Four Ge
pels* (Synopse des Quatre Evangiles) by Fathers Benoît and Bo
mard, teachers at the Biblical School of Jerusalem, (1972 e
tion) [2], informs us in volume II, pages 451 and 452, that the co
tradiction between Luke's Gospel and the Acts of the Apost
may be explained by a 'literary artifice': this is, to say the lea
difficult to follow!

In all probability, Father Roguet in his *Initiation to the Ge
pel*, 1973, (pg 187) has not been convinced by the above arg
ment. The explanation he gives us is curious, to say the least:

"Here, as in many similar cases, the problem only appears
superable if one takes Biblical statements literally, and forg
their religious significance. It is not a matter of breaking do
the factual reality into a symbolism which is inconsistent, b
rather of looking for the theological intentions of those reveali
these mysteries to us by providing us with facts we can app
hend with our senses and signs appropriate to our incarn
spirit."

How is it possible to be satisfied by an exegesis of this ki
Only a person who accepted everything unconditionally wo
find such apologetic set-phrases acceptable.

---

1. Pub. Desclée and Co., Paris.
2. Pub. Editions du Cerf, Paris

Another interesting aspect of Father Roguet's commentary is his admission that there are 'many similar cases'; similar, that is, to the Ascension in the Gospels. The problem therefore has to be approached as a whole, objectively and in depth. It would seem reasonable to look for an explanation by studying the conditions attendant upon the writing of the Gospels, or the religious atmosphere prevailing at the time. When adaptations of the original writings taken from oral traditions are pointed out, and we see the way texts handed down to us have been corrupted, the presence of obscure, incomprehensible, contradictory, improbable, and even absurd passages comes as much less of a surprise. The same may be said of texts which are incompatible with today's proven reality, thanks to scientific progress. Observations such as these denote the element of human participation in the writing and modification of the texts.

Admittedly, in the last few decades, objective research on the Scriptures has gained attention. In a recent book, *Faith in the Resurrection, Resurrection of Faith*[1] (Foi en la Résurrection, Résurrection de la foi), Father Kannengiesser, a professor at the Catholic Institute of Paris, outlines this profound change in the following terms: "The faithful are hardly aware that a revolution has taken place in methods of Biblical exegesis since the time of Pious XII"[2]. The 'Revolution' that the author mentions is therefore very recent. It is beginning to be extended to the teaching of the faithful, in the case of certain specialists at least, who are animated by this spirit of revival. "The overthrow of the most assured prospects of the pastoral tradition," the author writes, "has more or less begun with this revolution in methods of exegesis."

Father Kannengiesser warns that 'one should not take literally' facts reported about Jesus by the Gospels, because they are 'writings suited to an occasion' or 'to combat', whose authors 'are writing down the traditions of their own community about Jesus'. Concerning the Resurrection of Jesus, which is the subject of his book, he stresses that none of the authors of the Gospels can claim to have been an eye-witness. He intimates that, as far as the rest of Jesus's public life is concerned, the same must

1. Pub. Beauchesne, Coll. 'Le Point théologique', Paris, 1974
2. Pious XII was Pope from 1939 to 1959

be true because, according to the Gospels, none of the Apostles— apart from Judas Iscariot—left Jesus from the moment he firs followed Him until His last earthly manifestations.

We have come a long way from the traditional position, whic was once again solemnly confirmed by the Second Vatican Cour cil only ten years ago. This once again is resumed by moder works of popularization destined to be read by the faithfu Little by little the truth is coming to light however.

It is not easy to grasp, because the weight of such a bitterly de fended tradition is very heavy indeed. To free oneself from it, on has to strike at the roots of the problem, i.e. examine first th circumstances that marked the birth of Christianity.

Historical Reminder
Judeo-Christianity
and Saint Paul

The majority of Christians believe that the Gospels were written by direct witnesses of the life of Jesus and therefore constitute unquestionable evidence concerning the events high-lighting
his life and preachings. One wonders, in the presence of such
guarantees of authenticity, how it is possible to discuss the teachings derived from them and how one can cast doubt upon the
validity of the Church as an institution applying the general
instructions Jesus Himself gave. Today's popular editions of the
Gospels contain commentaries aimed at propagating these ideas
among the general public.

The value the authors of the Gospels have as eye-witnesses is
always presented to the faithful as axiomatic. In the middle of
the Second century, Saint Justin did, after all, call the Gospels
the 'Memoirs of the Apostles'. There are moreover so many details proclaimed concerning the authors that it is a wonder that
one could ever doubt their accuracy; Matthew was a well-known
character 'a customs officer employed at the tollgate or customs
house at Capharnaum'; it is even said that he spoke Aramaic and
Greek. Mark is also easily identifiable as Peter's colleague; there
is no doubt that he too was an eye-witness. Luke is the 'dear
physician' of whom Paul talks: information on him is very precise. John is the Apostle who was always near to Jesus, son of
Zebedee, fisherman on the Sea of Galilee.

Modern studies on the beginnings of Christianity show that this way of presenting things hardly corresponds to reality. We shall see who the authors of the Gospels really were. As far as the decades following Jesus's mission are concerned, it must be understood that events did not at all happen in the way they have been said to have taken place and that Peter's arrival in Rome in no way laid the foundations for the Church. On the contrary, from the time Jesus left earth to the second half of the Second century, there was a struggle between two factions. One was what one might call Pauline Christianity and the other Judeo-Christianity. It was only very slowly that the first supplanted the second, and Pauline Christianity triumphed over Judeo-Christianity.

A large number of very recent works are based on contemporary discoveries about Christianity. Among them we find Cardinal Daniélou's name. In December 1967 he published an article in the review *Studies* (Etudes) entitled: '*A New Representation of the Origins of Christianity: Judeo-Christianity*'. (Une vision nouvelle des origines chrétiennes, le judéo-christianisme). Here he reviews past works, retraces its history and enables us to place the appearance of the Gospels in quite a different context from the one that emerges on reading accounts intended for mass publication. What follows is a condensed version of the essential points made in his article, including many quotations from it.

After Jesus's departure, the "little group of Apostles" formed a "Jewish sect that remained faithful to the form of worship practised in the Temple". However, when the observances of converts from paganism were added to them, a 'special system' was offered to them, as it were: the Council of Jerusalem in A.D. exempted them from circumcision and Jewish observances "many Judeo-Christians rejected this concession". This group was quite separate from Paul's. What is more, Paul and the Judeo-Christians were in conflict over the question of pagans who had turned to Christianity, (the incident of Antioch, A.D.). "For Paul, the circumcision, Sabbath, and form of worship practised in the Temple were henceforth old fashioned even for the Jews. Christianity was to free itself from its poli

cal-cum-religious adherence to Judaism and open itself to the
Gentiles."

For those Judeo-Christians who remained 'loyal Jews,' Paul
was a traitor: Judeo-Christian documents call him an 'enemy',
accuse him of 'tactical double-dealing', . . . "Until 70 A.D.,
Judeo-Christianity represents the majority of the Church" and
"Paul remains an isolated case". The head of the community at
that time was James, a relation of Jesus. With him were Peter
(at the beginning) and John. "James may be considered to represent the Judeo-Christian camp, which deliberately clung to Judaism as opposed to Pauline Christianity." Jesus's family has a
very important place in the Judeo-Christian Church of Jerusalem. "James's successor was Simeon, son of Cleopas, a cousin
of the Lord".

Cardinal Danielou here quotes Judeo-Christian writings which
express the views on Jesus of this community which initially
formed around the apostles: the Gospel of the Hebrews (coming
from a Judeo-Christian community in Egypt), the writings of
Clement: Homilies and Recognitions, 'Hypotyposeis', the Second
Apocalypse of James, the Gospel of Thomas.' "It is to the Judeo-
Christians that one must ascribe the oldest writings of Christian
literature." Cardinal Daniélou mentions them in detail.

"It was not just in Jerusalem and Palestine that Judeo-Christianity predominated during the first hundred years of the
Church. The Judeo-Christian mission seems everywhere to have
developed before the Pauline mission. This is certainly the explanation of the fact that the letters of Paul allude to a conflict."
They were the same adversaries he was to meet everywhere: in
Galatia, Corinth, Colossae, Rome and Antioch.

The Syro-Palestinian coast from Gaza to Antioch was Judeo-
Christian "as witnessed by the Acts of the Apostles and Clementine writings". In Asia Minor, the existence of Judeo-Christians is indicated in Paul's letters to the Galatians and Colossians.
Papias's writings give us information about Judeo-Christianity
in Phrygia. In Greece, Paul's first letter to the Corinthians men-

---

1. One could note here that all these writings were later to be classed as
   Apocrypha, i.e. they had to be concealed by the victorious Church which
   was born of Paul's success. This Church made obvious excisions in the
   Gospel literature and retained only the four Canonic Gospels.

tions Judeo-Christians, especially at Apollos. According to Clement's letter and the Shepherd of Hermas, Rome was an 'important centre'. For Suetonius and Tacitus, the Christians represented a Jewish sect. Cardinal Daniélou thinks that the first evangelization in Africa was Judeo-Christian. The Gospel of the Hebrews and the writings of Clement of Alexandria link up with this.

It is essential to know these facts to understand the struggle between communities that formed the background against which the Gospels were written. The texts that we have today, after many adaptations from the sources, began to appear around 70 A.D., the time when the two rival communities were engaged in a fierce struggle, with the Judeo-Christians still retaining the upper hand. With the Jewish war and the fall of Jerusalem in 70 A.D. the situation was to be reversed. This is how Cardinal Daniélou explains the decline:

"After the Jews had been discredited in the Empire, the Christians tended to detach themselves from them. The Hellenistic peoples of Christian persuasion then gained the upper hand: Paul won a posthumous victory; Christianity separated itself politically and sociologically from Judaism; it became the third people. All the same, until the Jewish revolt in 140 A.D., Judeo-Christianity continued to predominate culturally."

From 70 A.D. to a period sometime before 110 A.D. the Gospels of Mark, Matthew, Luke and John were produced. They do not constitute the first written Christian documents: the letters of Paul date from well before them. According to O. Culmann, Paul probably wrote his letter to the Thessalonians in 50 A.D. He had probably disappeared several years prior to the completion of Mark's Gospel.

Paul is the most controversial figure in Christianity. He was considered to be a traitor to Jesus's thought by the latter's family and by the apostles who had stayed in Jerusalem in the circle around James. Paul created Christianity at the expense of those whom Jesus had gathered around him to spread his teachings. He had not known Jesus during his lifetime and he proved the legitimacy of his mission by declaring that Jesus, raised from the dead, had appeared to him on the road to Damascus. It is quite reasonable to ask what Christianity might have been without

Paul and one could no doubt construct all sorts of hypotheses on this subject. As far as the Gospels are concerned however, it is almost certain that if this atmosphere of struggle between communities had not existed, we would not have had the writings we possess today. They appeared at a time of fierce struggle bebetween the two communities. These 'combat writings', as Father Kannengiesser calls them, emerged from the multitude of writings on Jesus. These occurred at the time when Paul's style of Christianity won through definitively, and created its own collection of official texts. These texts constituted the 'Canon' which condemned and excluded as unorthodox any other documents that were not suited to the line adopted by the Church.

The Judeo-Christians have now disappeared as a community with any influence, but one still hears people talking about them under the general term of 'Judaïstic'. This is how Cardinal Daniélou describes their disappearance:

"When they were cut off from the Great Church, that gradually freed itself from its Jewish attachments, they petered out very quickly in the West. In the East however it is possible to find traces of them in the Third and Fourth Centuries A.D., especially in Palestine, Arabia, Transjordania, Syria and Mesopotamia. Others joined in the orthodoxy of the Great Church, at the same time preserving traces of Semitic culture; some of these still persist in the Churches of Ethiopia and Chaldea".

Paul in Romans refutes this!

The Four Gospels.
Sources and History.

In the writings that come from the early stages of Christianity, the Gospels are not mentioned until long after the works of Paul. It was not until the middle of the Second century A.D., after 140 A.D. to be precise, that accounts began to appear concerning a collection of Evangelic writings. In spite of this, "from the beginning of the Second century A.D., many Christian authors clearly intimate that they knew a great many of Paul's letters." These observations are set out in the Introduction to the *Ecumenical Translation of the Bible, New Testament* (Introduction à la Traduction oecuménique de la Bible, Nouveau Testament) edited 1972[1]. They are worth mentioning from the outset, and it is useful to point out here that the work referred to is the result of a collective effort which brought together more than one hundred Catholic and Protestant specialists.

The Gospels, later to become official, i.e. canonic, did not become known until fairly late, even though they were completed at the beginning of the Second century A.D. According to the Ecumenical Translation, stories belonging to them began to be quoted around the middle of the Second century A.D. Nevertheless, "it is nearly always difficult to decide whether the quotations come from written texts that the authors had next to them or if the latter were content to evoke the memory of fragments of the oral tradition."

"Before 140 A.D." we read in the commentaries this translation of the Bible contains, "there was, in any case, no account

---

1. Pub. Editions du Cerf et Les Bergers et les Mages, Paris.

by which one might have recognised a collection of evangelic writings". This statement is the opposite of what A. Tricot writes (1960) in the commentary to his translation of the New Testament: "Very early on, from the beginning of the Second century A.D., it became a habit to say 'Gospel' meaning the books that Saint Justin around 150 A.D. had also called 'The Memoirs of the Apostles'." Unfortunately, assertions of this kind are sufficiently common for the public to have ideas on the date of the Gospels which are mistaken.

The Gospels did not form a complete whole 'very early on'; it did not happen until more than a century after the end of Jesus's mission. The *Ecumenical Translation of the Bible* estimates the date the four Gospels acquired the status of canonic literature at around 170 A.D.

Justin's statement which calls the authors 'Apostles' is not acceptable either, as we shall see.

As far as the date the Gospels were written is concerned, A. Tricot states that Matthew's, Mark's and Luke's Gospels were written before 70 A.D.: but this is not acceptable, except perhaps for Mark. Following many others, this commentator goes out of his way to present the authors of the Gospels as the apostles or the companions of Jesus. For this reason he suggests dates of writing that place them very near to the time Jesus lived. As for John, whom A. Tricot has us believe lived until roughly 100 A.D., Christians have always been used to seeing him depicted as being very near to Jesus on ceremonial occasions. It is very difficult however to assert that he is the author of the Gospel that bears his name. For A. Tricot, as for other commentators, the Apostle John (like Matthew) was the officially qualified witness of the facts he recounts, although the majority of critics do not support the hypothesis which says he wrote the fourth Gospel.

If however the four Gospels in question cannot reasonably be regarded as the 'Memoirs' of the apostles or companions of Jesus, where do they come from?

O. Culmann, in his book *The New Testament* (Le Nouveau Testament)[1], says of this that the evangelists were only the "spokesmen of the early Christian community which wrote down the oral tradition. For thirty or forty years, the Gos-

---

1. Pub. Presses Universitaires de France, Paris, 1967

pel had existed as an almost exclusively oral tradition: the latter only transmitted sayings and isolated narratives. The evangelists strung them together, each in his own way according to his own character and theological preoccupations. They linked up the narrations and sayings handed down by the prevailing tradition. The grouping of Jesus's sayings and likewise the sequence of narratives is made by the use of fairly vague linking phrases such as 'after this', 'when he had' etc. In other words, the 'framework' of the Synoptic Gospels[1] is of a purely literary order and is not based on history."

The same author continues as follows:

"It must be noted that the needs of preaching, worship and teaching, more than biographical considerations, were what guided the early community when it wrote down the tradition of the life of Jesus. The apostles illustrated the truth of the faith they were preaching by describing the events in the life of Jesus. Their sermons are what caused the descriptions to be written down. The sayings of Jesus were transmitted, in particular, in the teaching of the catechism of the early Church."

This is exactly how the commentators of the *Ecumenical Translation of the Bible* (Traduction oecuménique de la Bible) describe the writing of the Gospels: the formation of an oral tradition influenced by the preachings of Jesus's disciples and other preachers; the preservation by preaching of this material, which is in actual fact found in the Gospels, by preaching, liturgy, and teaching of the faithful; the slender possibility of a concrete form given by writings to certain confessions of faith, sayings of Jesus, descriptions of the Passion for example; the fact that the evangelists resort to various written forms as well as data contained in the oral tradition. They resort to these to produce texts which "are suitable for various circles, which meet the needs of the Church, explain observations on the Scriptures, correct errors and even, on occasion, answer adversaries' objections. Thus the evangelists, each according to his own outlook, have collected and recorded in writing the material given to them by the oral tradition".

---

1. The three Gospels of Mark, Matthew and Luke.

This position has been collectively adopted by more than one hundred experts in the exegesis of the New Testament, both Catholic and Protestant. It diverges widely from the line established by the Second Vatican Council in its dogmatic constitution on the Revelation drawn up between 1962 and 1965. This conciliar document has already been referred to once above, when talking of the Old Testament. The Council was able to declare of the latter that the books which compose it "contain material which is imperfect and obsolete", but it has not expressed the same reservations about the Gospels. On the contrary, as we read in the following:

"Nobody can overlook the fact that, among all the Scriptures, even those of the New Testament, the Gospels have a well-deserved position of superiority. This is by virtue of the fact that they represent the most pre-eminent witness to the life and teachings of the Incarnate Word, Our Saviour. At all times and in all places the Church has maintained and still maintains the apostolic origin of the four Gospels. What the apostles actually preached on Christ's orders, both they and the men in their following subsequently transmitted, with the divine inspiration of the Spirit, in writings which are the foundation of the faith, i.e. the fourfold Gospel according to Matthew, Mark, Luke and John."

"Our Holy Mother, the Church, has firmly maintained and still maintains with the greatest constancy, that these four Gospels, which it unhesitatingly confirms are historically authentic, faithfully transmit what Jesus, Son Of God, actually did and taught during his life among men for their eternal salvation until the day when He was taken up into the heavens. . . . The sacred authors therefore composed the four Gospels in such a way as to always give us true and frank information on the life of Jesus".

This is an unambiguous affirmation of the fidelity with which the Gospels transmit the acts and sayings of Jesus.

There is hardly any compatibility between the Council's affirmation and what the authors quoted above claim. In particular the following:

The Gospels *"are not to be taken literally"* they are *"writings suited to an occasion"* or *"combat writings"*. Their authors *"are writing down the traditions of their own community concerning Jesus".* (Father Kannengiesser).

The Gospels are texts which "are suitable for various circles, meet the needs of the Church, explain observations on the Scriptures, correct errors and even, on occasion, answer adversaries' objections. Thus, the evangelists, each according to his own outlook, have collected and recorded in writing the material given to them by the oral tradition". (*Ecumenical Translation of the Bible*).

It is quite clear that we are here faced with contradictory statements: the declaration of the Council on the one hand, and more recently adopted attitudes on the other. According to the declaration of the Second Vatican Council, a faithful account of the actions and words of Jesus is to be found in the Gospels; but it is impossible to reconcile this with the existence in the text of contradictions, improbabilities, things which are materially impossible or statements which run contrary to firmly established reality.

If, on the other hand, one chooses to regard the Gospels as expressing the personal point of view of those who collected the oral traditions that belonged to various communities, or as writings suited to an occasion or combat-writings, it does not come as a surprise to find faults in the Gospels. All these faults are the sign that they were written by men in circumstances such as these. The writers may have been quite sincere, even though they relate facts without doubting their inaccuracy. They provide us with descriptions which contradict other authors' narrations, or are influenced by reasons of religious rivalry between communities. They therefore present stories about the life of Jesus from a completely different angle than their adversaries.

It has already been shown how the historical context is in harmony with the second approach to the Gospels. The data we have on the texts themselves definitively confirms it.

THE GOSPEL ACCORDING TO MATTHEW

Matthew's is the first of the four Gospels as they appear in the New Testament. This position is perfectly justified by the fact that it is a prolongation, as it were, of the Old Testament.

It was written to show that "Jesus fulfilled the history of Israel", as the commentators of the *Ecumenical Translation of the Bible* note and on which we shall be drawing heavily. To do so, Matthew constantly refers to quotations from the Old Testament which show how Jesus acted as if he were the Messiah the Jews were awaiting.

This Gospel begins with a genealogy of Jesus[1]. Matthew traces it back to Abraham via David. We shall presently see the fault in the text that most commentators silently ignore. Matthew's obvious intention was nevertheless to indicate the general tenor of his work straight away by establishing this line of descendants. The author continues the same line of thought by constantly bringing to the forefront Jesus's attitude toward Jewish law, the main principles of which (praying, fasting, and dispensing charity) are summarized here.

Jesus addresses His teachings first and foremost to His own people. This is how He speaks to the twelve Apostles: "Go nowhere among the Gentiles, and enter no town of the Samaritans[2] but go rather to the lost sheep of the house of Israel." (Matthew 10, 5-6). "I was sent only to the lost sheep of the house of Israel". (Matthew 15, 24). At the end of his Gospel, in second place, Matthew extends the apostolic mission of Jesus's first disciples to all nations. He makes Jesus give the following order: "Go therefore and make disciples of all nations" (Matthew 28, 19), but the primary destination must be the 'house of Israel'. A. Tricot says of this Gospel, "Beneath its Greek garb, the flesh and bones of this book are Jewish, and so is its spirit; it has a Jewish feel and bears its distinctive signs".

On the basis of these observations alone, the origins of Matthew's Gospel may be placed in the tradition of a Judeo-Christian community. According to O. Culmann, this community "was trying to break away from Judaism while at the same time preserving the continuity of the Old Testament. The main preoccupations and the general tenor of this Gospel point towards a strained situation."

---

1. The fact that it is in contradiction with Luke's Gospel will be dealt with in a separate chapter.
2. The Samaritans' religious code was the Torah or Pentateuch; they lived in the expectation of the Messiah and were faithful to most Jewish observances, but they had built a rival Temple to the one at Jerusalem.

There are also political factors to be found in the text. The Roman occupation of Palestine naturally heightened the desire of this country to see itself liberated. They prayed for God to intervene in favour of the people He had chosen among all others, and as their omnipotent sovereign who could give direct support to the affairs of men, as He had already done many times in the course of history.

What sort of person was Matthew? Let us say straight away that he is no longer acknowledged to be one of Jesus's companions. A. Tricot nevertheless presents him as such in his commentary to the translation of the New Testament, 1960: "Matthew alias, Levi, was a customs officer employed at the toll-gate or customs house at Capharnaum when Jesus called him to be one of His disciples." This is the opinion of the Fathers of the Church, Origen, Jerome and Epiphanes. This opinion is no longer held today. One point which is uncontested is that the author is writing "for people who speak Greek, but nevertheless know Jewish customs and the Aramaic language."

It would seem that for the commentators of the Ecumenical Translation, the origins of this Gospel are as follows:

"It is normally considered to have been written in Syria, perhaps at Antioch (. . .), or in Phoenicia, because a great many Jews lived in these countries.[1] (. . .) we have indications of a polemic against the orthodox Judaism of the Synagogue and the Pharasees such as was manifested at the synagogal assembly at Jamina circa 80 A.D." In such conditions, there are many authors who date the first of the Gospels at about 80-90 A.D., perhaps also a little earlier; it is not possible to be absolutely definite about this . . . since we do not know the author's exact name, we must be satisfied with a few outlines traced in the Gospel itself: the author can be recognized by his profession. He is well-versed in Jewish writings and traditions. He knows, respects, but vigorously challenges the religious leaders of his people. He is a past master in the art of teaching and making Jesus understandable to his listeners. He always insists on the practical consequences of his teachings. He would fit fairly well the description of an

---

1. It has been thought that the Judeo-Christian community that Matthew belonged to might just as easily have been situated at Alexandria. O. Culmann refers to this hypothesis along with many others.

lucated Jew turned Christian; a householder "who brings out of
s treasure what is new and what is old" as Matthew says
13,52). This is a long way from the civil servant at Caphar-
ium, whom Mark and Luke call Levi, and who had become one
the twelve Apostles ...

Everyone agrees in thinking that Matthew wrote his Gospel
sing the same sources as Mark and Luke. His narration is, as
e shall see, different on several essential points. In spite of this,
atthew borrowed heavily from Mark's Gospel although the
tter was not one of Jesus's disciples (O. Cullmann).

Matthew takes very serious liberties with the text. We shall
e this when we discuss the Old Testament in relation to the
enealogy of Jesus which is placed at the beginning of his Gospel.
e inserts into his book descriptions which are quite literally
credible. This is the adjective used in the work mentioned above
ァ Father Kannengiesser referring to an episode in the Resur-
ction; the episode of the guard. He points out the improbability
' the story referring to military guards at the tomb, "these
entile soldiers" who "report, not to their hierarchical superiors,
it to the high priests who pay them to tell lies". He adds how-
'er: "One must not laugh at him because Matthew's intention
as extremely serious. In his own way he incorporates ancient
ita from the oral tradition into his written work. The scenario
nevertheless worthy of *Jesus Christ Superstar.*[1]"

Let us not forget that this opinion on Matthew comes from
i eminent theologian teaching at the Catholic Institute of Paris
nstitut Catholique de Paris).

Matthew relates in his narration the events accompanying the
ath of Jesus. They are another example of his imagination.

"And behold, the curtain of the temple was torn in two, from
p to bottom; and the earth shook, and the rocks were split; the
mbs also were opened, and many bodies of the saints who had
llen asleep were raised, and coming out of tombs after his
surrection they went into the holy city and appeared to many."

This passage from Matthew (27, 51-53) has no corresponding
issage in the other Gospels. It is difficult to see how the bodies
' the saints in question could have raised from the dead *at the
me of Jesus's death* (according to the Gospels it was on the eve

---

. An American film which parodies the life of Jesus.

of the Sabbath) and only emerge from their tombs *after his res*
urrection (according to the same sources on the day after th
Sabbath).

The most notable improbability is perhaps to be found in Mat
thew. It is the most difficult to rationalize of all that the Gospe
authors claim Jesus said. He relates in chapter 12, 38-40 th
episode concerning Jonah's sign:

Jesus was among the scribes and pharisees who addressed hir
in the following terms:

"Teacher, we wish to see a sign from you." But he answere
them, "An evil and adulterous generation seeks for a sign; bu
no sign shall be given to it except the sign of the prophet Jonah
For as Jonah was three days and three nights in the belly of th
whale, so will the Son of Man be three days and three nights i
the heart of the earth."

Jesus therefore proclaims that he will stay in the earth thre
days and three nights. So Matthew, along with Luke and Mark
place the death and burial of Jesus on the eve of the Sabbath
This, of course, makes the time spent in the earth three day
(*treis émeras* in the Greek text), but this period can only includ
two and not three nights (*treis nuktas* in the Greek text[1]).

Gospel commentators frequently ignore this episode. Fathe
Roguet nevertheless points out this improbability when he note
that Jesus "only stayed in the tomb" three days (one of them
complete) and two nights. He adds however that "it is a set ex
pression and really means three days". It is disturbing to se
commentators reduced to using arguments that do not contair
any positive meaning. It would be much more satisfying intellec-
tually to say that a gross error such as this was the result of a
scribe's mistake!

Apart from these improbabilities, what mostly distinguishe
Matthew's Gospel is that it is the work of a Judeo-Christian
community in the process of breaking away from Judaism while
remaining in line with the Old Testament. From the point of
view of Judeo-Christian history it is very important.

---

1. In another part of his Gospel Matthew again refers to this episode but
   without being precise about the time (16, 1-4). The same is true for
   Luke (11, 29-32). We shall see later on how in Mark, Jesus is said to
   have declared that no sign would be given to that generation (Mark
   8, 11-12).

THE GOSPEL ACCORDING TO MARK

This is the shortest of the four Gospels. It is also the oldest, but in spite of this it is not a book written by an apostle. At best it was written by an apostle's disciple.

O. Culmann has written that he does not consider Mark to be a disciple of Jesus. The author nevertheless points out, to those who have misgivings about the ascription of this Gospel to the Apostle Mark, that "Matthew and Luke would not have used this Gospel in the way they did had they not known that it was indeed based on the teachings of an apostle". This argument is in no way decisive. O. Culmann backs up the reservations he expresses by saying that he frequently quotes from the New Testament the sayings of a certain 'John nicknamed Mark'. These quotations do not however mention the name of a Gospel author, and the text of Mark itself does not name any author.

The paucity of information on this point has led commentators to dwell on details that seem rather extravagant: using the pretext, for example, that Mark was the only evangelist to relate in his description of the Passion the story of the young man who had nothing but a linen cloth about his body and, when seized, left the linen cloth and ran away naked (Mark 14, 51-52), they conclude that the young man must have been Mark, "the faithful disciple who tried to follow the teacher" (Ecumenical Translation). Other commentators see in this "personal memory a sign of authenticity, an anonymous signature", which "proves that he was an eyewitness" (O. Culmann).

O. Culmann considers that "many turns of phrase corroborate the hypothesis that the author was of Jewish origin," but the presence of Latin expressions might suggest that he had written his Gospel in Rome. "He addresses himself moreover to Christians not living in Palestine and is careful to explain the Aramic expressions he uses."

Tradition has indeed tended to see Mark as Peter's companion in Rome. It is founded on the final section of Peter's first letter (always supposing that he was indeed the author). Peter wrote in his letter: "The community which is at Babylon, which is likewise chosen, sends you greetings; and so does my son Mark." "By Babylon, what is probably meant is Rome" we read in the commentary to the Ecumenical Translation. From this, the commentators then imagine themselves authorized to conclude that Mark, who was supposed to have been with Peter in Rome, was the Evangelist . . .One wonders whether it was not the same line of reasoning that led Papias, Bishop of Hierapolis in circa 150 A.D., to ascribe this Gospel to Mark as 'Peter's interpreter' and the possible collaborator of Paul.

Seen from this point of view, the composition of Mark's Gospel could be placed after Peter's death, i.e. at between 65 and 70 A.D. for the Ecumenical Translation and circa 70 A.D. for O. Culmann.

The text itself unquestionably reveals a major flaw; it is written with a total disregard to chronology. Mark therefore places, at the beginning of his narration (1, 16-20), the episode of the four fishermen whom Jesus leads to follow him by simply saying "I will make you become fishers of men", though they do not even know Him. The evangelist shows, among other things, a complete lack of plausibility.

As Father Roguet has said, Mark is 'a clumsy writer', 'the weakest of all the evangelists'; he hardly knows how to write a narrative. The commentator reinforces his observation by quoting a passage about how the twelve Apostles were selected.

Here is the literal translation:

"And he went up into the hills, and called to him those whom he desired; and they came to him. And he made that the twelve were to be with him, and to be sent out to preach and have authority to cast out demons; and he made the twelve and imposed the name Simon on Peter" (Mark, 3, 13-16).

He contradicts Matthew and Luke, as has already been noted above, with regard to the sign of Jonah. On the subject of signs given by Jesus to men in the course of His mission Mark (8, 11-13) describes an episode that is hardly credible:

"The Pharisees came and began to argue with him, seeking from him a sign from heaven, to test him. And he sighed deeply in his spirit, and said, 'Why does this generation seek a sign? Truly, I say to you, no sign shall be given to this generation.' And he left them, and getting into the boat again he departed to the other side."

There can be no doubt that this is an affirmation coming from Jesus Himself about his intention not to commit any act which might appear supernatural. Therefore the commentators of the

Ecumenical Translation, who are surprised that Luke says Jesus will only give one sign (the sign of Jonah; see Matthew's Gospel), consider it 'paradoxical' that Mark should say "no sign shall be given to this generation" seeing, as they note, the "miracles that Jesus himself gives as a sign" (Luke 7,22 and 11,20).

Mark's Gospel as a whole is officially recognised as being canonic. All the same, the final section of Mark's Gospel (16,19-20) is considered by modern authors to have been tacked on to the basic work: the Ecumenical Translation is quite explicit about this.

This final section is not contained in the two oldest complete manuscripts of the Gospels, the *Codex Vaticanus* and the *Codex Sinaiticus* that date from the Fourth century A.D. O. Gulmann notes on this subject that: "More recent Greek manuscripts and certain versions at this point added a conclusion on appearances which is not drawn from Mark but from the other Gospels." In fact, the versions of this added ending are very numerous. In the texts there are long and short versions (both are reproduced in the Bible, Revised Standard Version, 1952). Sometimes the long version has some additional material.

Father Kannengiesser makes the following comments on the ending: "The last verses must have been surpressed when his work was officially received (or the popular version of it) in the community that guaranteed its validity. Neither Matthew, Luke or a *fortiori* John saw the missing section. Nevertheless, the gap was unacceptable. A long time afterwards, when the writings of Matthew, Luke and John, all of them similar, had been in circulation, a worthy ending to Mark was composed. Its elements were taken from sources throughout the other Gospels. It would be easy to recognise the pieces of the puzzle by enumerating Mark (16,9-20). One would gain a more concrete idea of the free way in which the literary genre of the evangelic narration was handled until the beginnings of the Second century A.D."

What a blunt admission is provided for us here, in the thoughts of a great theologian, that human manipulation exists in the texts of the Scriptures!

THE GOSPEL ACCORDING TO LUKE

For O. Culmann, Luke is a 'chronicler', and for Father Kannengiesser he is a 'true novelist'. In his prologue to Theophilus, Luke warns us that he, in his turn, following on from others who have written accounts concerning Jesus, is going to write a narrative of the same facts using the accounts and information of eyewitnesses—implying that he himself is not one—including information from the apostles' preachings. It is therefore to be a methodical piece of work which he introduces in the following terms:

"Inasmuch as many have undertaken to compile a narrative of the things which have been accomplished among us, just as they were delivered to us by those who from the beginning were eyewitnesses and ministers of the word, it seemed good to me also, having informed myself about all things from their beginnings, to write an orderly account for you, most excellent Theophilus, that you may know the truth concerning things of which you have been informed."

From the very first line one can see all that separates Luke from the 'scribbler' Mark to whose work we have just referred. Luke's Gospel is incontestably a literary work written in classical Greek free from any barbarisms.

Luke was a cultivated Gentile convert to Christianity. His attitude towards the Jews is immediately apparent. As O. Culmann points out, Luke leaves out Mark's most Judaic verses and highlights the Jews' incredulity at Jesus's words, throwing into relief his good relations with the Samaritans, whom the Jews detested. Matthew, on the other hand, has Jesus ask the apostles to flee from them. This is just one of many striking examples of the fact that the evangelists make Jesus say whatever suits their own personal outlook. They probably do so with sincere conviction. They give us the version of Jesus's words that is adapted to the point of view of their own community. How can one deny in the face of such evidence that the Gospels are 'combat writings' or 'writings suited to an occasion', as has been mentioned already? The comparison between the general tone of Luke's Gospel and Matthew's is in this respect a good demonstration.

Who was Luke? An attempt has been made to identify him with the physician of the same name referred to by Paul in several of his letters. The Ecumenical Translation notes that "several commentators have found the medical occupation of the author of this Gospel confirmed by the precision with which he describes the sick". This assessment is in fact exaggerated out of all proportion. Luke does not properly speaking 'describe' things of this kind; "the vocabulary he uses is that of a cultivated man of his time". There was a Luke who was Paul's travelling companion, but was he the same person? O. Culmann thinks he was.

The date of Luke's Gospel can be estimated according to several factors: Luke used Mark's and Matthew's Gospels. From what we read in the Ecumenical Translation, it seems that he witnessed the siege and destruction of Jerusalem by Titus's armies in 70 A.D. The Gospel probably dates from after this time. Present-day critics situate the time it was written at circa 80-90 A.D., but several place it at an even earlier date.

The various narrations in Luke show important differences when compared to his predecessors. An outline of this has already been given. The Ecumenical Translation indicates them on pages 181 et sec. O. Culmann, in his book, *The New Testament* (Le Nouveau Testament) page 18, cites descriptions in Luke's Gospel that are not to be found anywhere else. And they are not about minor points of detail.

The descriptions of Jesus's childhood are unique to Luke's Gospel. Matthew describes Jesus's childhood differently from Luke, and Mark does not mention it at all.

Matthew and Luke both provide different genealogies of Jesus: the contradictions are so large and the improbabilities so great, from a scientific point of view, that a special chapter of this book has been devoted to the subject. It is possible to explain why Matthew, who was addressing himself to Jews, should begin the genealogy at Abraham, and include David in it, and that Luke, as a converted Gentile, should want to go back even farther. We shall see however that the two genealogies contradict each other from David onwards.

Jesus's mission is described differently on many points by Luke, Matthew and Mark.

An event of such great importance to Christians as the institution of the Eucharist gives rise to variations between Luke

and the other two evangelists.[1] Father Roguet notes in his book
Initiation to the Gospel (Initiation à l'Evangile) page 75, that
the words used to institute the Eucharist are reported by Luke
(22,19-24) in a form very different from the wording in Matthew
(26,26-29) and in Mark (14,22-24) which is almost identical.
"On the contrary" he writes, "the wording transmitted by Luke
is very similar to that evoked by Saint Paul" (First Letter to the
Corinthians, 11,23-25).

As we have seen, in his Gospel, Luke expresses ideas on the
subject of Jesus's Ascension which contradict what he says in
the Acts of the Apostles. He is recognized as their author and
they form an integral part of the New Testament. In his Gospel
he situates the Ascension on Easter Day, and in the Acts forty
days later. We already know to what strange commentaries this
contradiction has led Christian experts in exegesis.

Commentators wishing to be objective, such as those of the
Ecumenical Translation of the Bible, have been obliged to recognise as a general rule the fact that for Luke "the main preoccu-
pation was not to write facts corresponding to material accuracy". When Father Kannengiesser compares the descriptions in
the Acts of the Apostles written by Luke himself with the description of similar facts on Jesus raised from the dead by Paul,
he pronounces the following opinion on Luke: "Luke is the most
sensitive and literary of the four evangelists, he has all the qualities of a true novelist".

THE GOSPEL ACCORDING TO JOHN

John's Gospel is radically different from the three others; to
such an extent indeed that Father Roguet in his book *Initiation
to the Gospel* (Initiation à l'Evangile), having commented on the
other three, immediately evokes a startling image for the fourth.
He calls it ' different world'. It is indeed a unique book; different in the arrangement and choice of subject, description and
speech; different in its style, geography, chronology; there are
even differences in theological outlook (O. Culmann). Jesus's

---

1. It is not possible to establish a comparison with John because he does
not refer to the institution of the Eucharist during the Last Supper
prior to the Passion.

words are therefore differently recorded by John from the other evangelists: Father Roguet notes on this that whereas the synoptics record Jesus's words in a style that is "striking, much nearer to the oral style", in John all is meditation; to such an extent indeed that "one sometimes wonders if Jesus is still speaking or whether His ideas have not imperceptibly been extended by the Evangelist's own thoughts".

Who was the author? This is a highly debated question and extremely varying opinions have been expressed on this subject.

A. Tricot and Father Roguet belong to a camp that does not have the slightest misgivings: John's Gospel is the work of an eyewitness, its author is John, son of Zebedee and brother of James. Many details are known about this apostle and are set out in works for mass publication. Popular iconography puts him near Jesus, as in the Last Supper prior to the Passion. Who could imagine that John's Gospel was not the work of John the Apostle whose figure is so familiar?

The fact that the fourth Gospel was written so late is not a serious argument against this opinion. The definitive version was probably written around the end of the First century A.D. To situate the time it was written at sixty years after Jesus would be in keeping with an apostle who was very young at the time of Jesus and who lived to be almost a hundred.

Father Kannengiesser, in his study on the Resurrection, arrives at the conclusion that none of the New Testament authors, save Paul, can claim to have been eyewitnesses to Jesus's Resurrection. John nevertheless related the appearance to a number of the assembled apostles, of which he was probably a member, in the absence of Thomas (20,19-24), then eight days later to the full group of apostles (20,25-29).

O. Culmann in his work *The New Testament* does not subscribe to this view.

The *Ecumenical Translation of the Bible* states that the majority of critics do not accept the hypothesis that the Gospel was written by John, although this possibility cannot be entirely ruled out. Everything points however towards the fact that the text we know today had several authors: "It is probable that the Gospel as it stands today was put into circulation by the author's disciples who added chapter 21 and very likely several annotations (i.e. 4,2 and perhaps 4,1; 4,44; 7,37b; 11,2; 19,35). With regard to the story of the adulterous woman (7,53-8,11), everyone agrees that it is a fragment of unknown origin inserted later (but nevertheless belonging to canonic Scripture)". Passage 19,35 appears as a 'signature' of an 'eyewitness' (O. Culmann), the only explicit signature in the whole of John's Gospel; but commentators believe that it was probably added later.

O. Culmann thinks that latter additions are obvious in this Gospel; such as chapter 21 which is probably the work of a "disciple who may well have made slight alterations to the main body of the Gospel".

It is not necessary to mention all the hypotheses suggested by experts in exegesis. The remarks recorded here made by the most eminent Christian writers on the questions of the authorship of the fourth Gospel are sufficient to show the extent of the confusion reigning on the subject of its authorship.

The historical value of John's stories has been contested to a great extent. The discrepancy between them and the other three Gospels is quite blatant. O. Culman offers an explanation for this; he sees in John a different theological point of view from the other evangelists. This aim "directs the choice of stories from the Logia[1] recorded, as well as the way in which they are reproduced . . . Thus the author often prolongs the lines and makes the historical Jesus say what the Holy Spirit Itself revealed to Him". This, for the exegete in question, is the reason for the discrepancies.

It is of course quite conceivable that John, who was writing after the other evangelists, should have chosen certain stories suitable for illustrating his own theories. One should not be surprised by the fact that certain descriptions contained in the other Gospels are missing in John. The *Ecumenical Translation* picks out a certain number of such instances (page 282). Certain gaps hardly seem credible however, like the fact that the Institution of the Eucharist is not described. It is unthinkable that an episode so basic to Christianity, one indeed that was to be the mainstay of its liturgy, i.e. the mass, should not be mentioned by John, the most pre-eminently meditative evangelist. The fact is, he limits himself, in the narrative of the supper prior to the Passion, to

1. Words.

imply describing the washing of the disciples' feet, the predic-
ion of Judas's betrayal and Peter's denial.

In contrast to this, there are stories which are unique to John
and not present in the other three. The Ecumenical Translation
mentions these (page 283). Here again, one could infer that the
hree authors did not see the importance in these episodes that
John saw in them. It is difficult however not to be taken aback
when one finds in John a description of the appearance of Jesus
raised from the dead to his disciples beside the Sea of Tiberias
(John 21,1-14). The description is nothing less than the reproduction (with numerous added details) of the miracle catch of
fish which Luke (5,1-11) presents as an episode that occurred
during Jesus's life. In his description Luke alludes to the presence
of the Apostle John who, as tradition has it, was the evangelist.
Since this description in John's Gospel forms part of chapter 21,
agreed to be a later addition, one can easily imagine that the
reference to John's name in Luke could have led to its artificial
inclusion in the fourth Gospel. The necessity of transforming a
description from Jesus's life to a posthumous description in no
way prevented the evangelical text from being manipulated.

Another important point on which John's Gospel differs from
the other three is in the duration of Jesus's mission. Mark, Matthew and Luke place it over a period of one year. John spreads
it over two years. O. Culmann notes this fact. On this subject the
Ecumenical Translation expresses the following:

"The synoptics describe a long period in Galilee followed by a
march that was more or less prolonged towards Judea, and finally
a brief stay in Jerusalem. John, on the other hand, describes frequent journeys from one area to another and mentions a long
stay in Judea, especially in Jerusalem (1,19-51; 2,13-3,36; 5,1-
47; 14,20-31). He mentions several Passover celebrations (2,13;
5,1; 6,4; 11,55) and thus suggests a ministry that lasted more
than two years".

Which one of them should one believe—Mark, Matthew, Luke
or John?

SOURCES OF THE GOSPELS

The general outline that has been given here of the Gospels
and which emerges from a critical examination of the texts tends

to make one think of a literature which is "disjointed, with plan that lacks continuity" and "seemingly insuperable contra dictions". These are the terms used in the judgement passed o them by the commentators of the *Ecumenical Translation of th Bible*. It is important to refer to their authority because the con sequences of an appraisal of this subject are extremely serious It has already been seen how a few notions concerning the re ligious history of the time when the Gospels were written helpe to explain certain disconcerting aspects of this literature ap parent to the thoughtful reader. It is necessary to continue, how ever, and ascertain what present-day works can tell us about th sources the Evangelists drew on when writing their texts. It i also interesting to see whether the history of the texts once the were established can help to explain certain aspects they presen today.

The problem of sources was approached in a very simplistic fashion at the time of the Fathers of the Church. In the early centuries of Christianity, the only source available was the Gospel that the complete manuscripts provided first, i.e. Matthew's Gospel. The problem of sources only concerned Mark and Luke because John constituted a quite separate case. Saint Augustine held that Mark, who appears second in the traditional order of presentation, had been inspired by Matthew and had summarized his work. He further considered that Luke, who comes third in the manuscripts, had used data from both; his prologue suggests this, and has already been discussed.

The experts in exegesis at this period were as able as we are to estimate the degree of corroboration between the texts and find a large number of verses common to two or three synoptics. Today, the commentators of the *Ecumenical Translation of the Bible* provide the following figures :

        verses common to all three synoptics 330
        verses common to Mark and Matthew 178
        verses common to Mark and Luke 100
        verses common to Matthew and Luke 230

The verses unique to each of the first three Gospels are as follows: Matthew 330, Mark 53, and Luke 500.

From the Fathers of the Church until the end of the Eighteenth century A.D., one and a half millenia passed without any w problems being raised on the sources of the evangelists: ople continued to follow tradition. It was not until modern nes that it was realized, on the basis of these data, how each angelist had taken material found in the others and compiled own specific narration guided by his own personal views. eat weight was attached to actual collection of material for the rration. It came from the oral traditions of the communities m which it originated on the one hand, and from a common itten Aramaic source that has not been rediscovered on the er. This written source could have formed a compact mass or ve been composed of many fragments of different narrations d by each evangelist to construct his own original work.

More intensive studies in circa the last hundred years have led heories which are more detailed and in time will become even re complicated. The first of the modern theories is the so-called Itzmann Two Sources Theory', (1863). O. Culmann and the menical Translation explain that, according to this theory, tthew and Luke may have been inspired by Mark on the one d and on the other by a common document which has since n lost. The first two moreover each had his own sources. This ls to the following diagram:

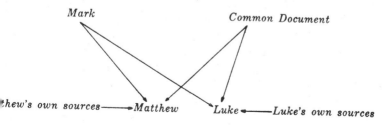

ulmann criticises the above on the following points:

Mark's work, used by both Luke and Matthew, was probably not the author's Gospel but an earlier version.

The diagram does not lay enough emphasis on the oral tradition. This appears to be of paramount importance because it alone preserved Jesus's words and the descriptions of his mission during a period of thirty or forty years, as each of the Evangelists was only the spokesman for the Christian community which wrote down the oral tradition.

This is how it is possible to conclude that the Gospels we possess today are a reflection of what the early Christian communities knew of Jesus's life and ministry. They also mirror their beliefs and theological ideas, of which the evangelists were the spokesmen.

The latest studies in textual criticism on the sources of the Gospels have clearly shown an even more complicated formation process of the texts. A book by Fathers Benoit and Boismard both professors at the Biblical School of Jerusalem (1972-1973) called the *Synopsis of the Four Gospels* (Synopse des quatre Evangiles) stresses the evolution of the text in stages parallel to the evolution of the tradition. This implies the conquences set out by Father Benoit in his introduction to Father Boismard' part of the work. He presents them in the following terms:

"(. . .) the wording and form of description that result from a long evolution of tradition are not as authentic as in the original. Some readers of this work will perhaps be surprised or embarrassed to learn that certain of Jesus sayings, parables, or predictions of His destiny were not expressed in the way we read them today, but were altered and adapted by those who transmitted them to us. This may come as a source of amazement and even scandal to those not used to this kind of historical investigation."

The alterations and adaptations to the texts made by those transmitting them to us were done in a way that Father Boismard explains by means of a highly complex diagram. It is development of the so-called 'Two Sources Theory', and is the product of examination and comparison of the texts which it not possible to summarize here. Those readers who are interested in obtaining further details should consult the original work published by Les Editions du Cerf, Paris.

Four basic documents—A, B, C and Q—represent the original sources of the Gospels (see general diagram). Page 76.

Document A comes from a Judeo-Christian source. Matthew and Mark were inspired by it.

Document B is a reinterpretation of document A, for use Pagan-cum-Christian churches: all the evangelists were inspired by it except Matthew.

Document C inspired Mark, Luke and John.

Document Q constitutes the majority of sources common to Matthew and Luke; it is the 'Common Document' in the 'Two Sources' theory referred to earlier.

None of these basic documents led to the production of the definitive texts we know today. Between them and the final version lay the intermediate versions: Intermediate Matthew, Intermediate Mark, Intermediate Luke and Intermediate John. These four intermediate documents were to lead to the final versions of the four Gospels, as well as to inspire the final corresponding versions of other Gospels. One only has to consult the diagram to see the intricate relationships the author has revealed.

The results of this scriptural research are of great importance. They show how the Gospel texts not only have a history (to be discussed later) but also a 'pre-history', to use Father Boismard's expression. What is meant is that before the final versions appeared, they underwent alterations at the Intermediate Document stage. Thus it is possible to explain, for example, how a well-known story from Jesus's life, such as the miracle catch of fish, is shown in Luke to be an event that happened during His life, and in John to be one of His appearances after His Resurrection.

The conclusion to be drawn from the above is that when we read the Gospel, we can no longer be at all sure that we are reading Jesus's word. Father Benoit addresses himself to the readers of the Gospel by warning them and giving them the following compensation: "If the reader is obliged in more than one case to give up the notion of hearing Jesus's voice directly, he still hears the voice of the Church and he relies upon it as the divinely appointed interpreter of the Master who long ago spoke to us on earth and who now speaks to us in His glory".

How can one reconcile this formal statement of the inauthenticity of certain texts with the phrase used in the dogmatic constitution on Divine Revelation by the Second Vatican Council assuring us to the contrary, i.e. the faithful transmission of Jesus's words: "These four Gospels, which it (the Church) unhesitatingly confirms are historically authentic, faithfully transmit what Jesus, Son of God, actually did and taught during his life among men for their eternal salvation, until the day when he was taken up into the heavens"?

It is quite clear that the work of the Biblical School of Jerusalem flatly contradicts the Council's declaration.

M. E. BOISMARD
SYNOPSIS OF THE FOUR GOSPELS[1]
GENERAL DIAGRAM
(1) Synopse des quatre Evangiles

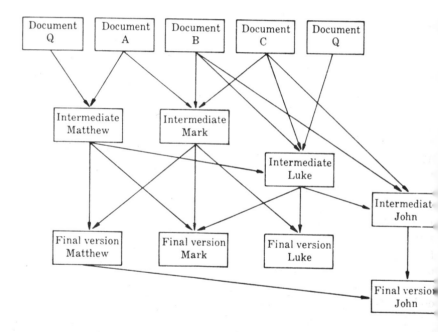

Documents A, B, C, Q = Basic documents used in the compiling of the texts.

Intermediate   = Intermediate version of the text

HISTORY OF THE TEXTS

One would be mistaken in thinking that once the Gospels were ~ritten they constituted the basic Scriptures of the newly born ~hristianity and that people referred to them the same way they ~eferred to the Old Testament. At that time, the foremost author-~y was the oral tradition as a vehicle for Jesus's words and the ~achings of the apostles. The first writings to circulate were ~aul's letters and they occupied a prevalent position long before ~e Gospels. They were, after all, written several decades earlier.

It has already been shown, that contrary to what certain com-~entators are still writing today, before 140 A.D. there was no ~itness to the knowledge that a collection of Gospel writings ~xisted. It was not until circa 170 A.D. that the four Gospels ac-~uired the status of canonic literature.

In the early days of Christianity, many writings on Jesus ~ere in circulation. They were not subsequently retained as being ~orthy of authenticity and the Church ordered them to be ~idden, hence their name 'Apocrypha'. Some of the texts of these ~orks have been well preserved because they "benefitted from ~e fact that they were generally valued", to quote the Ecumen-~al Translation. The same was true for the Letter of Barnabas, ~ut unfortunately others were "more brutally thrust aside" and ~nly fragments of them remain. They were considered to be the ~essengers of error and were removed from the sight of the ~aithful. Works such as the Gospels of the Nazarenes, the Gospels ~f the Hebrews and the Gospels of the Egyptians, known through ~uotations taken from the Fathers of the Church, were neverthe-~ss fairly closely related to the canonic Gospels. The same holds ~ood for Thomas's Gospel and Barnabas's Gospel.

Some of these apocryphal writings contain imaginary details, ~e product of popular fantasy. Authors of works on the Apoc-~ypha also quote with obvious satisfaction passages which are ~terally ridiculous. Passages such as these are however to be ~ound in *all* the Gospels. One has only to think of the imaginary ~escription of events that Matthew claims took place at Jesus's ~eath. It is possible to find passages lacking seriousness in all the ~arly writings of Christianity: One must be honest enough to ad-~it this.

The abundance of literature concerning Jesus led the Church to make certain excisions while the latter was in the process of becoming organized. Perhaps a hundred Gospels were suppressed. Only four were retained and put on the official list of neo-Testament writings making up what is called the 'Canon'.

In the middle of the Second century A.D., Marcion of Sinope put heavy pressure on the ecclesiastic authorities to take a stand on this. He was an ardent enemy of the Jews and at that time rejected the whole of the Old Testament and everything in writings produced after Jesus that seemed to him too close to the Old Testament or to come from the Judeo-Christian tradition. Marcion only acknowledged the value of Luke's Gospel because, he believed Luke to be the spokesman of Paul and his writings.

The Church declared Marcion a heretic and put into its canon all the Letters of Paul, but included the other Gospels of Matthew, Mark, Luke and John. They also added several other works such as the Acts of the Apostles. The official list nevertheless varies with time during the first centuries of Christianity. For a while, works that were later considered not to be valid (i.e. Apocrypha) figured in it, while other works contained in today's New Testament Canon were excluded from it at this time. These hesitations lasted until the Councils of Hippo Regius in 393 and Carthage in 397. The four Gospels always figured in it however.

One may join Father Boismard in regretting the disappearance of a vast quantity of literature declared apocryphal by the Church although it was of historical interest. The above author indeed gives it a place in his *Synopsis of the Four Gospels* alongside that of the official Gospels. He notes that these books still existed in libraries near the end of the Fourth century A.D.

This was the century that saw things put into serious order. The oldest manuscripts of the Gospels date from this period. Documents prior to this, i.e. papyri from the Third century A.D. and one possibly dating from the Second, only transmit fragments to us. The two oldest parchment manuscripts are Greek. Fourth century A.D. They are the *Codex Vaticanus*, preserved in the Vatican Library and whose place of discovery is unknown, and the *Codex Sinaiticus*, which was discovered on Mount Sinai and is now preserved in the British Museum, London. The second contains two apocryphal works.

According to the Ecumenical Translation, two hundred and fifty other known parchments exist throughout the world, the last of these being from the Eleventh century A.D. "Not all the copies of the New Testament that have come down to us are identical" however. "On the contrary, it is possible to distinguish differences of varying degrees of importance between them, but however important they may be, there is always a large number of them. Some of these only concern differences of grammatical detail, vocabulary or word order. Elsewhere however, differences between manuscripts can be seen which affect the meaning of whole passages". If one wishes to see the extent of textual differences, one only has to glance through the *Novum Testamentum Graece*.[1] This work contains a so-called 'middle-of-the-road' Greek text. It is a text of synthesis with notes containing all the variations found in the different versions.

The authenticity of a text, and of even the most venerable manuscript, is always open to debate. The *Codex Vaticanus* is a good example of this. The facsimile reproductions edited by the Vatican City, 1965, contains an accompanying note from its editors informing us that "several centuries after it was copied (believed to have been in circa the Tenth or Eleventh century), a scribe inked over all the letters except those he thought were a mistake". There are passages in the text where the original letters in light brown still show through, contrasting visibly with the rest of the text which is in dark brown. There is no indication that it was a faithful restoration. The note states moreover that "the different hands that corrected and annotated the manuscript over the centuries have not yet been definitively discerned; a certain number of corrections were undoubtedly made when the text was inked over." In all the religious manuals the text is presented as a Fourth century copy. One has to go to sources at the Vatican to discover that various hands may have altered the text centuries later.

One might reply that other texts may be used for comparison, but how does one choose between variations that change the meaning? It is a well known fact that a very old scribe's correc-

---

1. Nestlé-Aland Pub. United Bible Societies, London, 1971.

tion can lead to the definitive reproduction of the corrected te*
We shall see further on how a single word in a passage fr*
John concerning the Paraclete radically alters its meaning a*
completely changes its sense when viewed from a theologi*
point of view.

O. Culmann, in his book, *The New Testament*, writes the *
lowing on the subject of variations:

"Sometimes the latter are the result of inadvertant flaws: *
copier misses a word out, or conversely writes it twice, or a wh*
section of a sentence is carelessly omitted because in the ma*
script to be copied it appeared between two identical wor*
Sometimes it is a matter of deliberate corrections, either *
copier has taken the liberty of correcting the text according
his own ideas or he has tried to bring it into line with a para*
text in a more or less skilful attempt to reduce the number
discrepancies. As, little by little, the New Testament writi*
broke away from the rest of early Christian literature, and ca*
to be regarded as Holy Scripture, so the copiers became m*
and more hesitant about taking the same liberties as th*
predecessors: they thought they were copying the authen*
text, but in fact wrote down the variations. Finally, a cop*
sometimes wrote annotations in the margin to explain an *
scure passage. The following copier, thinking that the sente*
he found in the margin had been left out of the passage by *
predecessor, thought it necessary to include the margin notes
the text. This process often made the new text even m*
obscure."

The scribes of some manuscripts sometimes took exceedin*
great liberties with the texts. This is the case of one of the m*
venerable manuscripts after the two referred to above, t*
Sixth century *Codex Bezae Cantabrigiensis*. The scribe pr*
ably noticed the difference between Luke's and Matthew's ge*
alogy of Jesus, so he put Matthew's genealogy into his copy
Luke, but as the second contained fewer names than the fir*
he padded it out with extra names (without balancing them u*

Is it possible to say that the Latin translations, such as Sa*
Jerome's Sixth century Vulgate, or older translations (*Vet*
Itala), or Syriac and Coptic translations are any more faith*
than the basic Greek manuscripts? They might have been ma*

...m manuscripts older than the ones referred to above and sub-
...uently lost to the present day. We just do not know.

...t has been possible to group the bulk of these versions into
...nilies all bearing a certain number of common traits. Accord-
... to O. Culmann, one can define:

...a so-called Syrian text, whose constitution could have led to
... majority of the oldest Greek manuscripts; this text was
...lely disseminated throughout Europe from the Sixteenth
...ntury A.D. onwards thanks to printing; the specialists say that
...s probably the worst text.

...a so-called Western text, with old Latin versions and the *Codex
...zae Cantabrigiensis* which is in both Greek and Latin; accord-
... to the Ecumenical Translation, one of its characteristics is
...efinite tendency to provide explanations, paraphrases, inaccu-
...e data and 'harmonizations'.

...he so-called Neutral text, containing the *Codex Vaticanus* and
... *Codex Sinaiticus,* is said to have a fairly high level of purity;
...dern editions of the New Testament readily follow it, although
...oo has its flaws (Ecumenical Translation).

...ll that modern textual criticism can do in this respect is to
... and reconstitute "a text which has the most likelihood of
...ning near to the original. In any case, there can be no hope of
...ng back to the original text itself." (Ecumenical Translation)

The Gospels and Modern Science.

The Genealogies of Jesus.

The Gospels contain very few passages which give rise to confrontation with modern scientific data.

Firstly however, there are many descriptions referring to miracles which hardly lend themselves to scientific comment. T miracles concern people—the healing of the sick (the insar blind, paralytic; the healing of lepers, resurrection of Lazarus) as well as the purely material phenomena that lie outside t laws of nature (the description of Jesus walking on water th held him up, the changing of the water into wine). Sometim a natural phenomenom is seen from an unusual angle by virtue the fact that the time element is very short: the immediate cal ing of the storm, the instantaneous withering of the fig tre the miracle catch of fish, as if all the fish in the sea had con together at exactly the place where the nets were cast.

God intervenes in His Omnipotent Power in all these episod One need not be surprised by what He is able to achieve; human standards it is stupendous, but for Him it is not. This do not at all mean that a believer should forget science. A belief divine miracles and in science is quite compatible: one is on divine scale, the other on a human one.

Personally, I am very willing to believe that Jesus cured leper, but I cannot accept the fact that a text is declared authe tic and inspired by God when I read that only twenty genei tions existed between the first man and Abraham. Luke says th in his Gospel (3, 23-28). We shall see in a moment the reasons that show why Luke's text, like the Old Testament text on the same theme, is quite simply a product of human imagination.

The Gospels (like the Qur'an) give us the same description of Jesus's biological origins. The formation of Jesus in the maternal uterus occurred in circumstances which lay outside the laws of nature common to all human beings. The ovule produced by the mother's ovary did not need to join with a spermatozoon, which should have come from his father, to form the embryo and hence a viable infant. The phenomenon of the birth of a normal individual without the fertilizing action of the male is called 'parthenogenesis'. In the animal kingdom, parthenogenesis can be observed under certain conditions. This is true for various insects, certain invertebrates and, very occasionally, a select breed of bird. By way of experiment, it has been possible, for example, in certain mammals (female rabbits), to obtain the beginnings of a development of the ovule into an embryo at an extremely rudimentary stage without any intervention of spermatozoon. It was not possible to go any further however and an example of complete parthenogenesis, whether experimental or natural, is unknown. Jesus is an unique case. Mary was a virgin mother. She preserved her virginity and did not have any children apart from Jesus. Jesus is a biological exception.[1]

THE GENEALOGIES OF JESUS.

The two genealogies contained in Matthew's and Luke's Gospels give rise to problems of verisimilitude, and conformity with scientific data, and hence authenticity. These problems are a source of great embarassment to Christian commentators because the latter refuse to see in them what is very obviously the product of human imagination. The authors of the Sacerdotal text of Genesis, Sixth century B.C., had already been inspired by imagination for their genealogies of the first men. It again inspired

---

1. The Gospels sometimes refer to Jesus's 'brothers' and 'sisters' (Matthew 13, 46-50 and 54-58; Mark 6, 1-6; John 7, 3 and 2, 12). The Greek words used, *adelphoi* and *adelphai*, indeed signify biological brothers and sisters; they are most probably a defective translation of the original Semitic words which just mean 'kin'; in this instance they were perhaps cousins.

Matthew and Luke for the data they did not take from the Old
Testament.

One must straight away note that the male genealogies have
absolutely no relevance to Jesus. Were one to give a genealogy to
Mary's only son, who was without a biological father, it would
have to be the genealogy of his mother Mary.

Here is the text of the Revised Standard Version of the Bible
1952:

The genealogy according to Matthew is at the beginning of his
Gospel:

"THE BOOK OF THE GENEALOGY OF JESUS CHRIST, THE SON OF DAVID, THE SON OF ABRAHAM.

Abraham	was the father of Isaac
Isaac	was the father of Jacob
Jacob	was the father of Judah and his brothers
Judah	was the father of Perez and Zerah by Tamar
Perez	was the father of Hezron
Hezron	was the father of Ram
Ram	was the father of Amminadab
Amminadab	was the father of Nahshon
Nahshon	was the father of Salmon
Salmon	was the father of Boaz by Rahab
Boaz	was the father of Obed by Ruth
Obed	was the father of Jesse
Jesse	was the father of David the king
David	was the father of Solomon by the wife of Uriah
Solomon	was the father of Rehoboam
Rehoboam	was the father of Abijah
Abijah	was the father of Asa
Asa	was the father of Jehoshaphat
Jehoshaphat	was the father of Joram
Joram	was the father of Uzziah
Uzziah	was the father of Jotham
Jotham	was the father of Ahaz
Ahaz	was the father of Hezekiah
Hezekiah	was the father of Manasseh
Manasseh	was the father of Amos
Amos	was the father of Josiah
Josiah	was the father of Jechoniah and his brothers

at the time of the deportation to Babylon.

After the deportation to Babylon:

Jechoniah	was the father of Shealtiel
Shealtiel	was the father of Zerubbabel

Zerubbabel	was the father of Abiud
Abiud	was the father of Eliakim
Eliakim	was the father of Azor
Azor	was the father of Zadok
Zadok	was the father of Achim
Achim	was the father of Eliud
Eliud	was the father of Eleazar
Eleazar	was the father of Matthan
Matthan	was the father of Jacob
Jacob	was the father of Joseph the husband of Mary
	of whom Jesus was born, who was called Christ.

So all the generations from Abraham to David were fourteen generations, and from David to the deportation to Babylon fourteen generations, and from the deportation to Babylon to the Christ fourteen generations". (Matthew, I, 1-17)

The genealogy given by Luke (3, 23-38) is different from Matthew. The text reproduced here is from the Revised Standard Version of the Bible:

"Jesus, when he began his ministry, was about thirty years of age, being the son (as was supposed) of Joseph, the son of Heli, the son of Matthat, the son of Levi, the son of Melchi, the son of Jannai, the son of Joseph, the son of Mattathias, the son of Amos, the son of Nahum, the son of Esli, the son of Naggai, the son of Maath, the son of Mattathias, the son of Semein, the son of Josech, the son of Joda, the son of Joanan, the son of Rhesa, the son of Zerubbabel, the son of Shealtiel, the son of Neri, the son of Melchi, the son of Addi, the son of Cosam, the son of Elmadam, the son of Er, the son of Joshua, the son of Eliezer, the son of Jorim, the son of Matthat, the son of Levi, the son of Simeon, the son of Judah, the son of Joseph, the son of Jonam, the son of Eliakim, the son of Melea, the son of Menna, the son of Mattatha, the son of Nathan, the son of David, the son of Jesse, the son of Obed, the son of Boaz, the son of Sala, the son of Nahshon, the son of Amminadab, the son of Admin, the son of Arni, the son of Hezron, the son of Perez, the son of Judah, the son of Jacob, the son of Isaac, the son of Abraham, the son of Terah, the son of Nahor, the son of Serug, the son of Reu, the son of Peleg, the son of Eber, the son of Shelah, the son of Cainan, the son of Arphaxad, the son of Shem, the son of Noah, the son of Lamech, the son of Methuselah, the son of Enoch, the son of

Jared, the son of Mahalaleel, the son of Cainan, the son of Enos. the son of Seth, the son of Adam, the son of God."

The genealogies appear more clearly when presented in two tables, one showing the genealogy before David and the other after him.

GENEALOGY OF JESUS, BEFORE DAVID
(Through Mary)

According to Matthew	According to Luke	
Traces the Royal line of Jesus Ancestry and his Jewishness: Stops/starts at Abraham (through Joseph)	1	Adam
	2	Seth
	3	Enos
	4	Cainan
	5	Mahalaleel
	6	Jared
	7	Enoch
	8	Methuselah
	9	Lamech
Matthew does not mention any name before Abraham.	10	Noah
	11	Shem
	12	Arphaxad
	13	Cainan
	14	Shelah
	15	Eber
	16	Peleg
	17	Reu
	18	Serug
	19	Nahor
	20	Terah
1 Abraham	21	Abraham
2 Isaac	22	Isaac
3 Jacob	23	Jacob
4 Judah	24	Judah
5 Perez	25	Perez
6 Hezron	26	Hezron
7 Ram	27	Arni
	28	Admin
8 Amminadab	29	Amminadab
9 Nahshon	30	Nahshon
10 Salmon	31	Sala
11 Boaz	32	Boaz
12 Obed	33	Obed
13 Jesse	34	Jesse
14 David	35	David

GENEALOGY OF JESUS, AFTER DAVID

According to Matthew	According to Luke
14 David	35 David
15 Solomon	36 Nathan
16 Rehoboam	37 Mattatha
17 Abijah	38 Menna
18 Asa	39 Melea
19 Jehoshaphat	40 Eliakim
20 Joram	41 Jonam
21 Uzziah	42 Joseph
22 Jotham	43 Judah
23 Ahaz	44 Simeon
24 Hezekiah	45 Levi
25 Manasseh	46 Matthat
26 Amos	47 Jorim
27 Josiah	48 Eliezer
28 Jechoniah	49 Joshua
	50 Er
Deportation to Babylon	51 Elmadam
	52 Cosam
29 Shealtiel	53 Addi
30 Zerubbabel	54 Melchi
31 Abiud	55 Neri
32 Eliakim	56 Shealtiel
33 Azor	57 Zerubbabel
34 Zadok	58 Rhesa
35 Achim	59 Joanan
36 Eliud	60 Joda
37 Eleazar	61 Josech
38 Matthan	62 Semein
39 Jacob	63 Mattathias
40 Joseph	64 Maath
41 Jesus	65 Naggai
	66 Esli
	67 Nahum
	68 Amos
	69 Mattathias
	70 Joseph
	71 Jannai
	72 Melchi
	73 Levi
	74 Matthat
	75 Heli
	76 Joseph
	77 Jesus

VARIATIONS IN THE MANUSCRIPTS AND IN RELATION TO THE OLD TESTAMENT.

Apart from variations in spelling, the following must be mentioned:

a) *Matthew's Gospel*

The genealogy has disappeared from the *Codex Bezae Cantabrigiensis*, a very important Six century manuscript in both Greek and Latin. It has completely disappeared from the Greek text and also a large part of the Latin text. It may quite simply be that the first pages were lost.

One must note here the great liberties Matthew has taken with the Old Testament. He has pared down the genealogies for the sake of a strange numerical demonstration (which, in the end, he does not give, as we shall see).

b) *Luke's Gospel*

1.—Before Abraham: Luke mentions 20 names; the Old Testament only mentions 19 (see table of Adam's descendants in the Old Testament section of this work). After Arphaxad (No. 12), Luke has added a person called Cainan (No. 13), who is not mentioned in Genesis as the son of Arphaxad.

2.—From Abraham to David: 14 to 16 names are found according to the manuscripts.

3.—From David to Jesus.

The most important variation is the *Codex Bezae Cantabrigiensis* which attributes to Luke a whimsical genealogy taken from Matthew and to which the scribe has added five names. Unfortunately, the genealogy of Matthew's Gospel has disappeared from this manuscript, so that comparison is no longer possible.

CRITICAL EXAMINATION OF THE TEXTS.

We are here faced with two different genealogies having one essential point in common, i.e. they both pass via Abraham and David. To make this examination easier, we shall separate the whole into three critical sections:

—From Adam to Abraham.

· —From Abraham to David.

—From David to Jesus.

1. The Period from Adam to Abraham

Matthew began his genealogy with Abraham so we are not concerned with his text here. Luke alone provides information on Abraham's ancestors going back to Adam: 20 names, 19 of which are to be found in Genesis (chapters 4, 5 and 11), as has already been stated.

Is it possible to believe that only 19 or 20 generations of human beings existed before Abraham? The problem has been examined in the discussion of the Old Testament. If one looks at the table of Adam's descendants, based on Genesis and giving figures for the time element contained in the Biblical text, one can see that roughly nineteen centuries passed between man's appearance on earth and the birth of Abraham. Today it is estimated that Abraham was alive in circa 1850 B.C. and it has been deduced from this that the information provided by the Old Testament places man's appearance on earth at roughly thirty-eight centuries B.C. Luke was obviously guided by these data for his Gospel. He expresses a blatant untruth for having copied them down and we have already seen the decisive historical arguments leading to this statement.

The idea that Old Testament data are unacceptable in the present day is duly admitted; they belong to the 'obsolete' material referred to by the Second Vatican Council. The fact, however that the Gospels take up the same scientifically incompatible data is an extremely serious observation which may be used to oppose those who defend the historical accuracy of the Gospel texts.

Commentators have quickly sensed this danger. They try to get round the difficulty by saying that it is not a complete genealogical tree, that the evangelist has missed names out. They claim that this was done quite deliberately, and that his sole "intention was to establish the broad lines or essential elements of a line of descent based on historical reality."[1] There is nothing in the texts that permits them to form this hypothesis. In the text it says quite clearly: A was the father of B, or B was the son of A. For the part preceding Abraham in particular, the

---

1. A. Tricot, *Little Dictionary of the New Testament* (Petit Dictionnaire du Nouveau Testament in "La Sainte Bible", Desclée, Pub. Paris)

evangelist draws moreover on the Old Testament where the genealogies are set out in the following form:

When X had lived n years, he became the father of Y . . . When Y had lived n years, he became the father of Z. . . .

There is therefore no break.

The part of Jesus's genealogy according to Luke, which precedes Abraham, is not acceptable in the light of modern knowledge. why not.?

2. The Period from Abraham to David.

Here the two genealogies tally (or almost), excepting one or two names: the difference may be explained by copiers' errors.

Does this mean that the evangelists are to be considered accurate?

History situates David at circa 1000 B.C. and Abraham at 1800-1850 B.C.: 14 to 16 generations for roughly eight centuries. Can one believe this? One might say that for this period the Gospel texts are at the very limit of the admissible. why?

3. The Post-David Period.

It is a great pity, but unfortunately the texts no longer tally at all when it comes to establishing Joseph's line from David, and figuratively speaking, Jesus's, for the Gospel.

Leaving aside the obvious falsification in the Codex Bezae Cantabrigiensis concerning Luke, let us now compare what the two most venerable manuscripts have to offer: the Codex Vaticanus and the Codex Sinaiticus.

In the genealogy according to Luke 42 names are placed after David (No. 35) down to Jesus (No. 77). In the genealogy according to Matthew 27 are mentioned after David (No. 14) down to Jesus (No. 41). The number of (fictitious) ancestors given to Jesus after David is therefore different in the two Gospels. The names themselves are different as well.

This is not all.

Matthew tells us that he discovered how Jesus's genealogy split up after Abraham into three groups of 14 names; first group from Abraham to David; second from David to the deportation to Babylon; third from the deportation to Jesus. His text does indeed contain 14 names in the first two groups, but in the third—from the deportation to Jesus—there are only 13 and not 14, as expected; the table shows that Shealthiel is No. 29 and Jesus No. 41. There is no variation of Matthew that gives 14 names for this group.

To enable himself to have 14 names in his second group, Matthew takes very great liberties with the Old Testament text. The names of the first six descendants of David (No. 15 to 20) tally with the data in the Old Testament, but the three descendants of Ioram (No. 20), given in Chronicles II of the Bible as Ahaziah, Joash, and Amaziah, are suppressed by Matthew. Elsewhere, Jechoniah (No. 28) is for Matthew the son of Josiah, although Kings II of the Bible tells us that Eliakim comes between Josiah and Jechoniah.

It may be seen from this that Matthew has altered the genealogical lines in the Old Testament to present an artificial group of 14 names between David and the deportation to Babylon. There is also the fact that one name is missing in Matthew's third group, so that none of the present-day Gospel texts contains the 42 names mentioned. What is surprising is not so much the existence of the omission itself (explained perhaps by a very old scribe's error that was subsequently perpetuated), but the almost total silence of commentators on this subject. How can one miss this omission? W. Trilling breaks this pious conspiracy of silence in his book *The Gospel According to Matthew* (L'Evangile selon Matthieu)[1] by devoting one line to it. It is a fact which is of considerable importance because the commentators of this Gospel, including the Ecumenical Translation and Cardinal Daniélou among others, stress the great symbolical significance of Matthew's 3 × 14. This significance was so important for the evangelist that he suppressed Biblical names without hesitation to arrive at his numerical demonstration.

To make this hold good, commentators will, no doubt, construct some reassuring statements of an apologetic nature, justifying the fact that names have been craftily suppressed and carefully avoiding the omission that undermines the whole point of what the evangelist was trying to show.

---

1. Pub. Desclée, coll. 'Parole et Prière', Paris.

COMMENTARIES OF MODERN EXPERTS IN EXEGESIS.
In his book *The Gospels of Childhood* (1967) Les Evangiles de
l'Enfance)[1], Cardinal Daniélou invests Matthew's 'numerical
schematisation' with a symbolic value of paramount importance
since it is this that establishes Jesus's ancestry, which is asserted
also by Luke. For him Luke and Matthew are 'historians' who
have completed their 'historical investigations', and the 'genealogy' has been 'taken down from the archives of Jesus family'.
It must be added here that the archives have never been found.[2]

Cardinal Daniélou condemns out of hand anyone who criticizes
his point of view: "It is the Western mentality, ignorance of
Judeo-Christianity and the absence of a Semitic outlook that have
made so many experts in exegesis loose their way when inter-
preting the Gospels. They have projected their own categories
onto them: (sic) Platonic, Cartesian, Hegelian and Heidegger-
ian. It is easy to see why everything is mixed up in their minds."
Plato, Descartes, Hegel and Heidegger obviously have nothing
to do with the critical attitude one may have towards these whimsical genealogies.

In his search for the meaning of Matthew's 3 × 14, the author
expands on strange suppositions. They are worth quoting here:
"What may be meant are the common ten weeks of the Jewish
Apocalypse. The first three, corresponding to the time from
Adam to Abraham, would have been subtracted; seven weeks of
years would then remain, the first six would correspond to the
six times seven representing the three groups of fourteen and
leaving the seventh, started by Christ with whom the seventh age
of the world begins." Explanations like this are beyond comment!

The commentators of the *Ecumenical Translation—New Testament*—also give us numerical variations of an apologetic nature
which are equally unexpected:
For Matthew's 3 × 14:

---

1. Pub. Editions du Seuil, Paris.
2. Although the author assures us that he knows of the existence of these
   supposed family archives from the Ecclesiastic History by Eusebius
   Pamphili (about whose respectabiiity much could be said), it is difficult
   to see why Jesus's family should have two genealogical trees that were
   necessarily different just because each of the two so-called 'historians'
   gave a genealogy substantially different from the other concerning the
   names of those who figure among Jesus's ancestors.

14 could be the numerical total of the 3 consonants in the Hebrew name David (D=4, V=6), hence $4+6+4=14$.

$3 \times 14 = 6 \times 7$ and "Jesus came at the end of the sixth week of Holy history beginning with Abraham."

For Luke, this translation gives 77 names from Adam to Jesus, owing the number 7 to come up again, this time by dividing by 7 ($7 \times 11 = 77$). It is quite apparent that for Luke the mber of variations where words are added or subtracted is ch that a list of 77 names is completely artificial. It does how- er have the advantage of adapting itself to these numerical mes.

The genealogies of Jesus as they appear in the Gospels may rhaps be the subject that has led Christian commentators to rform their most characteristic feats of dialectic acrobatics, par indeed with Luke's and Matthew's imagination.

Contradictions and Improbabilities in the Descriptions.

Each of the four Gospels contains a large number of descri tions of events that may be unique to one single Gospel or con mon to several if not all of them. When they are unique to on Gospel, they sometimes raise serious problems. Thus, in the ca of an event of considerable importance, it is surprising to fin the event mentioned by only one evangelist; Jesus's Ascensio into heaven on the day of Resurrection, for example. Elsewhei numerous events are differently described—sometimes very di fently indeed—by two or more evangelists. Christians are ver often astonished at the existence of such contradictions betwee the Gospels—if they ever discover them. This is because the have been repeatedly told in tones of the greatest assurance tha the New Testament authors were the eyewitnesses of the even they describe!

Some of these disturbing improbabilities and contradiction have been shown in previous chapters. It is however the late events of Jesus's life in particular, along with the events follov ing the Passion, that form the subject of varying or contradicto descriptions.

DESCRIPTIONS OF THE PASSION

Father Roguet himself notes that Passover is placed at diffe ent times in relation to Jesus's Last Supper with His disciples i e Synoptic Gospels and John's Gospel. John places the Last pper 'before the Passover celebrations' and the other three angelists place it during the celebrations themselves. Obvious probabilities emerge from this divergence: a certain episode comes impossible because of the position of Passover in relation it. When one knows the importance it had in the Jewish liturgy d the importance of the meal where Jesus bids farewell to his sciples, how is it possible to believe that the memory of one ent in relation to the other could have faded to such an extent the tradition recorded later by the evangelists?

On a more general level, the descriptions of the Passion differ om one evangelist to another, and more particularly between hn and the first three Gospels. The Last Supper and the Pason in John's Gospel are both very long, twice as long as in ark and Luke, and roughly one and a half times as long as atthew's text. John records a very long speech of Jesus to His sciples which takes up four chapters (14 to 17) of his Gospel. uring this crowning speech, Jesus announces that He will leave is last instructions and gives them His last spiritual testament. here is no trace of this in the other Gospels. The same process n work the other way however; Matthew, Luke and Mark all late Jesus's prayer in the Garden of Gethsemane, but John does ot mention it.

JOHN'S GOSPEL DOES NOT DESCRIBE THE INSTITUTION OF THE EUCHARIST.

The most important fact that strikes the reader of the Passion John's Gospel is that he makes absolutely no reference to the stitution of the Eucharist during the Last Supper of Jesus ith His Apostles.

There is not a single Christian who does not know the icongraphy of the Last Supper, where Jesus is for the last time eated among His Apostles at table. The world's greatest painters ave always represented this final gathering with John sitting ear Jesus, John whom we are accustomed to considering as the uthor of the Gospel bearing that name.

However astonishing it may appear to many, the majority of pecialists do not consider John to have been the author of the fourth Gospel, nor does the latter mention the institution of tl Eucharist. The consecration of the bread and wine, which b come the body and blood of Jesus, is the most essential act the Christian liturgy. The other evangelists refer to it, even they do so in differing terms, as we have noted above. John do not say anything about it. The four evangelists' descriptions ha' only two single points in common: the prediction of Peter's d nial and of the betrayal by one of the Apostles (Judas Iscariot only actually named in Matthew and John). John's descriptic is the only one which refers to Jesus washing his disciple feet at the beginning of the meal.

How can this omission in John's Gospel be explained?

If one reasons objectively, the hypothesis that springs immed ately to mind (always supposing the story as told by the othe three evangelists is exact) is that a passage of John's Gosp relating the said episode was lost. This is not the conclusio arrived at by Christian commentators.

Let us now examine some of the positions they have adopted

In his *Little Dictionary of the New Testament* (Petit Di tionnaire du Nouveau Testament) A. Tricot makes the followin entry under *Last Supper* (Cène) : "Last meal Jesus partook with the Twelve Disciples during which he instituted the Eucha ist. It is described in the Synoptic Gospels" (references to Matth ew, Mark and Luke). ". . . and the fourth Gospel gives us furthe details" (references to John). In his entry on the Eucharis (Eucharistie), the same author writes the following: "The insti tution of the Eucharist is briefly related in the first three Gos pels: it was an extremely important part of the Apostolic syster of religious instruction. Saint John has added an indispensabl complement to these brief descriptions in his account of Jesus' speech on the bread of life (6, 32-58)." The commentator conse quently fails to mention that John does not describe Jesus's in titution of the Eucharist. The author speaks of 'complementar details', but they are not complementary to the institution o the Eucharist (he basically describes the ceremony of the wash ing of the Apostles' feet). The commentator speaks of the 'brea of life', but it is Jesus's reference (quite separate from the Las Supper) to God's daily gift of manna in the wilderness at th time of the Jews' exodus led by Moses. John is the only one o

▪e evangelists who records this allusion. In the following pass-
▪e of his Gospel, John does, of course, mention Jesus's reference
▪ the Eucharist in the form of a digression on the bread, but no
▪her evangelist speaks of this episode.

One is surprised therefore both by John's silence on what the
▪her three evangelists relate and their silence on what, accord-
▪g to John, Jesus is said to have predicted.

The commentators of the *Ecumenical Translation of the Bible,
'ew Testament*, do actually acknowledge this omission in John's
▪ospel. This is the explanation they come up with to account for
▪e fact that the description of the institution of the Eucharist
▪ missing: "In general, John is not very interested in the tradi-
▪ons and institutions of a bygone Israel. This may have dis-
▪aded him from showing the establishment of the Eucharist in
▪e Passover liturgy". Are we seriously to believe that it was a
▪ck of interest in the Jewish Passover liturgy that led John not
▪ describe the institution of the most fundamental act in the
▪turgy of the new religion?

The experts in exegesis are so embarrassed by the problem
▪hat theologians rack their brains to find prefigurations or equiv-
lents of the Eucharist in episodes of Jesus's life recorded by
▪ohn. O. Culmann for example, in his book, *The New Testament*
Le Nouveau Testament), states that "the changing of the water
▪nto wine and the feeding of the five thousand prefigure the
▪acrament of the Last Supper (the 'Eucharist')". It is to be re-
▪embered that the water was changed into wine because the
▪atter had failed at a wedding in Cana. (This was Jesus's first
▪iracle, described by John in chapter 2, 1-12. He is the only
▪vangelist to do so). In the case of the feeding of the five thou-
▪and, this was the number of people who were fed on 5 barley
▪oaves that were miraculously multiplied. When describing these
▪vents, John makes no special comment, and the parallel exists
▪nly in the mind of this expert in exegesis. One can no more
▪nderstand the reasoning behind the parallel he draws than his
▪iew that the curing of a paralized man and of a man born blind
predict the baptism' and that 'the water and blood issuing from
▪esus's side after his death unite in a single fact' a reference to
▪oth baptism and the Eucharist.

Another parallel drawn by the same expert in exegesis co
concerning the Eucharist is quoted by Father Roguet in his bo
Initiation to the Gospel (Initiation à l'Evangile). "Some the
logians, such as Oscar Culmann, see in the description of t
washing of the feet before the Last Supper a symbolical equiv
lent to the institution of the Eucharist . . ."

It is difficult to see the cogency of all the parallels that co
mentators have invented to help people accept more readily t
most disconcerting omission in John's Gospel.

APPEARANCES OF JESUS RAISED FROM THE DEAD.

A prime example of imagination at work in a description h
already been given in the portrayal of the abnormal phenomer
said to have accompanied Jesus's death given in Matthew's Go
pel. The events that followed the Resurrection provided materi
for contradictory and even absurd descriptions on the part of a
the evangelists.

Father Roguet in his *Initiation to the Gospel* (Initiation
l'Evangile), page 182, provides examples of the confusion, di
order and contradiction reigning in these writings:

"The list of women who came to the tomb is not exactly th
same in each of the three Synoptic Gospels. In John only on
woman came: Mary Magdalene. She speaks in the plural how
ever, as if she were accompanied: 'we do not know where the
have laid him.' In Matthew the Angel predicts to the women tha
they will see Jesus in Galilee. A few moments later howeve
Jesus joins them beside the tomb. Luke probably sensed thi
difficulty and altered the source a little. The Angel says: "Re
member how he told you, while he was still in Galilee . . .' I
fact, Luke only actually refers to three appearances . . ."—"Joh
places two appearances at an interval of one week in the uppe
room at Jerusalem and the third beside the lake, in Galilee there
fore. Matthew records only one appearance in Galilee." Th
commentator excludes from this examination the last section o
Mark's Gospel concerning the appearances because he believe
this was 'probably written by another hand'.

All these facts contradict the mention of Jesus's appearances
contained in *Paul's First Letter to the Corinthians* (15, 5-7), t

ore than five hundred people at once, to James, to all the
postles and, of course, to Paul himself.

After this, it is surprising therefore to find that Father Roguet
tigmatizes, in the same book, the 'grandiloquent and puerile
hantasms of certain Apocrypha' when talking of the Resurrec-
ion. Surely these terms are perfectly appropriate to Matthew
nd Paul themselves: they are indeed in complete contradiction
/ith the other Apostles on the subject of the appearances of
esus raised from the dead.

Apart from this, there is a contradiction between Luke's de-
cription, in the Acts of the Apostles, of Jesus's appearance to
'aul and what Paul himself succinctly tells us of it. This has led
'ather Kannengiesser in his book, *Faith in the Resurrection,
Resurrection of Faith* (Foi en la Résurrection, Résurrection
le la Foi), 1974, to stress that Paul, who was 'the sole eyewitness
f Christ's resurrection, whose voice comes directly to us from
iis writings[1], never speaks of his personal encounter with Him
Vho was raised from the dead—'. . . except for three extremely
liscreet references . . .'—'he refrains moreover from describing
t.'

The contradiction between Paul, who was the sole eyewitness
)ut is dubious, and the Gospels is quite obvious.

O. Culmann in his book, *The New Testament* (Le Nouveau
Testament), notes the contradictions between Luke and Matthew.
The first situates Jesus's appearances in Judea, the second in
Galilee.

One should also remember the Luke-John contradiction. ?
John (21, 1-14) relates an episode in which Jesus raised from
he dead appears to the fishermen beside the Sea of Tiberias;
they subsequently catch so many fish that they are unable to
bring them all in. This is nothing other than a repetition of the
miracle catch of fish episode which took place at the same spot
and was also described by Luke (5, 1-11), as an event of Jesus's
life. NOT THE SAME EVENT

When talking of these appearances, Father Roguet assures
us in his book that 'their disjointed, blurred and disordered
character inspires confidence' because all these facts go to show

---

1. 'No other New Testament author can claim that distinction', he notes.

that there was no connivance between the evangelists[1], othe
wise they would definitely have co-ordinated their stories. Th
is indeed a strange line of argument. In actual fact, they cou.
all have recorded, with complete sincerity, traditions of the com
munities which (unknown to them) all contained elements c
fantasy. This hypothesis in unavoidable when one is faced wit
so many contradictions and improbabilities in the description c
of events.

ASCENSION OF JESUS

Contradictions are present until the very end of the descrip
tions because neither John nor Matthew refer to Jesus's Ascen
sion. Mark and Luke are the only one to speak of it.

For Mark (16, 19), Jesus was 'taken up into heaven, and sa
down at the right hand of God' without any precise date bein
given in relation to His Resurrection. It must however be note
that the final passage of Mark containing this sentence is, fo
Father Roguet, an 'invented' text, although for the Church it i
canonic!

There remains Luke, the only evangelist to provide an undis
puted text of the Ascension episode (24, 51): 'he parted from
them[2] and was carried up into heaven'. The evangelist places th
event at the end of the description of the Resurrection and ap
pearance to the eleven Apostles: the details of the Gospel de
scription imply that the Ascension took place on the day of the
Resurrection. In the Acts of the Apostles, Luke (whom every
body believes to be their author) describes in chapter 1, 3 Jesus's
appearance to the Apostles, between the Passion and the Ascen
sion, in the following terms:

"To them he presented himself alive after his passion by many
proofs, appearing to them during forty days, and speaking of the
kingdom of God."

The placing of the Christian festival of the Ascension at forty
days after Easter, the Festival of the Resurrection, originates
from this passage in the Acts of the Apostles. The date is there-

---

1. It is difficult to see how there could have been!

2. i.e. the eleven Apostles; Judos, the twelfth, was already dead.

fore set in contradiction to Luke's Gospel: none of the other Gospel texts say anything to justify this in a different way.

The Christian who is aware of this situation is highly disconcerted by the obviousness of the contradiction. The *Ecumenical Translation of the Bible, New Testament,* acknowledges the facts but does not expand on the contradiction. It limits itself to noting the relevance the forty days may have had to Jesus's mission.

Commentators wishing to explain everything and reconcile the irreconcilable provide some strange interpretations on this subject.

The *Synopsis of the Four Gospels* edited in 1972 by the Biblical School of Jerusalem (vol. 2, page 451) contains, for example, some very strange commentaries.

The very word 'Ascension' is criticized as follows: "In fact there was no ascension in the actual physical sense because God is no more 'on high' than he is 'below' " (sic). It is difficult to grasp the sense of this comment because one wonders how Luke could otherwise have expressed himself.

Elsewhere, the author of this commentary sees a 'literary artifice' in the fact that "in the Acts, the Ascension is said to have taken place forty days after the resurrection"; this 'artifice' is "intended to stress the notion that the period of Jesus's appearances on earth is at an end". He adds however, in relation to the fact that in Luke's Gospel, "the event is situated during the evening of Easter Sunday, because the evangelist does not put any breaks between the various episodes recorded following the discovery of the empty tomb on the morning of the resurrection . . ."—". . . surely this is also a literary artifice, intended to allow a certain lapse of time before the appearance of Jesus raised from the dead." (sic)

The feeling of embarrassment that surrounds these interpretations is even more obvious in Father Roguet's book. He discerns not one, but two Ascensions!

"Whereas from Jesus's point of view the Ascension coincides with the Resurrection, from the disciples' point of view it does not take place until Jesus ceases definitely to present Himself to them, so that the Spirit may be given to them and the period of the Church may begin."

To those readers who are not quite able to grasp the theological subtlety of his argument (which has absolutely no Scriptural basis whatsoever), the author issues the following general warning, which is a model of apologetical verbiage:

"Here, as in many similar cases, the problem only appears insuperable if one takes Biblical statements literally, and forgets their religious significance. It is not a matter of breaking down the factual reality into a symbolism which is inconsistent, but rather of looking for the theological intentions of those revealing these mysteries to us by providing us with facts we can apprehend with our senses and signs appropriate to our incarnate spirit."

JESUS'S LAST DIALOGUES.
THE PARACLETE OF JOHN'S GOSPEL.

John is the only evangelist to report the episode of the last dialogue with the Apostles. It takes place at the end of the Last Supper and before Jesus's arrest. It ends in a very long speech: four chapters in John's Gospel (14 to 17) are devoted to this narration which is not mentioned anywhere in the other Gospels. These chapters of John nevertheless deal with questions of prime importance and fundamental significance to the future outlook. They are set out with all the grandeur and solemnity that characterizes the farewell scene between the Master and His disciples.

This very touching farewell scene which contains Jesus's spiritual testament, is entirely absent from Matthew, Mark and Luke. How can the absence of this description be explained? One might ask the following: did the text initially exist in the first three Gospels? Was it subsequently suppressed? Why? It must be stated immediately that no answer can be found; the mystery surrounding this huge gap in the narrations of the first three evangelists remains as obscure as ever.

The dominating feature of this narration—seen in the crowning speech—is the view of man's future that Jesus describes, His care in addressing His disciples, and through them the whole of humanity, His recommendations and commandments and His concern to specify the guide whom man must follow after His departure. The text of John's Gospel is the only one to designate him as *Parakletos* in Greek, which in English has become 'Paraclete'. The following are the essential passages:

"If you love me, you will keep my commandments. And I will pray the Father, and he will give you another Paraclete." (14, 15-16)

What does 'Paraclete' mean? The *present* text of John's Gospel explains its meaning as follows:

"But the Paraclete, the Holy Spirit, whom the Father will send in my name, he will teach you all things, and bring to your remembrance all that I have said to you" (14, 26).

"he will bear witness to me" (15, 26).

"it is to your advantage that I go away, for if I do not go away, the Paraclete will not come to you; but if I go, I will send him to you. And when he comes, he will convince the world of sin and of righteousness and of judgment . . ." (16, 7-8).

"When the Spirit of truth comes, he will guide you into all the truth; for he will not speak on his own authority, but whatever he hears he will speak, and he will declare to you the things that are to come. He will glorify me . . ." (16, 13-14).

(It must be noted that the passages in John, chapters 14-17, which have not been cited here, in no way alter the general meaning of these quotations).

On a cursory reading, the text which identifies the Greek word 'Paraclete' with the Holy Spirit is unlikely to attract much attention. This is especially true when the subtitles of the text are generally used for translations and the terminology commentators employ in works for mass publication direct the reader towards the meaning in these passages that an exemplary orthodoxy would like them to have. Should one have the slightest difficulty in comprehension, there are many explanations available, such as those given by A. Tricot in his *Little Dictionary of the New Testament* (Petit Dictionnaire du Nouveau Testament) to enlighten one on this subject. In his entry on the Paraclete this commentator writes the following:

"This name or title translated from the Greek is only used in the New Testament by John: he uses it four times in his account of Jesus's speech after the Last Supper[1] (14, 16 and 26; 15, 26; 16, 7) and once in his First Letter (2, 1). In John's Gospel the word is applied to the Holy Spirit; in the Letter it refers to Christ. 'Paraclete' was a term in current usage among the Hellenist Jews, First century A.D., meaning 'intercessor', 'defender' (. . .) Jesus predicts that the Spirit will be sent by the Father and Son. Its mission will be to take the place of the Son in the role he played during his mortal life as a helper for the benefit of his disciples. The Spirit will intervene and act as a substitute for Christ, adopting the role of Paraclete or omnipotent intercessor."

This commentary therefore makes the Holy Spirit into the ultimate guide of man after Jesus's departure. How does it square with John's text?

It is a necessary question because *a priori* it seems strange to ascribe the last paragraph quoted above to the Holy Spirit: "for he will not speak on his own authority, but whatever he hears he will speak, and he will declare to you the things that are to come." It seems inconceivable that one could ascribe to the Holy Spirit the ability to speak and declare whatever he hears . . . Logic demands that this question be raised, but to my knowledge, it is not usually the subject of commentaries.

To gain an exact idea of the problem, one has to go back to the basic Greek text. This is especially important because John is universally recognized to have written in Greek instead of another language. The Greek text consulted was the *Novum Testamentum Graece*[2].

Any serious textual criticism begins with a search for variations. Here it would seem that in all the known manuscripts of John's Gospel, the only variation likely to change the meaning of the sentence is in passage 14, 26 of the famous Palimpsest version written in Syriac[3]. Here it is not the Holy Spirit that is mentioned, but quite simply the Spirit. Did the scribe merely

---

1. In fact, for John it was during the Last Supper itself that Jesus delivered the long speech that mentions the Paraclete.
2. Nestlé and Aland. Pub. United Bibles Societies, London, 1971.
3. This manuscript was written in the Fourth or Fifth century A.D. It was discovered in 1812 on Mount Sinai by Agnes S.-Lewis and is so named because the first text had been covered by a later one which, when obliterated, revealed the original.

miss out a word or, knowing full well that the text he was to copy claimed to make the Holy Spirit hear and speak, did he perhaps lack the audacity to write something that seemed absurd to him? Apart from this observation there is little need to labour the other variations, they are grammatical and do not change the general meaning. The important thing is that what has been demonstrated here with regard to the exact meaning of the verbs 'to hear' and 'to speak' should apply to all the other manuscripts of John's Gospel, as is indeed the case.

The verb 'to hear, in the translation is the Greek verb '*akouô*' meaning to perceive sounds. It has, for example, given us the word 'acoustics', the science of sounds.

The verb 'to speak' in the translation is the Greek verb '*laleô*' which has the general meaning of 'to emit sounds' and the specific meaning of 'to speak'. This verb occurs very frequently in the Greek text of the Gospels. It designates a solemn declaration made by Jesus during His preachings. It therefore becomes clear that the communication to man which He here proclaims does not in any way consist of a statement inspired by the agency of the Holy Spirit. It has a very obvious material character moreover, which comes from the idea of the emission of sounds conveyed by the Greek word that defines it.

The two Greek verbs '*akouô*' and '*laleô*' therefore define concrete actions which can only be applied to a being with hearing and speech organs. It is consequently impossible to apply them to the Holy Spirit. *If the Holy Spirit is God: He invented speech!*

For this reason, the text of this passage from John's Gospel, as *why could* handed down to us in Greek manuscripts, is quite incomprehensible if one takes it as a whole, including the words 'Holy Spirit' *He not* in passage 14, 26: "But the Paraclete, the Holy Spirit, whom the *speak* Father will send in my name" etc. It is the only passage in John's *without* Gospel that identifies the Paraclete with the Holy Spirit. *organ*

If the words 'Holy Spirit' (*to pneuma to agion*) are ommitted from the passage, the complete text of John then conveys a meaning which is perfectly clear. It is confirmed moreover, by another text by the same evangelist, the First Letter, where John uses the same word 'Paraclete' simply to mean Jesus, the intercessor

at God's side[1]. According to John, when Jesus says (14, 16) :
"And I will pray the Father, and he will give you another Paraclete", what He is saying is that 'another' intercessor will be sent
to man, as He Himself was at God's side on man's behalf during
His earthly life.

According to the rules of logic therefore, one is brought to
see in John's Paraclete a human being like Jesus, possessing the
faculties of hearing and speech formally implied in John's Greek
text. Jesus therefore predicts that God will later send a human
being to Earth to take up the role defined by John, i.e. to be a
prophet who hears God's word and repeats his message to man.
This is the logical interpretation of John's texts arrived at if
one attributes to the words their proper meaning.

The presence of the term 'Holy Spirit' in today's text could
easily have come from a later addition made quite deliberately.
It may have been intended to change the original meaning which
predicted the advent of a prophet subsequent to Jesus and was
therefore in contradiction with the teachings of the Christian
churches at the time of their formation; these teachings maintained that Jesus was the last of the prophets.

---

1. Many translations and commentaries of the Gospel, especially older
ones, use the word 'Consoler' to translate this, but it is totally inaccurate.

Conclusions

The facts recorded here and the commentaries quoted from several extremely eminent Christian experts in exegesis have refuted affirmations of orthodoxy supported by the line adopted by the last Council on the absolute historical authenticity of the Gospels. These are said to have faithfully transmitted what Jesus actually did and taught.

Several different kinds of argument have been given.

Firstly, quotations from the Gospels themselves show flat contradictions. It is impossible to believe two facts that contradict each other. Neither can one accept certain improbabilities and affirmations that go against the cast-iron data provided by modern knowledge. In this respect, the two genealogies of Jesus given in the Gospels and the untruths implied in them are quite conclusive.

These contradictions, improbabilities and incompatibilities pass unnoticed by many Christians. They are astonished when they discover them because they have been influenced by their reading of commentaries that provide subtle explanations calculated to reassure them and orchestrated by an apologetic lyricism. Some very typical examples have been given of the skill employed by certain experts in exegesis in camouflaging what they modestly call 'difficulties'. There are very few passages indeed in the Gospels that have been acknowledged as inauthentic although the Church declares them canonic.

According to Father Kannengiesser, works of modern textual criticism have revealed data which constitute a 'revolution in methods of Biblical exegesis' so that the facts relating to Jesus recorded in the Gospels are no longer 'to be taken literally', they

are 'writings suited to an occasion' or 'combat writings'. Modern
knowledge has brought to light the history of Judeo-Christianity
and the rivalry between communities which accounts for the
existence of facts that today's readers find disconcerting. The
concept of eyewitness evangelists is no longer defensible, although numerous Christians still retain it today. The work done
at the Biblical School of Jerusalem (Fathers Benoit and Boismard) shows very clearly that the Gospels were written, revised
and corrected several times. They also warn the reader that he is
"obliged in more than one case to give up the notion of hearing
Jesus's voice directly". ? really

The historical nature of the Gospels is beyond question.
Through descriptions referring to Jesus however, these documents provide us above all with information about the character
of their authors, the spokesmen for the tradition of the early
Christian communities to which they belonged, and in particular
about the struggle between the Judeo-Christians and Paul: Cardinal Daniélou's work is authoritative on these points.

Why be surprised by the fact that some evangelists distort
certain events in Jesus's life with the object of defending a personal point of view? Why be surprised by the omission of certain
events? Why be surprised by the fictitious nature of other events
described? where ?

This leads us to compare the Gospels with the narrative poems
found in Medieval literature. A vivid comparison could be made
with the *Song of Roland* (Chanson de Roland), the most well-
known of all poems of this kind, which relates a real event in a
fictitious light. It will be remembered that it describes an actual
episode: Roland was leading Charlemagne's rear-guard when it
was ambushed on the pass at Roncevaux. The episode which was
of minor importance, is said to have taken place on the 15th
August, 778 according to historical records (Eginhard). It was
raised to the stature of a great feat of arms, a battle in a war of
religion. It is a whimsical description, but the imaginary element
does not obliterate one of the real battles that Charlemagne had
to fight in order to protect his frontiers against the attempts
made by neighbouring peoples to penetrate his borders. That is
the element of truth and the epic style of narrative does not re-
move it.

The same holds true for the Gospels: Matthew's phantasms, the flat contradictions between Gospels, the improbabilities, the incompatibilities with modern scientific data, the successive distortions of the text—all these things add up to the fact that the Gospels contain chapters and passages that are the sole product of the human imagination. These flaws do not however cast doubt on the existence of Jesus's mission: the doubt is solely confined to the course it took.

The Qur'an and Modern Science

Introduction

The relationship between the Qur'an and science is *a priori* a surprise, especially when it turns out to be one of harmony and not of discord. A confrontation between a religious book and the secular ideas proclaimed by science is perhaps, in the eyes of many people today, something of a paradox. The majority of today's scientists, with a small number of exceptions of course, are indeed bound up in materialist theories, and have only indifference or contempt for religious questions which they often consider to be founded on legend. In the West moreover, when science and religion are discussed, people are quite willing to mention Judaism and Christianity among the religions referred to, but they hardly ever think of Islam. So many false judgements based on inaccurate ideas have indeed been made about it, that today it is very difficult to form an exact notion of the reality of Islam.

As a prelude to any confrontation between the Islamic Revelation and science, it would seem essential that an outline be given of a religion that is so little known in the West.

The totally erroneous statements made about Islam in the West are sometimes the result of ignorance, and sometimes of systematic denigration. The most serious of all the untruths told about it are however those dealing with facts; for while mistaken opin-

•ns are excusable, the presentation of facts running contrary to
ιe reality is not. It is disturbing to read blatant untruths in
ninently respectable works written by authors who *a priori* are
ighly qualified. The following is an example taken from the
niversalis Encyclopedia (Encyclopedia Universalis) vol.6. Un-
:r the heading *Gospels* (Evangiles) the author alludes to the
fferences between the latter and the Qur'an: "The evangelists
. .) do not (. . .), as in the Qur'an, claim to transmit an
ιtobiography that God miraculously dictated to the Prophet
.". In fact, the Qur'an has nothing to do with an autobiogra-
ιy: it is a preaching; a consultation of even the worst trans-
tion would have made that clear to the author. The statement
e have quoted is as far from reality as if one were to define
Gospel as an account of an evangelist's life. The person re-
ιonsible for this untruth about the Qur'an is a professor at the
:suit Faculty of Theology, Lyon! The fact that people utter such
ιtruths helps to give a false impression of the Qur'an and
Jam.

There is hope today however because religions are no longer
; inward-looking as they were and many of them are seeking
ιr mutual understanding. One must indeed be impressed by a
nowledge of the fact that an attempt is being made on the
ighest level of the hierarchy by Roman Catholics to establish
ιntact with Muslims; they are trying to fight incomprehension
ιd are doing their utmost to change the inaccurate views on
Jam that are so widely held.

In the Introduction to this work, I mentioned the great change
ιat has taken place in the last few years and I quoted a document
roduced by the Office for Non-Christian Affairs at the Vatican
ιder the title *Orientations for a Dialogue between Christians
ιd Muslims* (Orientations pour un dialogue entre chrétiens et
usulmans). It is a very important document in that it shows
ιe new position adopted towards Islam. As we read in the third
lition of this study (1970), this new position calls for 'a revi-
on of our attitude towards it and a critical examination of our
·ejudices' . . . 'We should first set about progressively changing
ιe way our Christian brothers see it. This is the most important
' all.' . . . We must clear away the 'out-dated image inherited
·om the past, or distorted by prejudice and slander' . . . , and

'recognize the past injustice towards the Muslims for which th
West, with its Christian education, is to blame.'[1] The Vatica
document is nearly 150 pages long. It therefore expands on th
refutation of classic views held by Christians on Islam and set
out the reality.

Under the title *Emancipating ourselves from our worst prej
udices* (Nous libérer de nos préjugés les plus notables) th
authors address the following suggestions to Christians: "Her
also, we must surrender to a deep purification of our attitude. I
particular, what is meant by this are certain 'set judgement
that are all too often and too lightly made about Islam. It i
essential not to cultivate in the secret of our hearts views suc
as these, too easily or arbitrarily arrived at, and which th
sincere Muslim finds confusing."

One extremely important view of this kind is the attitude which
leads people to repeatedly use the term 'Allah' to mean the Go
of the Muslims, as if the Muslims believed in a God who wa
different from the God of the Christians. *Al lâh* means 'th
Divinity' in Arabic: it is a single God, implying that a correc
transcription can only render the exact meaning of the word wit
the help of the expression 'God'. For the Muslim, *al lâh* is non
other than the God of Moses and Jesus.

The document produced by the Office for Non-Christian Affair
at the Vatican stresses this fundamental point in the followin
terms:

"It would seem pointless to maintain that Allâh is not reall
God, as do certain people in the West! The conciliar document
have put the above assertion in its proper place. There is n
better way of illustrating Islamic faith in God than by quotin

---

1. At a certain period of history, hostility to Islam, in whatever shape o
   form, even coming from declared enemies of the church, was received
   with the most heartfelt approbation by high dignitaries of the Catholi
   Church. Thus Pope Benedict XIV, who is reputed to have been the
   greatest Pontiff of the Eighteenth century, unhesitatingly sent his blessing to Voltaire. This was in thanks for the dedication to him of the
   tragedy *Mohammed or Fanaticism* (Mahomet ou le Fanatisme) 1741, a
   coarse satire that any clever scribbler of bad faith could have written
   on any subject. In spite of a bad start, the play gained sufficient pres-
   tige to be included in the repertoire of the Comédie-Francaise.

the following extracts from *Lumen Gentium*[1]: 'The Muslims profess the faith of Abraham and worship with us the sole merciful God, who is the future judge of men on the Day of Reckoning . . . ' "

One can therefore understand the Muslims' protest at the all too frequent custom in European languages of saying '*Allâh*' instead of 'God' . . . Cultivated Muslims have praised D. Masson's French translation of the Qur'an for having 'at last' written 'Dieu'[2] instead of 'Allah'.

The Vatican document points out the following: "Allâh is the only word that Arabic-speaking Christians have for God."

Muslims and Christians worship a single God.

The Vatican document then undertakes a critical examination of the other false judgements made on Islam.

'Islamic fatalism' is a widely-spread prejudice; the document examines this and quoting the Qur'an for support, it puts in opposition to this the notion of the responsibility man has, who is to be judged by his actions. It shows that the concept of an Islamic legalism is false; on the contrary, it opposes the sincerity of faith to this by quoting two phrases in the Qur'an that are highly misunderstood in the West:

"There is no compulsion in religion"   (sura 2, verse 256)

"(God) has not laid upon you in religion any hardship"

(sura 22, verse 78)

The document opposes the widely-spread notion of 'Islam, religion of fear' to 'Islam, religion of love'—love of one's neighbor based on faith in God. It refutes the falsely spread notion that Muslim morality hardly exists and the other notion, shared by so many Jews and Christians, of Islamic fanaticism. It makes the following comment on this: "In fact, Islam was hardly any more fanatical during its history than the sacred bastions of Christianity whenever the Christian faith took on, as it were, a political value." At this point, the authors quote expressions from the Qur'an that show how, in the West, the expression 'Holy

---

1. *Lumen Gentium* is the title of a document produced by the Second Vatican Council (1962-1965)

2. God.

War'[1] has been mis-translated; "in Arabic it is *Al jihâd fî sab* *Allâh*, the effort on God's road", "the effort to spread Islam an defend it against its aggressors." The Vatican document con tinues as follows: "The *jihâd* is not at all the Biblical *kherem* it does not lead to extermination, but to the spreading of God' and man's rights to new lands."—"The past violence of the *jihâ* generally followed the rules of war; at the time of the Crusade moreover, it was not always the Muslims that perpetrated th worst slaughters."

Finally, the document deals with the prejudice according t which "Islam is a hide-bound religion which keeps its followers i a kind of superannuated Middle Ages, making them unfit t adapt to the technical conquests of the modern age." It com pares analogous situations observed in Christian countries an states the following: "we find, (...) in the traditional expansio of Muslim thought, a principle of possible evolution in civilia society."

I am certain that this defense of Islam by the Vatican wil surprise many believers today, be they Muslims, Jews or Chris tians. It is a demonstration of sincerity and open-mindednes that is singularly in contrast with the attitudes inherited from the past. The number of people in the West who are aware o the new attitudes adopted by the highest authorities in the Catholic Church is however very small.

Once one is aware of this fact, it comes as less of a surprise to learn of the actions that sealed this reconciliation: firstly, there was the official visit made by the President of the Office for Non-Christian Affairs at the Vatican to King Faisal of Saudi

---

1. Translators of the Qur'an, even famous ones, have not resisted the secular habit of putting into their translations things that are not really in the Arabic text at all. One can indeed add titles to the text that are not in the original without changing the text itself, but this addition changes the general meaning. R. Blachère, for example, in his well-known translation (Pub. Maisonneuve et Larose, Paris, 1966, page 115) inserts a title that does not figure in the Qur'an: *Duties of the Holy War* (Obligations de la guerre sainte). This is at the beginning of a passage that is indisputably a call to arms, but does not have the character that has been ascribed to it. After reading this, how can the reader who only has access to the Qur'an via translations fail to think that a Muslim's duty is to wage holy war?

Arabia; then the official reception given by Pope Paul VI to the Grand Ulema of Saudi Arabia in the course of 1974. Henceforth, one understands more clearly the spiritual significance of the fact that His Grace Bishop Elchinger received the Grand Ulema at his cathedral in Strasbourg and invited them during their visit to pray in the choir. This they did before the altar, turned towards Makka.

Thus the representatives of the Muslim and Christian worlds at their highest level, who share a faith in the same God and a mutual respect for their differences of opinion, have agreed to open a dialogue. This being so, it is surely quite natural for other aspects of each respective Revelation to be confronted. The subject of this confrontation is the examination of the Scriptures in the light of scientific data and knowledge concerning the authenticity of the texts. This examination is to be undertaken for the Qur'an as it was for the Judeo-Christian Revelation.

The relationship between religions and science has not always been the same in any one place or time. It is a fact that there is no writing belonging to a monotheistic religion that condemns science. In practise however, it must be admitted that scientists have had great difficulties with the religious authorities of certain creeds. For many centuries, in the Christian world, scientific development was opposed by the authorities in question, on their own initiative and without reference to the authentic Scriptures. We already know the measures taken against those who sought to enlarge science, measures which often made scientists go into exile to avoid being burnt at the stake, unless they recanted, changed their attitude and begged for pardon. The case of Galileo is always cited in this context: he was tried for having accepted the discoveries made by Copernicus on the rotation of the Earth. Galileo was condemned as the result of a mistaken interpretation of the Bible, since not a single Scripture could reasonably be brought against him. *YES THIS IS TRUE*

In the case of Islam, the attitude towards science was, generally speaking, quite different. Nothing could be clearer than the famous Hadith of the Prophet: "Seek for science, even in China", or the other hadith which says that the search for knowledge is a strict duty for every Muslim man and woman. As we shall see further on in this section, another crucial fact is that the

Qur'an, while inviting us to cultivate science, itself contains many observations on natural phenomena and includes explanatory details which are seen to be in total agreement with modern scientific data. There is no equal to this in the Judeo-Christian Revelation.

It would nevertheless be wrong to imagine that, in the history of Islam, certain believers had never harboured a different attitude towards science. It is a fact that, at certain periods, the obligation to educate oneself and others was rather neglected. It is equally true that in the Muslim world, as elsewhere, an attempt was sometimes made to stop scientific development. All the same it will be remembered that at the height of Islam, between the Eighth and Twelfth centuries A.D., i.e. at a time when restrictions on scientific development were in force in the Christian world, a very large number of studies and discoveries were being made at Islamic universities. It was there that the remarkable cultural resources of the time were to be found. The Calif's library at Cordoba contained 400,000 volumes. Averroës was teaching there, and Greek, Indian and Persian sciences were taught. This is why scholars from all over Europe went to study at Cordoba, just as today people go to the United States to perfect their studies. A very great number of ancient manuscripts have come down to us thanks to cultivated Arabs who acted as the vehicle for the culture of conquered countries. We are also greatly indebted to Arabic culture for mathematics (algebra was an Arabic invention), astronomy, physics (optics), geology, botany, medicine (Avicenna) etc. For the very first time, science took on an international character in the Islamic universities of the Middle Ages. At this time, men were more steeped in the religious spirit than they are today; but in the Islamic world, this did not prevent them from being both believers and scientists. Science was the twin of religion and it should never have ceased to be so.

The Medieval period was, for the Christian world, a time of stagnation and absolute conformity. It must be stressed that scientific research was not slowed down by the Judeo-Christian Revelation itself, but rather by those people who claimed to be its servants. Following the Renaissance, the scientists' natural reaction was to take vengeance on their former enemies; this vengeance still continues today, to such an extent indeed that in the West, anyone who talks of God in scientific circles really does stand out. This attitude affects the thinking of all young people who receive a university education, Muslims included.

Their thinking could hardly be different from what it is considering the extreme positions adopted by the most eminent scientists. A Nobel prize winner for Medicine has tried in the last few years to persuade people, in a book intended for mass publication, that living matter was able to create itself by chance from several basic components. Starting, he says, with this primitive living matter, and under the influence of various external circumstances, organized living beings were formed, resulting in the formidable complex being that constitutes man.

Surely these marvels of contemporary scientific knowledge in the field of life should lead a thinking person to the opposite conclusion. The organization presiding over the birth and maintenance of life surely appears more and more complicated as one studies it; the more details one knows, the more admiration it commands. A knowledge of this organization must surely lead one to consider as less and less probable the part chance has to play in the phenomenon of life. The further one advances along the road to knowledge, especially of the infinitely small, the more eloquent are the arguments in favor of the existence of a Creator. Instead of being filled with humility in the face of such facts, man is filled with arrogance. He sneers at any idea of God, in the same way he runs down anything that detracts from his pleasure and enjoyment. This is the image of the materialist society that is flourishing at present in the West.

What spiritual forces can be used to oppose this pollution of thought practised by many contemporary scientists?

Judaism and Christianity make no secret of their inability to cope with the tide of materialism and invasion of the West by atheism. Both of them are completely taken off guard, and from one decade to the next one can surely see how seriously diminished their resistance is to this tide that threatens to sweep everything away. The materialist atheist sees in classic Christianity nothing more than a system constructed by men over the last two thousand years designed to ensure the authority of a minority over their fellow men. He is unable to find in Judeo-Christian writings any language that is even vaguely similar to his own; they contain so many improbabilities, contradictions and incompatibilities with modern scientific data, that he refuses to take texts into consideration that the vast majority of theologians would like to see accepted as an inseparable whole.

When one mentions Islam to the materialist atheist, he smiles with a complacency that is only equal to his ignorance of the subject. In common with the majority of western intellectuals, of whatever religious persuasion, he has an impressive collection of false notions about Islam.

One must, on this point, allow him one or two excuses: Firstly, apart from the newly-adopted attitudes prevailing among the highest Catholic authorities, Islam has always been subject in the West to a so-called 'secular slander'. Anyone in the West who has acquired a deep knowledge of Islam knows just to what extent its history, dogma, and aims have been distorted. One must also take into account the fact that documents published in European languages on this subject (leaving aside highly specialized studies) do not make the work of a person willing to learn any easier.

A knowledge of the Islamic Revelation is indeed fundamental from this point of view. Unfortunately, passages from the Qur'an, especially those relating to scientific data, are badly translated and interpreted, so that a scientist has every right to make criticisms—with apparent justification—that the Book does not actually deserve at all. This detail is worth noting henceforth: inaccuracies in translation or erroneous commentaries (the one is often associated with the other), which would not have surprised anybody one or two centuries ago, offend today's scientists. When faced with a badly translated phrase containing a scientifically unacceptable statement, the scientist is prevented from taking the phrase into serious consideration. In the chapter on human reproduction, a very typical example will be given of this kind of error.

Why do such errors in translation exist? They may be explained by the fact that modern translators often take up, rather uncritically, the interpretations given by older commentators. In their day, the latter had an excuse for having given an inappropriate definition to an Arabic word containing several possible meanings; they could not possibly have understood the real sense of the word or phrase which has only become clear in the present day thanks to scientific knowledge. In other words, the problem is raised of the necessary revision of translations and commentaries. It was not possible to do this at a certain period in the past, but nowadays we have knowledge that enables us to render their true sense. These problems of translation are not present for the texts of the Judeo-Christian Revelation: the case described here is absolutely unique to the Qur'an.

These scientific considerations, which are very specific to the Qur'an, greatly surprised me at first. Up until then, I had not thought it possible for one to find so many statements in a text compiled more than thirteen centuries ago referring to extremely diverse subjects and all of them totally in keeping with modern scientific knowledge. In the beginning, I had no faith whatsoever in Islam. I began this examination of the texts with a completely open mind and a total objectivity. If there was any influence acting upon me, it was gained from what I had been taught in my youth; people did not speak of Muslims, but of 'Muhammadans', to make it quite clear that what was meant was a religion founded by a man and which could not therefore have any kind of value in terms of God. Like many in the West, I could have retained the same false notions about Islam; they are so widely-spread today, that I am indeed surprised when I come across anyone, other than a specialist, who can talk in an enlightened manner on this subject. I therefore admit that before I was given a view of Islam different from the one received in the West, I was myself extremely ignorant.

I owe the fact that I was able to realize the false nature of the judgements generally made in the West about Islam to exceptional circumstances. It was in Saudi Arabia itself that an inkling was given to me of the extent to which opinions held in the West on this subject are liable to error.

The debt of gratitude I owe to the late King Faisal, whose memory I salute with deepest respect, is indeed very great: the fact that I was given the signal honour of hearing him speak on Islam and was able to raise with him certain problems concerning the interpretation of the Qur'an in relation to modern science is a very cherished memory. It was an extremely great privilege for me to have gathered so much precious information from him personally and those around him.

Since I had now seen the wide gap separating the reality of Islam from the image we have of it in the West, I experienced a great need to learn Arabic (which I did not speak) to be sufficiently well-equipped to progress in the study of such a misunderstood religion. My first goal was to read the Qur'an and to make a sentence-by-sentence analysis of it with the help of various commentaries essential to a critical study. My approach was to pay special attention to the description of numerous natural phenomena given in the Qur'an; the highly accurate nature of certain details referring to them in the Book, which was only apparent in the original, struck me by the fact that they were in keeping with present-day ideas, although a man living at the time of Muhammad could not have suspected this at all. I subsequently read several works written by Muslim authors on the scientific aspects of the Qur'anic text: they were extremely helpful in my appreciation of it, but I have not so far discovered a general study of this subject made in the West.

What initially strikes the reader confronted for the first time with a text of this kind is the sheer abundance of subjects discussed: the Creation, astronomy, the explanation of certain matters concerning the earth, and the animal and vegetable kingdoms, human reproduction. Whereas monumental errors are to be found in the Bible, I could not find a single error in the Qur'an. I had to stop and ask myself: if a man was the author of the Qur'an, how could he have written facts in the Seventh century A.D. that today are shown to be in keeping with modern scientific knowledge? There was absolutely no doubt about it: the text of the Qur'an we have today is most definitely a text of the period, if I may be allowed to put it in these terms (in the next chapter of the present section of the book I shall be dealing with this problem). What human explanation can there be for this observation? In my opinion there is no explanation; there is no special reason why an inhabitant of the Arabian Peninsula should, at a time when King Dagobert was reigning in France (629-639 A.D.), have had scientific knowledge on certain subjects that was ten centuries ahead of our own.

It is an established fact that at the time of the Qur'anic Revelation, i.e. within a period of roughly twenty years straddling Hegira (622 A.D.), scientific knowledge had not progressed for centuries and the period of activity in Islamic civilization, with its accompanying scientific upsurge, came *after* the close of the Qur'anic Revelation. Only ignorance of such religious and secular data can lead to the following bizarre suggestion I have heard several times: if surprising statements of a scientific nature exist in the Qur'an, they may be accounted for by the fact that Arab scientists were so far ahead of their time and Muhammad was influenced by their work. Anyone who knows anything about Islamic history is aware that the period of the Middle Ages which saw the cultural and scientific upsurge in the Arab world came after Muhammad, and would not therefore indulge in such whims. Suggestions of this kind are particularly off the mark because the majority of scientific facts which are either suggested or very clearly recorded in the Qur'an have only been confirmed in modern times.

It is easy to see therefore how for centuries commentators on the Qur'an (including those writing at the height of Islamic culture) have inevitably made errors of interpretation in the case of certain verses whose exact meaning could not possibly have been grasped. It was not until much later, at a period not far from our own, that it was possible to translate and interpret them correctly. This implies that a thorough linguistic knowledge is not in itself sufficient to understand these verses from the Qur'an. What is needed along with this is a highly diversified knowledge of science. A study such as the present one embraces many disciplines and is in that sense encyclopedic. As the questions raised are discussed, the variety of scientific knowledge essential to the understanding of certain verses of the Qur'an will become clear.

The Qur'an does not aim at explaining certain laws governing the Universe, however; it has an absolutely basic religious objective. The descriptions of Divine Omnipotence are what principally incite man to reflect on the works of Creation. They are accompanied by references to facts accessible to human observation or to laws defined by God who presides over the organization of the universe both in the sciences of nature and as regards man.

One part of these assertions is easily understood, but the meaning of the other can only be grasped if one has the essential scientific knowledge it requires. This means that in former times, man could only distinguish an apparent meaning which led him to draw the wrong conclusions on account of the inadequacy of his knowledge at the time in question.

It is possible that the choice of verses from the Qur'an which are to be studied for their scientific content may perhaps seem too small for certain Muslim writers who have already drawn attention to them before I have. In general, I believe I have retained a slightly smaller number of verses than they have. On the other hand, I have singled out several verses which until now have not, in my opinion, been granted the importance they deserve from a scientific point of view. Wherever I may have mistakenly failed to take verses into consideration for this study that were selected by these writers, I hope that they will not hold it against me. I have also found, on occasion, that certain books contain scientific interpretations which do not appear to me to be correct; it is with an open mind and a clear conscience that I have provided personal interpretations of such verses.

By the same token, I have tried to find references in the Qur'an to phenomena accessible to human comprehension but which have not been confirmed by modern science. In this context, I think I may have found references in the Qur'an to the presence of planets in the Universe that are similar to the Earth. It must be added that many scientists think this is a perfectly feasible fact, although modern data cannot provide any hint of certainty. I thought I owed it to myself to mention this, whilst retaining all the attendant reservations that might be applied.

Had this study been made thirty years ago, it would have been necessary to add another fact predicted by the Qur'an to what would have been cited concerning astronomy; this fact is the conquest of space. At that time, subsequent to the first trials of ballistic missiles, people imagined a day when man would perhaps have the material possibility of leaving his earthly habitat and exploring space. It was then known that a verse existed in the Qur'an predicting how one day man would make this conquest. This statement has now been verified.

The present confrontation between Holy Scripture and science brings ideas into play, both for the Bible and the Qur'an, which concern scientific truth. For this confrontation to be valid, the scientific arguments to be relied upon must be quite soundly established and must leave no room for doubt. Those who balk at the idea of accepting the intervention of science in an appreciation of the Scriptures deny that it is possible for science to constitute a valid term of comparison (whether it be the Bible, which does not escape the comparison unscathed—and we have seen why—or the Qur'an, which has nothing to fear from science). Science, they say, is changing with the times and a fact accepted today may be rejected later.

This last comment calls for the following observation: a distinction must be drawn between scientific theory and duly controlled observed fact. Theory is intended to explain a phenomenon or a series of phenomena not readily understandable. In many instances theory changes: it is liable to be modified or replaced by another theory when scientific progress makes it easier to analyse facts and invisage a more viable explanation. On the other hand, an observed fact checked by experimentation is not liable to modification: it becomes easier to define its characteristics, but it remains the same. It has been established that the Earth revolves around the Sun and the Moon around the Earth, and this fact will not be subject to revision; all that may be done in the future is to define the orbits more clearly.

A regard for the changing nature of theory is, for example, what made me reject a verse from the Qur'an thought by a Muslim physicist to predict the concept of anti-matter, a theory which is at present the subject of much debate. One can, on the other hand, quite legitimately devote great attention to a verse from the Qur'an describing the aquatic origins of life, a phenomenon we shall never be able to verify, but which has many arguments that speak in its favour. As for observed facts such as the evolution of the human embryo, it is quite possible to confront different stages described in the Qur'an with the data of modern embryology and find complete concordance between modern science and the verses of the Qur'an referring to this subject.

This confrontation between the Qur'an and science has been completed by two other comparisons: one is the confrontation of modern knowledge with Biblical data on the same subjects; and the other is the comparison from the same scientific point of view between the data in the Qur'an, the Book of Revelation transmitted by God to the Prophet, and the data in the Hadīths, books narrating the deeds and sayings of Muhammad that lie outside the written Revelation.

At the end of this, the third section of the present work, the detailed results of the comparison between the Biblical and Qur'anic description of a single event are given, along with an account of how the passage fared when subjected to the scientific criticism of each description. An examination has, for example, been made in the case of the Creation and of the Flood. In each instance, the incompatibilities with science in the Biblical description have been made clear. Also to be seen is the complete agreement between science and the descriptions in the Qur'an referring to them. We shall note precisely those differences that make one description scientifically acceptable in the present day and the other unacceptable.

This observation is of prime importance, since in the West, Jews, Christians and Atheists are unanimous in stating (without a scrap of evidence however) that Muhammad wrote the Qur'an or had it written as an imitation of the Bible. It is claimed that stories of religious history in the Qur'an resume Biblical stories. This attitude is as thoughtless as saying that Jesus Himself duped His contemporaries by drawing inspiration from the Old Testament during His preachings: the whole of Matthew's Gospel is based on this continuation of the Old Testament, as we have indeed seen already. What expert in exegesis would dream of depriving Jesus of his status as God's envoy for this reason? This is nevertheless the way that Muhammad is judged more often than not in the West: "all he did was to copy the Bible". It is a summary judgement that does not take account of the fact that the Qur'an and the Bible provide different versions of a single event. People prefer not to talk about the difference in the descriptions. They are pronounced to be the same and thus scientific knowledge need not be brought in. We shall enlarge on these problems when dealing with the description of the Creation and the Flood.

The collection of hadiths are to Muhammad what the Gospels re to Jesus: descriptions of the actions and sayings of the 'rophet. Their authors were not eyewitnesses. (This applies at east to the compilers of the collections of hadiths which are said o be the most authentic and were collected much later than the ime when Muhammad was alive). They do not in any way con- titute books containing the written Revelation. They are not the word of God, but the sayings of the Prophet. In these books, which are very widely read, statements are to be found containing errors from a scientific point of view, especially medical remedies. We naturally discount anything relating to problems of a relig- ous kind, since they are not discussed here in the context of the adiths. Many hadiths are of doubtful authenticity; they are discussed by Muslim scientists themselves. When the scientific ature of one of the hadiths is touched upon in the present work, t is essentially to put into relief all that distinguishes them from he Qur'an itself when seen from this point of view, since the atter does not contain a single scientific statement that is unac- ceptable. The difference, as we shall see, is quite startling.

The above observation makes the hypothesis advanced by those who see Muhammad as the author of the Qur'an quite untenable. How could a man, from being illiterate, become the most impor- ant author, in terms of literary merit, in the whole of Arabic iterature? How could he then pronounce truths of a scientific nature that no other human being could possibly have developed at the time, and all this without once making the slightest error in his pronouncements on the subject?

The ideas in this study are developed from a purely scientific point of view. They lead to the conclusion that it is inconceivable for a human being living in the Seventh century A.D. to have made statements in the Qur'an on a great variety of subjects that do not belong to his period and for them to be in keeping with what was to be known only centuries later. For me, there can be no human explanation to the Qur'an.

Authenticity of the Qur'an.

How It Came To Be Written.

Thanks to its undisputed authenticity, the text of the Qur'an holds a unique place among the books of Revelation, shared neither by the Old nor the New Testament. In the first two sections of this work, a review was made of the alterations undergone by the Old Testament and the Gospels before they were handed down to us in the form we know today. The same is not true for the Qur'an for the simple reason that it was written down at the time of the Prophet; we shall see how it came to be written, i.e. the process involved.

In this context, the differences separating the Qur'an from the Bible are in no way due to questions essentially concerned with date. Such questions are constantly put forward by certain people without regard to the circumstances prevailing at the time when the Judeo-Christian and the Qur'anic Revelations were written; they have an equal disregard for the circumstances surrounding the transmission of the Qur'an to the Prophet. It is suggested that a Seventh century text had more likelihood of coming down to us unaltered than other texts that are as many as fifteen centuries older. This comment, although correct, does not constitute a sufficient reason; it is made more to excuse the alterations made in the Judeo-Christian texts in the course of centuries than to underline the notion that the text of the Qur'an, which was more recent, had less to fear from being modified by man.

In the case of the Old Testament, the sheer number of authors who tell the same story, plus all the revisions carried out on the text of certain books from the pre-Christian era, constitute as many reasons for inaccuracy and contradiction. As for the Gospels, nobody can claim that they invariably contain faithful accounts of Jesus's words or a description of his actions strictly in keeping with reality. We have seen how successive versions of the texts showed a lack of definite authenticity and moreover that their authors were not eyewitnesses.

Also to be underlined is the distinction to be made between the Qur'an, a book of written Revelation, and the hadiths, collections of statements concerning the actions and sayings of Muhammad. Some of the Prophet's companions started to write them down from the moment of his death. As an element of human error could have slipped in, the collection had to be resumed later and subjected to rigorous criticism so that the greatest credit is in practise given to documents that came along after Muhammad. Their authenticity varies, like that of the Gospels. Not a single Gospel was written down at the time of Jesus (they were all written long after his earthly mission had come to an end), and not a single collection of hadiths was compiled during the time of the Prophet.

The situation is very different for the Qur'an. As the Revelation progressed, the Prophet and the believers following him recited the text by heart and it was also written down by the scribes in his following. It therefore starts off with two elements of authenticity that the Gospels do not possess. This continued up to the Prophet's death. At a time when not everybody could write, but everyone was able to recite, recitation afforded a considerable advantage because of the double-checking possible when the definitive text was compiled.

The Qur'anic Revelation was made by Archangel Gabriel to Muhammad. It took place over a period of more than twenty years of the Prophet's life, beginning with the first verses of Sura 96, then resuming after a three-year break for a long period of twenty years up to the death of the Prophet in 632 A.D., i.e. ten years before Hegira and ten years after Hegira.[1]

---

1. Muhammad's departure from Makka to Madina, 622 A.D.

The following was the first Revelation (sura 96, verses 1 to 5)
"Read: In the name of thy Lord who created,
Who created man from something which clings
Read! Thy Lord is the most Noble
Who taught by the pen
Who taught man what he did not know."

Professor Hamidullah notes in the Introduction to his Fren‹
translation of the Qur'an that one of the themes of this fir
Revelation was the 'praise of the pen as a means of huma
knowledge' which would 'explain the Prophet's concern for tl
preservation of the Qur'an in writing.'

Texts formally prove that long before the Prophet left Makl
for Madina (i.e. long before Hegira), the Qur'anic text so fa
revealed had been written down. We shall see how the Qur'a
is authentic in this. We know that Muhammad and the Believel
who surrounded him were accustomed to reciting the reveal‹
text from memory. It is therefore inconceivable for the Qur'a
to refer to facts that did not square with reality because tl
latter could so easily be checked with people in the Prophet
following, by asking the authors of the transcription.

Four suras dating from a period prior to Hegira refer to th
writing down of the Qur'an before the Prophet left Makka i
622 (sura 80, verses 11 to 16):
"By no means! Indeed it is a message of instruction
Therefore whoever wills, should remember
On leaves held in honor
Exalted, purified
In the hands of scribes
Noble and pious."

Yusuf Ali, in the commentary to his translation, 1934, wrot
that when the Revelation of this sura was made, forty-two o
forty-five others had been written and were kept by Muslims i
Makka (out of a total of 114).

---

1. Muhammad was totally overwhelmed by these words. We shall return ‼
   an interpretation of them, especially with regard to the fact that Mu
   hammad could neither read nor write.

—Sura 85, verses 21 and 22:
"Nay, this is a glorious reading[1]
On a preserved tablet"
—Sura 56, verses 77 to 80:
"This is a glorious reading[1]
In a book well kept
Which none but the purified teach.
This is a Revelation from the Lord of the Worlds."
—Sura 25, verse 5:
"They said: Tales of the ancients which he has caused to be
written and they are dictated to him morning and evening."
Here we have a reference to the accusations made by the
rophet's enemies who treated him as an imposter. They spread
e rumour that stories of antiquity were being dictated to him
nd he was writing them down or having them transcribed (the
eaning of the word is debatable, but one must remember that
uhammad was illiterate). However this may be, the verse refers
> this act of making a written record which is pointed out by
uhammad's enemies themselves.
A sura that came after Hegira makes one last mention of the
aves on which these divine instructions were written:
—Sura 98, verses 2 and 3:
"An (apostle) from God recites leaves
Kept pure where are decrees right and straight."
The Qur'an itself therefore provides indications as to the fact
hat it was set down in writing at the time of the Prophet. It is
known fact that there were several scribes in his following,
he most famous of whom, Zaid Ibn Thâbit, has left his name to
osterity.
In the preface to his French translation of the Qur'an (1971),
rofessor Hamidullah gives an excellent description of the condi-
ions that prevailed when the text of the Qur'an was written,
asting up until the time of the Prophet's death:
"The sources all agree in stating that whenever a fragment of
e Qur'an was revealed, the Prophet called one of his literate
ompanions and dictated it to him, indicating at the same time
he exact position of the new fragment in the fabric of what
ad already been received . . . Descriptions note that Muhammad

---

1. In the text: *Qur'ān* which also means 'reading'.

asked the scribe to reread to him what had been dictated so th
he could correct any deficiencies . . . Another famous story te.
how every year in the month of Ramadan, the Prophet wou
recite the whole of the Qur'an (so far revealed) to Gabriel . .
that in the Ramadan preceding Muhammad's death, Gabriel h:
made him recite it twice . . . It is known how since the Prophet
time, Muslims acquired the habit of keeping vigil during Ram
dan, and of reciting the whole of the Qur'an in addition to t]
usual prayers expected of them. Several sources add that Muhar
mad's scribe Zaid was present at this final bringing-together (
the texts. Elsewhere, numerous other personalities are mention(
as well."

Extremely diverse materials were used for this first recor
parchment, leather, wooden tablets, camels' scapula, soft stor
for inscriptions, etc.

At the same time however, Muhammad recommended that th
faithful learn the Qur'an by heart. They did this for a part 1
not all of the text recited during prayers. Thus there wer
Hafizūn who knew the whole of the Qur'an by heart and sprea
it abroad. The method of doubly preserving the text both in writ
ing and by memorization proved to be extremely precious.

Not long after the Prophet's death (632), his successor Ab
Bakr, the first Caliph of Islam, asked Muhammad's former hea
scribe, Zaid Ibn Thâbit, to make a copy; this he did. On Omar'
initiative (the future second Caliph), Zaid consulted all the in
formation he could assemble at Madina: the witness of th
Hafizūn, copies of the Book written on various materials belong
ing to private individuals, all with the object of avoiding possibl
errors in transcription. Thus an extremely faithful copy of th
Book was obtained.

The sources tell us that Caliph Omar, Abu Bakr's successor ir
634, subsequently made a single volume *(mushaf)* that he pre
served and gave on his death to his daughter Hafsa, the Prophet':
widow.

The third Caliph of Islam, Uthman, who held the caliphate
from 644 to 655, entrusted a commission of experts with the
preparation of the great recension that bears his name. It checked
the authenticity of the document produced under Abu Bakr which
had remained in Hafsa's possession until that time. The commis-

ion consulted Muslims who knew the text by heart. The critical analysis of the authenticity of the text was carried out very rigorously. The agreement of the witnesses was deemed necessary before the slightest verse containing debatable material was retained. It is indeed known how some verses of the Qur'an correct others in the case of prescriptions: this may be readily explained when one remembers that the Prophet's period of apostolic activity stretched over twenty years (in round figures). The result is a text containing an order of suras that reflects the order followed by the Prophet in his complete recital of the Qur'an during Ramadan, as mentioned above.

One might perhaps ponder the motives that led the first three Caliphs, especially Uthman, to commission collections and recensions of the text. The reasons are in fact very simple: Islam's expansion in the very first decades following Muhammad's death was very rapid indeed and it happened among peoples whose native language was not Arabic. It was absolutely necessary to ensure the spread of a text that retained its original purity: Uthman's recension had this as its objective.

Uthman sent copies of the text of the recension to the centres of the Islamic Empire and that is why, according to Professor Hamidullah, copies attributed to Uthman exist in Tashkent and Istanbul. Apart from one or two possible mistakes in copying, the oldest documents known to the present day, that are to be found throughout the Islamic world, are identical; the same is true for documents preserved in Europe (there are fragments in the Bibliothèque Nationale in Paris which, according to the experts, date from the Eighth and Ninth centuries A.D., i.e. the Second and Third Hegirian centuries). The numerous ancient texts that are known to be in existence all agree except for very minor variations which do not change the general meaning of the text at all. If the context sometimes allows more than one interpretation, it may well have to do with the fact that ancient writing was simpler than that of the present day.[1]

---

1. The absence of diacritical marks, for example, could make a verb either active or passive and in some instances, masculine or feminine. More often than not however, this was hardly of any great consequence since the context indicated the meaning in many instances.

The 114 suras were arranged in decreasing order of length,
there were nevertheless exceptions. The chronological sequence
of the Revelation was not followed. In the majority of cases however, this sequence is known. A large number of descriptions are
mentioned at several points in the text, sometimes giving rise to
repetitions. Very frequently a passage will add details to a description that appears elsewhere in an incomplete form. Everything connected with modern science is, like many subjects dealt
with in the Qur'an, scattered throughout the book without any
semblance of classification.

III

The Creation of the Heavens and the Earth.

DIFFERENCES FROM AND RESEMBLANCES TO THE BIBLICAL DESCRIPTION.

In contrast to the Old Testament, the Qur'an does not provide a unified description of the Creation. Instead of a continuous narration, there are passages scattered all over the Book which deal with certain aspects of the Creation and provide information on the successive events marking its development with varying degrees of detail. To gain a clear idea of how these events are presented, the fragments scattered throughout a large number of suras have to be brought together.

This dispersal throughout the Book of references to the same subject is not unique to the theme of the Creation. Many important subjects are treated in the same manner in the Qur'an: earthly or celestial phenomena, or problems concerning man that are of interest to scientists. For each of these themes, the same effort has been made here to bring all the verses together.

For many European commentators, the description of the Creation in the Qur'an is very similar to the one in the Bible and they are quite content to present the two descriptions side by side. I believe this concept is mistaken because there are very obvious differences. On subjects that are by no means unimportant from a scientific point of view, we find statements in the Qur'an whose equivalents we search for in vain in the Bible. The latter contains descriptions that have no equivalent in the Qur'an.

The obvious resemblances between the two texts are well known; among them is the fact that, at first glance, the number

133

given to the successive stages of the Creation is identical: the six days in the Bible correspond to the six days in the Qur'an. In fact however, the problem is more complex than this and it is worth pausing to examine it.

The Six Periods of the Creation.

There is absolutely no ambiguity whatsoever in the Biblical[1] description of the Creation in six days followed by a day of rest, the sabbath, analogous with the days of the week. It has been shown how this mode of narration practiced by the priests of the Sixth century B.C. served the purpose of encouraging the people to observe the sabbath. All Jews were expected to rest[2] on the sabbath as the Lord had done after he had laboured during the six days of the week.

The way the Bible interprets it, the word 'day' means the interval of time between two successive sunrises or sunsets for an inhabitant of the Earth. When defined in this way, the day is conditioned by the rotation of the Earth on its own axis. It is obvious that logically-speaking there can be no question of 'days' as defined just now, if the mechanism that causes them to appear—i.e. the existence of the Earth and its rotation around the Sun—has not already been fixed in the early stages of the Creation according to the Biblical description. This impossibility has already been emphasized in the first part of the present book.

When we refer to the majority of translations of the Qur'an, we read that—analogous with the Biblical description—the process of the Creation for the Islamic Revelation also took place over a period of six days. It is difficult to hold against the translators the fact that they have translated the Arabic word by its most common meaning. This is how it is usually expressed in translations so that in the Qur'an, verse 54, sura 7 reads as follows:

"Your Lord is God Who created the heavens and the earth in six days."

---

1. The Biblical description mentioned here is taken from the so-called Sacerdotal version discussed in the first part of this work; the description taken from the so-called Yahvist version has been compressed into the space of a few lines in today's version of the Bible and is too insubstantial to be considered here.
2. 'Sabbath' in Hebrew means 'to rest'.

There are very few translations and commentaries of the Qur'an that note how the word 'days' should really be taken to mean 'periods'. It has moreover been maintained that if the Qur'anic texts on the Creation divided its stages into 'days', it was with the deliberate intention of taking up beliefs held by all the Jews and Christians at the dawn of Islam and of avoiding a head-on confrontation with such a widely-held belief.

Without in any way wishing to reject this way of seeing it, one could perhaps examine the problem a little more closely and scru-. tinize *in the Qur'an itself*, and more generally in the language of the time, the possible meaning of the word that many translators themselves still continue to translate by the word 'day': *yaum*, plural *ayyām* in Arabic.[1]

Its most common meaning is 'day' but it must be stressed that it tends more to mean the diurnal light than the length of time that lapses between one day's sunset and the next. The plural *ayyām* can mean, not just 'days', but also 'long length of time', an indefinite period of time (but always long). The meaning 'period of time' that the word contains is to be found elsewhere in the Qur'an. Hence the following:

—sura 32, verse 5:

". . . in a period of time (*yaum*) whereof the measure is a thousand years of your reckoning."

(It is to be noted that the Creation in six periods is precisely what the verse preceding verse 5 refers to).

—sura 70, verse 4:

". . . in a period of time (*yaum*) whereof the measure is 50,000 years."

The fact that the word '*yaum*' could mean a period of time that was quite different from the period that we mean by the word 'day' struck very early commentators who, of course, did not have the knowledge we possess today concerning the length of the stages in the formation of the Universe. In the Sixteenth century A.D. for example, Abu al Sū'ud, who could not have had any idea of the day as defined astronomically in terms of the Earth's rotation, thought that for the Creation a division must

---

1. See table on last page of present work for equivalence between Latin and Arabic letters.

be considered that was not into days as we usually understand the word, but into 'events' (in Arabic *nauba*).

Modern commentators have gone back to this interpretation. Yusuf Ali (1934), in his commentary on each of the verses that deals with the stages in the Creation, insists on the importance of taking the word, elsewhere interpreted as meaning 'days', to mean in reality 'very long Periods, or Ages, or Aeons'.

It is therefore possible to say that in the case of the Creation of the world, the Qur'an allows for long periods of time numbering six. It is obvious that modern science has not permitted man to establish the fact that the complicated stages in the process leading to the formation of the Universe numbered six, but it has clearly shown that long periods of time were involved compared to which 'days' as we conceive them would be ridiculous.

One of the longest passages of the Qur'an, which deals with the Creation, describes the latter by juxtaposing an account of earthly events and one of celestial events. The verses in question are verses 9 to 12, sura 41:

(God is speaking to the Prophet)

"Say: Do you disbelieve Him Who created the earth in two periods? Do you ascribe equals to Him. He is the Lord of the Worlds.

"He set in the (earth) mountains standing firm. He blessed it. He measured therein its sustenance in four periods, in due proportion, in accordance with the needs of those who ask for (sustenance? or information?).

"Moreover (*tumma*) He turned to heaven when it was smoke and said to it and to the earth: come willingly or unwillingly! They said: we come in willing obedience.

"Then He ordained them seven heavens in two periods, and He assigned to each heaven its mandate by Revelation. And We adorned the lower heaven with luminaries and provided it a guard. Such is the decree of the All Mighty, the Full of Knowledge."

These four verses of sura 41 contain several points to which we shall return: the initially gaseous state of celestial matter and the highly symbolic definition of the number of heavens as seven. We shall see the meaning behind this figure. Also of a symbolic nature is the dialogue between God on the one hand

and the primordial sky and earth on the other: here however it is only to express the submission of the Heavens and Earth, once they were formed, to divine orders.

Critics have seen in this passage a contradiction with the statement of the six periods of the Creation. By adding the two periods of the formation of the Earth to the four periods of the spreading of its sustenance to the inhabitants, plus the two periods of the formation of the Heavens, we arrive at eight periods. This would then be in contradiction with the six periods mentioned above.

In fact however, this text, which leads man to reflect on divine Omnipotence, beginning with the Earth and ending with the Heavens, provides two sections that are expressed by the Arabic word '*tumma*', translated by 'moreover', but which also means 'furthermore' or 'then'. The sense of a 'sequence' may therefore be implied referring to a sequence of events or a series of man's reflections on the events mentioned here. It may equally be a simple reference to events juxtaposed without any intention of bringing in the notion of the one following the other. However this may be, the periods of the Creation of the Heavens may just as easily coincide with the two periods of the Earth's creation. A little later we shall examine how the basic process of the formation of the Universe is presented in the Qur'an and we shall see how it can be jointly applied to the Heavens and the Earth in keeping with modern ideas. We shall then realize how perfectly reasonable this way is of conceiving the simultaneous nature of the events here described.

There does not appear to be any contradiction between the passage quoted here and the concept of the formation of the world in six stages that is to be found in other texts in the Qur'an.

THE QUR'AN DOES NOT LAY DOWN A SEQUENCE FOR THE CREATION OF THE EARTH AND HEAVENS.

In the two passages from the Qur'an quoted above, reference was made in one of the verses to the Creation of the Heavens and the Earth (sura 7, verse 54), and elsewhere to the Creation of the Earth and the Heavens (sura 41, verses 9 to 12). The Qur'an does not therefore appear to lay down a sequence for the Creation of the Heavens and the Earth.

The number of verses in which the Earth is mentioned first is quite small, e.g. sura 2, verse 29 and sura 20, verse 4, where a reference is made to "Him Who created the earth and the high heavens". The number of verses where the Heavens are mentioned before the Earth is, on the other hand, much larger: (sura 7, verse 54; sura 10, verse 3; sura 11, verse 7; sura 25, verse 59; sura 32, verse 4; sura 50, verse 38; sura 57, verse 4; sura 79, verses 27 to 33; sura 91, verses 5 to 10).

In actual fact, apart from sura 79, there is not a single passage in the Qur'an that lays down a definite sequence; a simple co-ordinating conjunction (wa) meaning 'and' links two terms, or the word tumma which, as has been seen in the above passage, can indicate either a simple juxtaposition or a sequence.

There appears to me to be only one passage in the Qur'an where a definite sequence is plainly established between different events in the Creation. It is contained in verses 27 to 33, sura 79:

"Are you the harder to create or is it the heaven that (God) built? He raised its canopy and fashioned it with harmony. He made dark the night and he brought out the forenoon. And after that (ba' da dalika) He spread it out. Therefrom he drew out its water and its pasture. And the mountains He has fixed firmly. Goods for you and your cattle."

This list of earthly gifts from God to man, which is expressed in a language suited to farmers or nomads on the Arabian Peninsula, is preceded by an invitation to reflect on the creation of the heavens. The reference to the stage when God spreads out the earth and renders it arable is very precisely situated in time after the alternating of night and day has been achieved. Two groups are therefore referred to here, one of celestial phenomena, and the other of earthly phenomena articulated in time. The reference made here implies that the earth must necessarily have existed before being spread out and that it consequently existed when God created the Heavens. The idea of a concomitance therefore arises from the heavenly and earthly evolutions with the interlocking of the two phenomena. Hence, one must not look for any special significance in the reference in the Qur'anic text to the Creation of the Earth before the Heavens or the Heavens before the Earth: the position of the words does not influence the order in which the Creation took place, unless however it is specifically stated.

THE BASIC PROCESS OF THE FORMATION OF THE UNIVERSE AND THE RESULTING COMPOSITION OF THE WORLDS.

The Qur'an presents in two verses a brief synthesis of the phenomena that constituted the basic process of the formation of the Universe.

—sura 21, verse 30:

"Do not the Unbelievers see that the heavens and the earth were joined together, then We clove them asunder and We got every living thing out of the water. Will they not then believe?"

—sura 41, verse 11: God orders the Prophet to speak after inviting him to reflect on the subject of the earth's creation:

"Moreover (God) turned to the Heaven when it was smoke and said to it and to the earth . . ."

There then follow the orders to submit, referred to on page 136.

We shall come back to the aquatic origins of life and examine them along with other biological problems raised by the Qur'an. The important things to remember at present are the following:

a) The statement of the existence of a gaseous mass with fine particles, for this is how the word 'smoke' (*dukān* in Arabic) is to be interpreted. Smoke is generally made up of a gaseous substratum, plus, in more or less stable suspension, fine particles that may belong to solid and even liquid states of matter at high or low temperature;

b) The reference to a separation process (*fatq*) of an primary single mass whose elements were initially fused together (*ratq*). It must be noted that in Arabic '*fatq*' is the action of breaking, diffusing, separating, and that '*ratq*' is the action of fusing or binding together elements to make a homogenous whole.

This concept of the separation of a whole into several parts is noted in other passages of the Book with reference to multiple worlds. The first verse of the first sura in the Qur'an proclaims, after the opening invocation, the following: "In the name of God, the Beneficent, the Merciful", "Praise be to God, Lord of the Worlds."

The terms 'worlds' reappears dozens of times in the Qur'an. The Heavens are referred to as multiple as well, not only on account of their plural form, but also because of their symbolic numerical quantity: 7.

This number is used 24 times throughout the Qur'an for various numerical quantities. It often carries the meaning of 'many' although we do not know exactly why this meaning of the figure was used. The Greeks and Romans also seem to have used the number 7 to mean an undefined idea of plurality. In the Qur'an, the number 7 refers to the Heavens themselves (samāwāt). It alone is understood to mean 'Heavens'. The 7 roads of the Heavens are mentioned once:

—sura 2, verse 29:

"(God) is the One Who created for you all that is on the earth. Moreover He turned to the heaven and fashioned seven heavens with harmony. He is Full of Knowledge of all things."

—sura 23, verse 17:

"And We have created above you seven paths: We have never been unmindful of the Creation."

—sura 67, verse 3:

"(God) is the One Who created seven heavens one above another. Thou canst see no fault in the creation of the Beneficent. Turn the vision again! Canst thou see any rift?"

—sura 71, verse 15-16:

"Did you see how God created seven heavens one above another and made the moon a light therein and made the sun a lamp?[1]"

—sura 78, verse 12:

"We have built above you seven strong (heavens) and placed a blazing lamp."

Here the blazing lamp is the Sun.

The commentators on the Qur'an are in agreement on all these verses: the number 7 means no more than plurality.[2]

---

1. It is to be noted that while the Bible calls both Sun and Moon 'lights', here, as always in the Qur'an, they are differently named; the first is called 'Light' (nūr) and the second is compared in this verse to a 'lamp (sirāj) producing light'. We shall see later how other epithets are applied to the Sun.

2. Apart from the Qur'an, we often find the number 7 meaning plurality in texts from Muhammad's time, or from the first centuries following him, which record his words (hadiths).

There are therefore many Heavens and Earths, and it comes as no small surprise to the reader of the Qur'an to find that earths such as our own may be found in the Universe, a fact that has not yet been verified by man in our time.

Verse 12 of sura 65 does however predict the following:

"God is the One Who created seven heavens and of the earth (*ard*) a similar number. The Command descends among them so that you know that God has power over all things and comprehends all things in His knowledge."

Since 7 indicates an indefinite plurality (as we have seen), it is possible to conclude that the Qur'anic text clearly indicates the existence of more than one single Earth, our own Earth (*ard*) ; there are others like it in the Universe.

Another observation which may surprise the Twentieth century reader of the Qur'an is the fact that verses refer to three groups of things created, i.e.

—things in the Heavens
—things on the Earth
—things between the Heavens and the Earth

Here are several of these verses:

—sura 20, verse 6;

"To Him (God) belongs what is in the heavens, on earth, between them and beneath the soil."

—sura 25, verse 59:

". . . the One Who created the heavens, the earth and what is between them in six periods."

—sura 32, verse 4:

"God is the One Who created the heavens, the earth and what is between them in six periods."

—sura 50, verse 38:

"We created the heavens, the earth and what is between them in six periods, and no weariness touched Us."[1]

The reference in the Qur'an to 'what is between the Heavens and the Earth' is again to be found in the following verses: sura

---

1. This statement that the Creation did not make God at all weary stands out as an obvious reply to the Biblical description, referred to in the first part of the present book, where God is said to have rested on the seventh day from the preceding days' work!

21, verse 16; sura 44, verses 7 and 38; sura 78, verse 37; sura 15, verse 85; sura 46, verse 3; sura 43, verse 85.

This Creation outside the Heavens and outside the Earth, mentioned several times, is *a priori* difficult to imagine. To understand these verses, reference must be made to the most recent human observations on the existence of cosmic extra-galactic material and one must indeed go back to ideas established by contemporary science on the formation of the Universe, starting with the simplest and proceeding to the most complex. These are the subject of the following paragraph.

Before passing on to these purely scientific matters however, it is advisable to recapitulate the main points on which the Qur'an gives us information about the Creation. According to the preceding quotations, they are as follows:

1) Existence of six periods for the Creation in general.
2) Interlocking of stages in the Creation of the Heavens and the Earth.
3) Creation of the Universe out of an initially unique mass forming a block that subsequently split up.
4) Plurality of the Heavens and of the Earths.
5) Existence of an intermediary creation 'between the Heavens and the Earth'.

SOME MODERN SCIENTIFIC DATA CONCERNING THE FORMATION OF THE UNIVERSE.

The Solar System.

The Earth and planets rotating around the Sun constitute an organized world of dimensions which, to our human scale, appear quite colossal. The Earth is, after all, roughly 93 million miles from the Sun. This is a very great distance for a human being, but it is very small in comparison to the distance separating the Sun from the furthermost planet from it in the solar system (Pluto); in round numbers it is 40 times the distance from the Earth to the Sun, i.e. approximately 3,672 million miles away. This distance, when doubled, represents the largest dimension of our solar system. The Sun's light takes nearly 6 hours to reach

Pluto, and yet the journey is made at the terrifying speed of over 186,000 miles per second. The light coming from stars on the very confines of the known celestial world therefore takes billions of years to reach us.

The Galaxies.

The Sun, of which we are a satellite like the other planets surrounding it, is itself an infinitesmally small element among a hundred billion stars that form a whole, called a galaxy. On a fine summer night, the whole of space seems to be filled with stars that make up what is known as the Milky Way. This group has extremely large dimensions. Whereas light could cross the solar system in units of one hour, it would require something like 90,000 years to go from one extreme to the other of the most compact group of stars that make up our galaxy.

The galaxy that we belong to however, even though it is so incredibly huge, is only a small part of the Heavens. There are giant agglomerates of stars similar to the Milky Way that lie outside our galaxy. They were discovered a little over fifty years ago, when astronomy was able to make use of an optical instrument as sophisticated as the one that made possible the construction of the Mount Wilson telescope in the United States. Thus a very large number indeed of isolated galaxies and masses of galaxies have been discovered that are so far away that it was necessary to institute a special unit of light-years, the 'parsec' (the distance light travels in 3.26 years at 186,000 miles per second).

Formation and Evolution of Galaxies, Stars and Planetary Systems.

What was there originally in the immensely large space the galaxies now occupy? Modern science can only answer this question as of a certain period in the evolution of the Universe; it cannot put into numbers the length of time that separates this period from us.

At the earliest time it can provide us with, modern science has every reason to maintain that the Universe was formed of a gaseous mass principally composed of hydrogen and a certain amount of helium that was slowly rotating. This nebula subsequently split up into multiple fragments with very large dimensions and masses, so large indeed, that specialists in astrophysics are able to estimate their mass from 1 to 100 billion times the present mass of the Sun (the latter represents a mass that is over 300,000 times that of the Earth). These figures give an idea of the large size of the fragments of primary gaseous mass that were to give birth to the galaxies.

A new fragmentation was to form the stars. There then followed the intervention of a condensing process where gravitational forces came into play, (since these bodies were moving and rotating more and more quickly), along with pressures and the influence of magnetic fields and of radiations. The stars became shiny as they contracted and transformed the gravitational forces into thermal energy. Thermonuclear reactions came into play, and heavier atoms were formed by fusion at the expense of others that were lighter; this is how the transition was made from hydrogen to helium, then to carbon and oxygen, ending with metals and metalloids. Thus the stars have a life of their own and modern astronomy classifies them according to their present stage of evolution. The stars also have a death; in the final stage of their evolution, the violent implosion of certain stars has been observed so that they become veritable 'corpses'.

The planets, and in particular the Earth, originated in a separation process starting from an initial constituent that in the beginning was the primary nebula. A fact that has no longer been contested for over twenty-five years is that the Sun condensed inside the single nebula and that the planets did the same inside the surrounding nebular disc. One must stress—and this is of prime importance for the subject in hand—that there was no sequence in the formation of the celestial elements such as the Sun nor in the formation of an earthly element. There is an evolutionary parallelism with the identity of origin.

Here, science can give us information on the period during which the events just mentioned took place. Having estimated the age of our galaxy at roughly ten billion years, according to this hypothesis, the formation of the solar system took place a little over five billion years later. The study of natural radio activity makes it possible to place the age of the Earth and the time the Sun was formed at 4.5 billion years ago, to within a present-day accuracy of 100 million years, according to some scientists' calculations. This accuracy is to be admired, since 100 million years may represent a long time to us but the ratio 'maximum error/total time-to-be-measured' is 0.1/4.5, i.e. 2.2%.

Specialists in astrophysics have therefore attained a high degree of knowledge concerning the general process involved in the formation of the solar system. It may be summarized as follows: condensation and contraction of a rotating gaseous mass, splitting up into fragments that leave the Sun. and planets in their places, among them the Earth.[1] The knowledge that science has gained on the primary nebula and the way it split up into an incommensurable quantity of stars grouped into galaxies leaves absolutely no doubt as to the legitimacy of a concept of the plurality of worlds. It does not however provide any kind of certainty concerning the existence in the Universe of anything that might, either closely or vaguely, resemble the Earth.

The Concept of the Plurality of the Worlds.

In spite of the above, modern specialists in astrophysics consider it highly likely that planets similar to Earth are present in the Universe. As far as the solar system is concerned, nobody seriously entertains the possibility of finding general conditions similar to those on Earth on another planet in this system. We must therefore seek for them outside the solar system. The likelihood of their existing outside it is considered quite probable for the following reasons: .

It is thought that in our galaxy half of the 100 billion stars must, like the Sun, have a planetary system. The fifty billion stars do indeed, like the Sun, rotate very slowly; a characteristic which suggests that they are surrounded by planets that are their satellites. These stars are so far away that the possible planets are unobservable, but their existence is thought to be highly probable on account of certain trajectory characteristics; a slight undulation of the star's trajectory indicates the presence

---

1. As regards the Moon, its gradual separation from the Earth following the deceleration of its rotation is an acknowledged probability.

of a companion planetary satellite. Thus the Barnard Star probably has at least one planetary companion with a mass greater than that of Jupiter and may even have two satellites. As P. Guérin writes: "All the evidence points to the fact that planetary systems are scattered in profusion all over the universe. The solar system and the Earth are not unique." And as a corollary: "Life, like the planets that harbour it, is scattered throughout the universe, in those places where the physico-chemical conditions necessary for its flowering and development are to be found."

Interstellar Material.

The basic process in the formation of the Universe therefore lay in the condensation of material in the primary nebula followed by its division into fragments that originally constituted galactic masses. The latter in their turn split up into stars that provided the sub-product of the process, i.e. the planets. These successive separations left among the groups of principle elements what one might perhaps call 'remains'. Their more scientific name is 'interstellar galactic material'. It has been described in various ways; there are bright nebulae that reflect the light received from other stars and are perhaps composed of 'dusts' or 'smokes', to use the terminology of experts in astrophysics, and then there are the dark nebulae that are less dense, consisting of interstellar material that is even more modest, known for its tendency to interfere with photometric measurements in astronomy. There can be no doubt about the existence of 'bridges' of material between the galaxies themselves. Although these gases may be very rarefied, the fact that they occupy such a colossal space, in view of the great distance separating the galaxies, could make them correspond to a mass possibly greater than the total mass of the galaxies in spite of the low density of the former. A. Boichot considers the presence of these intergalactic masses to be of prime importance which could "considerably alter ideas on the evolution of the Universe."

We must now go back to the basic ideas on the Creation of the Universe that were taken from the Qur'an and look at them in the light of modern scientific data.

CONFRONTATION WITH THE DATA IN THE QUR'AN CONCERNING THE CREATION.

We shall examine the five main points on which the Qur'an gives information about the Creation.

1) The six periods of the Creation of the Heavens and the Earth covered, according to the Qur'an, the formation of the celestial bodies and the Earth, and the development of the latter until (with its 'sustenance') it became inhabitable by man. In the case of the Earth, the events described in the Qur'an happened over four periods. One could perhaps see in them the four geological periods described by modern science, with man's appearance, as we already know, taking place in the quaternary era. This is purely a hypothesis since nobody has an answer to this question.

It must be noted however, that the formation of the heavenly bodies and the Earth, as explained in verses 9 to 12, sura 41 (see page 136) required two phases. If we take the Sun and its sub-product the Earth as an example (the only one accessible to us), science informs us that their formation occurred by a process of condensation of the primary nebula and then their separation. This is exactly what the Qur'an expresses very clearly when it refers to the processes that produced a fusion and subsequent separation starting from a celestial 'smoke'. Hence there is complete correspondence between the facts of the Qur'an and the facts of science.

2) Science showed the interlocking of the two stages in the formation of a star (like the Sun) and its satellite (like the Earth). This interconnection is surely very evident in the text of the Qur'an examined.

3) The existence at an early stage of the Universe of the 'smoke' referred to in the Qur'an, meaning the predominantly gaseous state of the material that composes it, obviously corresponds to the concept of the primary nebula put forward by modern science.

4) The plurality of the heavens, expressed in the Qur'an by the number 7, whose meaning we have discussed, is confirmed by modern science due to the observations experts in astrophysics have made on galactic systems and their very large number. On the other hand the plurality of earths that are similar to ours

(from certain points of view at least) is an idea that arises in the text of the Qur'an but has not yet been demonstrated to be true by science; all the same, specialists consider this to be quite feasible.

5) The existence of an intermediate creation between 'the Heavens' and 'the Earth' expressed in the Qur'an may be compared to the discovery of those bridges of material present outside organized astronomic systems.

Although not all the questions raised by the descriptions in the Qur'an have been completely confirmed by scientific data, there is in any case absolutely no opposition between the data in the Qur'an on the Creation and modern knowledge on the formation of the Universe. This fact is worth stressing for the Qur'anic Revelation, whereas it is very obvious indeed that the present-day text of the Old Testament provides data on the same events that are unacceptable from a scientific point of view. It is hardly surprising, since the description of the Creation in the Sacerdotal version of the Bible[1] was written by priests at the time of the deportation to Babylon who had the legalist intentions already described and therefore compiled a description that fitted their theological views. The existence of such an enormous difference between the Biblical description and the data in the Qur'an concerning the Creation is worth underlining once again on account of the totally gratuitous accusations leveled against Muhammad since the beginnings of Islam to the effect that he copied the Biblical descriptions. As far as the Creation is concerned, this accusation is totally unfounded. *How could a man living fourteen hundred years ago have made corrections to the existing description to such an extent that he eliminated scientifically inaccurate material and, on his own initiative, made statements that science has been able to verify only in the present day? This hypothesis is completely untenable. The description of the Creation given in the Qur'an is quite different from the one in the Bible.*

---

1. This text completely overshadows the few lines contained in the Yahvist version. The latter is too brief and too vague for the scientist to take account of it.

ANSWERS TO CERTAIN OBJECTIONS

Indisputably, resemblances do exist between narrations dealing with other subjects, particularly religious history, in the Bible and in the Qur'an. It is moreover interesting to note from this point of view how nobody holds against Jesus the fact that he takes up the same sort of facts and Biblical teachings. This does not, of course, stop people in the West from accusing Muhammad of referring to such facts in his teaching with the suggestion that he is an imposter because he presents them as a Revelation. As for the proof that Muhammad reproduced in the Qur'an what he had been told or dictated by the rabbis, it has no more substance than the statement that a Christian monk gave him a sound religious education. One would do well to re-read what R. Blachère in his book, *The Problem of Muhammad* (Le Problème de Mahomet)[1], has to say about this 'fable'.

A hint of a resemblance is also advanced between other statements in the Qur'an and beliefs that go back a very long way, probably much further in time than the Bible.

More generally speaking, the traces of certain cosmogonic myths have been sought in the Holy Scriptures; for example the belief held by the Polynesians in the existence of primeval waters that were covered in darkness until they separated when light appeared; thus Heaven and Earth were formed. This myth is compared to the description of the Creation in the Bible, where there is undoubtedly a resemblance. It would however be superficial to then accuse the Bible of having copied this from the cosmogonic myth.

It is just as superficial to see the Qur'anic concept of the division of the primeval material constituting the Universe at its initial stage—a concept held by modern science—as one that comes from various cosmogonic myths in one form or another that express something resembling it.

It is worth analysing these mythical beliefs and descriptions more closely. Often an initial idea appears among them which is reasonable in itself, and is in some cases borne out by what we today know (or think we know) to be true, except that fantastic descriptions are attached to it in the myth. This is the case of

1. Pub. Presses Universitaries de France, Paris, 1952.

the fairly widespread concept of the Heavens and the Earth originally being united then subsequently separated. When, as in Japan, the image of the egg plus an expression of chaos is attached to the above with the idea of a seed inside the egg (as for all eggs), the imaginative addition makes the concept lose all semblance of seriousness. In other countries, the idea of a plant is associated with it; the plant grows and in so doing raises up the sky and separates the Heavens from the Earth. Here again, the imaginative quality of the added detail lends the myth its very distinctive character. Nevertheless a common characteristic remains, i.e. the notion of a single mass at the beginning of the evolutionary process leading to the formation of the Universe which then divided to form the various 'worlds' that we know today.

The reason these cosmogonic myths are mentioned here is to underline the way they have been embroidered by man's imagination and to show the basic difference between them and the statements in the Qur'an on the same subject. The latter are free from any of the whimsical details accompanying such beliefs on the contrary, they are distinguished by the sober quality of the words in which they are made and their agreement with scientific data.

Such statements in the Qur'an concerning the Creation, which appeared nearly fourteen centuries ago, obviously do not lend themselves to a human explanation.

IV

Astronomy In the Qur'an

The Qur'an is full of reflections on the Heavens. In the preced-
ng chapter on the Creation, we saw how the plurality of the
Ieavens and Earths was referred to, as well as what the Qur'an
alls an intermediary creation 'between the Heavens and the
Iarth': modern science has verified the latter. The verses refer-
-ing to the Creation already contain a broad idea of what is to
)e found in the heavens, i.e. of everything outside the earth.

Apart from the verses that specifically describe the Creation,
here are roughly another forty verses in the Qur'an which
rovide information on astronomy complementing what has
already been given. Some of them are not much more than
-eflections on the glory of the Creator, the Organizer of all the
stellar and planetary systems. These we know to be arranged
according to balancing positions whose stability Newton explained in his law of the mutual attraction of bodies.

The first verses to be quoted here hardly furnish much material for scientific analysis: the aim is simply to draw attention
to God's Omnipotence. They must be mentioned however to give
a realistic idea of the way the Qur'anic text described the organization of the Universe fourteen centuries ago.

These references constitute a new fact of divine Revelation.
The organization of the world is treated in neither the Gospels
nor the Old Testament (except for a few notions whose general
inaccuracy we have already seen in the Biblical description of
the Creation). The Qur'an however deals with this subject in
depth. What it describes is important, but so is what it does not
contain. It does not in fact provide an account of the theories
prevalent *at the time* of the Revelation that deal with the organi-

zation of the celestial world, theories that science was later †
show were inaccurate. An example of this will be given late
This negative consideration must however be pointed out.[1]

A. GENERAL REFLECTIONS CONCERNING THE SKY.

—sura 50, verse 6. The subject is man in general.
"Do they not look at the sky above them, how We have bui
it and adorned it, and there are no rifts in it."
—sura 31, verse 10:
"(God) created the heavens without any pillars that you ca
see . . ."
—sura 13, verse 2:
"God is the One Who raised the heavens without any pilla
that you can see, then He firmly established Himself on th
throne and He subjected the sun and moon . . ."
These two verses refute the belief that the vault of the heaven
was held up by pillars, the only things preventing the former fro
crushing the earth.
—sura 55, verse 7:
"the sky (God) raised it . . ."
—sura 22, verse 65:
"(God) holds back the sky from falling on the earth unles
by His leave . . ."
It is known how the remoteness of celestial masses at grea
distance and in proportion to the magnitude of their mass itsel
constitutes the foundation of their equilibrium. The more remot
the masses are, the weaker the force is that attracts one to th
other. The nearer they are, the stronger the attraction is tha
one has to the other: this is true for the Moon, which is near t

---

1. I have often heard those who go to great lengths to find a human ex
planation—and no other—to all the problems raised by the Qur'an sa
the following: "if the Book contains surprising statements on astron
omy, it is because the Arabs were very knowledgeable on this subject.
In so doing they forget the fact that, in general, science in Islami
countries is very much post-Qur'an, and that the scientific knowledge o
this great period would in any case not have been sufficient for a huma
being to write some of the verses to be found in the Qur'an. This wi
be shown in the following paragraphs.

e Earth (astronomically speaking), and exercises an influence
laws of attraction on the position occupied by the waters of
e sea, hence the phenomenon of the tides. If two celestial bodies
me too close to one another, collision is inevitable. The fact
at they are subjected to an order is the *sine qua non* for the
sence of disturbances.

The subjection of the Heavens to divine order is often referred
as well:

-sura 23, verse 86: God is speaking to the Prophet.
"Say: Who is Lord of the seven heavens and Lord of the
tremendous throne?"
We have already seen how by 'seven heavens' what is meant
not 7, but an indefinite number of Heavens.

-sura 45, verse 13:
"For you (God) subjected all that is in the heavens and on
the earth, all from Him. Behold! In that are signs for
people who reflect."

-sura 55, verse 5:
"The sun and moon (are subjected) to calculations"

-sura 6, verse 96:
"(God) appointed the night for rest and the sun and the moon
for reckoning."

-sura 14, verse 33:
"For you (God) subjected the sun and the moon, both dil-
igently pursuing their courses. And for you He subjected the
night and the day."

Here one verse completes another: the calculations referred to
esult in the regularity of the course described by the heavenly
odies in question, this is expressed by the word *dā'ib*, the present
articiple of a verb whose original meaning was 'to work eagerly
nd assiduously at something'. Here it is given the meaning of
o apply oneself to something with care in a perseverant, invari-
ble manner, in accordance with set habits'.

—sura 36, verse 39: God is speaking:
"And for the moon We have appointed mansions till she returns like an old shriveled palm branch."

This is a reference to the curled form of the palm bran
which, as it shrivels up, takes on the moon's crescent. This cor
mentary will be completed later.

—sura 16, verse 12:

"For you (God) subjected the night and the day, the sun a
the moon; the stars are in subjection to His Comman
Verily in this are signs for people who are wise."

The practical angle from which this perfect celestial order
seen is underlined on account of its value as an aid to man
travel on earth and by sea, and to his calculation of time. Th
comment becomes clear when one bears in mind the fact th
the Qur'an was originally a preaching addressed to men who on
understood the simple language of their everyday lives. Th
explains the presence of the following reflections:

—sura 6, verse 97:

"(God) is the One Who has set out for you the stars, that yo
may guide yourselves by them through the darkness of tl
land and of the sea. We have detailed the signs for peop
who know."

—sura 16, verse 16:

"(God sets on the earth) landmarks and by the stars (men
guide themselves."

—sura 10, verse 5:

"God is the One Who made the sun a shining glory and th
moon a light and for her ordained mansions, so that yo
might know the number of years and the reckoning (of th
time). God created this in truth. He explains the signs i
detail for people who know."

This calls for some comment. Whereas the Bible calls the Su
and Moon 'lights', and merely adds to one the adjective 'greate
and to the other 'lesser', the Qur'an ascribes differences othe
than that of dimension to each respectively. Agreed, this i
nothing more than a verbal distinction, but how was one t
communicate to men at this time without confusing them, whil
at the same time expressing the notion that the Sun and Moo
were not absolutely identical 'lights'?

B. NATURE OF HEAVENLY BODIES.

The Sun and the Moon.

The Sun is a shining glory (*ḍiyā'*) and the Moon a light (*nūr*). This translation would appear to be more correct than those given by others, where the two terms are inverted. In fact there is little difference in meaning since *ḍiyā'* belongs to a root (*ḍw'*) which, according to Kazimirski's authoritative Arabic/French dictionary, means 'to be bright, to shine' (e.g. like a fire). The same author attributes to the substantive in question the meaning of 'light'.

The difference between Sun and Moon will be made clearer by further quotes from the Qur'an.

—sura 25, verse 61:

"Blessed is the One Who placed the constellations in heaven and placed therein a lamp and a moon giving light."

—sura 71, 15-16:

"Did you see how God created seven heavens one above another and made the moon a light therein and made the sun a lamp?"

—sura 78, verses 12-13:

"We have built above you seven strong (heavens) and placed a blazing lamp."

The blazing lamp is quite obviously the sun.

Here the moon is defined as a body that gives light (*munīr*) from the same root as *nūr* (the light applied to the Moon). The Sun however is compared to a torch (*sirāj*) or a blazing (*wahhāj*) lamp.

A man of Muhammad's time could easily distinguish between the Sun, a blazing heavenly body well known to the inhabitants of the desert, and the Moon, the body of the cool of the night. The comparisons found in the Qur'an on this subject are therefore quite normal. What is interesting to note here is the sober quality of the comparisons, and the absence in the text of the Qur'an of any elements of comparison that might have prevailed at the time and which in our day would appear as phantasmagorial.

It is known that the Sun is a star that generates intense heat and light by its internal combustions, and that the Moon, which does not give off light itself, and is an inert body (on its external layers at least) merely reflects the light received from the Sun.

There is nothing in the text of the Qur'an that contradicts what we know today about these two celestial bodies.

The Stars.

As we know, the stars are heavenly bodies like the Sun. They are the scene of various physical phenomena of which the easiest to observe is their generation of light. They are heavenly bodies that produce their own light.

The word 'star' appears thirteen times in the Qur'an (*najm*, plural *nūjūm*) ; it comes from a root meaning to appear, to come into sight. The word designates a visible heavenly body without saying of what kind, i.e. either generator of light or mere reflector of light received. To make it clear that the object so designated is a star, a qualifying phrase is added as in the following sura :

—sura 86, verses 1-3 :

"By the sky and the Night-Visitor, who will tell thee what the Night-Visitor is, the Star of piercing brightness."[1]

The evening star is qualified in the Qur'an by the word *tākib* meaning 'that which pierces through something' (here the night shadows). The same word is moreover used to designate shooting stars (sura 37, verse 10) : the latter are the result of combustion.

The Planets.

It is difficult to say whether these are referred to in the Qur'an with the same exact meaning that is given to the heavenly bodies in the present day.

The planets do not have their own light. They revolve around the Sun, Earth being one of them. While one may presume that others exist elsewhere, the only ones known are those in the solar system.

Five planets other than Earth were known to the ancients : Mercury, Venus, Mars, Jupiter and Saturn. Three have been discovered in recent times : Uranus, Neptune and Pluto.

---

1. Here, the sky and a star are used to bear witness to the importance of what is to come in the text.

The Qur'an would seem to designate these by the word *kaukab* plural *kawākib*) without stating their number. Joseph's dream sura 12) refers to eleven of them, but the description is, by efinition, an imaginary one.

A good definition of the meaning of the word *kaukab* in the ur'an seems to have been given in a very famous verse. The minently spiritual nature of its deeper meaning stands forth, nd is moreover the subject of much debate among experts in xegesis. It is nevertheless of great interest to offer an account f the comparison it contains on the subject of the word that rould seem to designate a 'planet'.

Here is the text in question: (sura 24, verse 35)

"God is the light of the heavens and the earth. The similitude f His light is as if there were a niche and within it a luminary. he luminary is in a glass. The glass is as if it were a planet littering like a pearl."

Here the subject is the projection of light onto a body that re-lects it (glass) and gives it the glitter of a pearl, like a planet hat is lit by the sun. This is the only explanatory detail referring o this word to be found in the Qur'an.

The word is quoted in other verses. In some of them it is diffi-ult to distinguish which heavenly bodies are meant (sura 6, erse 76; sura 82, verses 1-2).

In one verse however, when seen in the light of modern science, t would seem very much that these can only be the heavenly odies that we know to be planets. In sura 37, verse 6, we see the ollowing:

"We have indeed adorned the lowest heaven with an ornament, the planets."

Is it possible that the expression in the Qur'an 'lowest heaven' means the 'solar system'? It is known that among the celestial elements nearest to us, there are no other permanent elements apart from the planets: the Sun is the only star in the system that bears its name. It is difficult to see what other heavenly bodies could be meant if not the planets. The translation given would therefore seem to be correct and the Qur'an to refer to the existence of the planets as defined in modern times.

The Lowest Heaven.

The Qur'an mentions the lowest heaven several times along with the heavenly bodies of which it is composed. The first among these would seem to be the planets, as we have just seen. When however the Qur'an associates material notions intelligible to us, enlightened as we are today by modern science, with statements of a purely spiritual nature, their meaning becomes obscure.

Thus the verse quoted could easily be understood, except that the following verse (7) of the same sura 37 speaks of a 'guard against every rebellious evil spirit', 'guard' again being referred to in sura 21, verse 32 and sura 41, verse 12, so that we are confronted by statements of quite a different kind.

What meaning can one attach moreover to the 'projectiles for the stoning of demons' that according to verse 5, sura 67 are situated in the lowest heaven? Do the 'luminaries' referred to in the same verse have something to do with the shooting stars mentioned above?[1]

All these observations seem to lie outside the subject of this study. They have been mentioned here for the sake of completeness. At the present stage however, it would seem that scientific data are unable to cast any light on a subject that goes beyond human understanding.

C. CELESTIAL ORGANIZATION.

The information the Qur'an provides on this subject mainly deals with the solar system. References are however made to phenomena that go beyond the solar system itself: they have been discovered in recent times.

There are two very important verses on the orbits of the Sun and Moon:

—sura 21, verse 33:

"(God is) the One Who created the night, the day, the sun and the moon. Each one is travelling in an orbit with its own motion."

---

1. It is known that when a meteorite arrives at the upper layers of the atmosphere, it may produce the luminous phenomenon of a 'shooting star'.

—sura 36, verse 40:

"The sun must not catch up the moon, nor does the night outstrip the day. Each one is travelling in an orbit with its own motion."

Here an essential fact is clearly stated: the existence of the Sun's and Moon's orbits, plus a reference is made to the travelling of these bodies in space with their own motion.

A negative fact also emerges from a reading of these verses: it is shown that the Sun moves in an orbit, but no indication is given as to what this orbit might be in relation to the Earth. At the time of the Qur'anic Revelation, it was thought that the Sun moved while the Earth stood still. This was the system of geocentrism that had held sway since the time of Ptolemy, Second century B.C., and was to continue to do so until Copernicus in the Sixteenth century A.D. Although people supported this concept at the time of Muhammad, it does not appear anywhere in the Qur'an, either here or elsewhere.

The Existence of the Moon's and the Sun's Orbits.

The Arabic word *falak* has here been translated by the word 'orbit'; many French translators of the Qur'an attach to it the meaning of a 'sphere'. This is indeed its initial sense. Hamidullah translates it by the word 'orbit'.

The word caused concern to older translators of the Qur'an who were unable to imagine the circular course of the Moon and the Sun and therefore retained images of their course through space that were either more or less correct, or hopelessly wrong. Si Hamza Boubekeur in his translation of the Qur'an cites the diversity of interpretations given to it: "A sort of axle, like an iron rod, that a mill turns around; a celestial sphere, orbit, sign of the zodiac, speed, wave . . .", but he adds the following observation made by Tabari, the famous Tenth century commentator: "It is our duty to keep silent when we do not know." (XVII, 15). This shows just how incapable men were of understanding this concept of the Sun's and Moon's orbit. It is obvious that if the word had expressed an astronomical concept common in Muhammad's day, it would not have been so difficult to interpret these verses. A new concept therefore existed in the Qur'an that was not to be explained until centuries later.

1. *The Moon's Orbit.*

Today, the concept is widely spread that the Moon is a satellite of the Earth around which it revolves in periods of twenty-nine days. A correction must however be made to the absolutely circular form of its orbit, since modern astronomy ascribes a certain eccentricity to this, so that the distance between the Earth and the Moon (240,000 miles) is only the average distance.

We have seen above how the Qur'an underlined the usefulness of observing the Moon's movements in calculating time (sura 10, verse 5, quoted at the beginning of this chapter.)

This system has often been criticized for being archaic, impractical and unscientific in comparison to our system based on the Earth's rotation around the Sun, expressed today in the Julian calendar.

This criticism calls for the following two remarks:

a) Nearly fourteen centuries ago, the Qur'an was directed at the inhabitants of the Arabian Peninsula who were used to the lunar calculation of time. It was advisable to address them in the only language they could understand and not to upset the habits they had of locating spatial and temporal reference-marks which were nevertheless quite efficient. It is known how well-versed men living in the desert are in the observation of the sky; they navigated according to the stars and told the time according to the phases of the Moon. Those were the simplest and most reliable means available to them.

b) Apart from the specialists in this field, most people are unaware of the perfect correlation between the Julian and the lunar calendar: 235 lunar months correspond exactly to 19 Julian years of 365¼ days. Then length of our year of 365 days is not perfect because it has to be rectified every four years (with a leap year). With the lunar calendar, the same phenomena occur every 19 years (Julian). This is the Metonic cycle, named after the Greek astronomer Meton, who discovered this exact correlation between solar and lunar time in the Fifth century B.C.

2. *The Sun.*

It is more difficult to conceive of the Sun's orbit because we are so used to seeing our solar system organized around it. To understand the verse from the Qur'an, the position of the Sun in our galaxy must be considered, and we must therefore call on modern scientific ideas.

Our galaxy includes a very large number of stars spaced so as to form a disc that is denser at the centre than at the rim. The Sun occupies a position in it which is far removed from the centre of the disc. The galaxy revolves on its own axis which is its centre with the result that the Sun revolves around the same centre in a circular orbit. Modern astronomy has worked out the details of this. In 1917, Shapley estimated the distance between the Sun and the centre of our galaxy at 10 kiloparsecs i.e., in miles, circa the figure 2 followed by 17 zeros. To complete one revolution on its own axis, the galaxy and Sun take roughly 250 million years. The Sun travels at roughly 150 miles per second in the completion of this.

The above is the orbital movement of the Sun that was already referred to by the Qur'an fourteen centuries ago. The demonstration of the existence and details of this is one of the achievements of modern astronomy.

Reference to the Movement of the Moon and the Sun in Space With Their Own Motion.

This concept does not appear in those translations of the Qur'an that have been made by men of letters. Since the latter know nothing about astronomy, they have translated the Arabic word that expresses this movement by one of the meanings the word has: 'to swim'. They have done this in both the French translations and the, otherwise remarkable, English translation by Yusuf Ali.[1]

The Arabic word referring to a movement with a self-propelled motion is the verb *sabaha* (*yasbahūna* in the text of the two verses). All the senses of the verb imply a movement that is associated with a motion that comes from the body in question. If the movement takes place in water, it is 'to swim'; it is 'to move by the action of one's own legs' if it takes place on land. For a movement that occurs in space, it is difficult to see how else this meaning implied in the word could be rendered other than

---

1. Pub. Sh. Muhammad Ashraf, Lahore (Pakistan)

by employing its original sense. Thus there seems to have been
no mistranslation, for the following reasons:
—The Moon completes its rotating motion on its own axis at the
same time as it revolves around the Earth, i.e. 29½ days (ap
prox.), so that it always has the same side facing us.
—The Sun takes roughly 25 days to revolve on its own axis
There are certain differences in its rotation at its equator and
poles, (we shall not go into them here) but as a whole, the Sun
is animated by a rotating motion.

It appears therefore that a verbal nuance in the Qur'an refers
to the Sun and Moon's own motion. These motions of the two
celestial bodies are confirmed by the data of modern science
and it is inconceivable that a man living in the Seventh century
A.D.—however knowledgeable he might have been in his day
(and this was certainly not true in Muhammad's case)—could
have imagined them.

This view is sometimes contested by examples from great
thinkers of antiquity who indisputably predicted certain data
that modern science has verified. They could hardly have relied
on scientific deduction however; their method of procedure was
more one of philosophical reasoning. Thus the case of the Pythagoreans is often advanced. In the Sixth century B.C., they defended the theory of the rotation of the Earth on its own axis
and the movement of the planets around the Sun. This theory
was to be confirmed by modern science. By comparing it with
the case of the Pythagoreans, it is easy to put forward the
hypothesis of Muhammad as being a brilliant thinker, who was
supposed to have imagined all on his own what modern science
was to discover centuries later. In so doing however, people
quite simply forget to mention the other aspect of what these
geniuses of philosophical reasoning produced, i.e. the colossal
blunders that litter their work. It must be remembered for
example, that the Pythagoreans also defended the theory whereby
the Sun was fixed in space; they made it the centre of the world
and only conceived of a celestial order that was centered on it.
It is quite common in the works of the great philosophers of
antiquity to find a mixture of valid and invalid ideas about the
Universe. The brilliance of these human works comes from the
advanced ideas they contain, but they should not make us over-

took the mistaken concepts which have also been left to us. From a strictly scientific point of view, this is what distinguished them from the Qur'an. In the latter, many subjects are referred to that have a bearing on modern knowledge without one of them containing a statement that contradicts what has been established by present-day science.

The Sequence of Day and Night.

At a time when it was held that the Earth was the centre of the world and that the Sun moved in relation to it, how could any one have failed to refer to the Sun's movement when talking of the sequence of night and day? This is not however referred to in the Qur'an and the subject is dealt with as follows:

—sura 7, verse 54:

"(God) covers the day with the night which is in haste to follow it . . ."

—sura 36, verse 37:

"And a sign for them (human beings) is the night. We strip it of the day and they are in darkness."

—sura 31, verse 29:

"Hast thou not seen how God merges the night into the day and merges the day into the night."

—sura 39, verse 5:

". . . He coils the night upon the day and He coils the day upon the night."

The first verse cited requires no comment. The second simply provides an image.

It is mainly the third and fourth verses quoted above that provide interesting material on the process of interpenetration and especially of winding the night upon the day and the day upon the night. (sura 39, verse 5)

'To coil' or 'to wind' seems, as in the French translation by R. Blachère, to be the best way of translating the Arabic verb *kawwara*. The original meaning of the verb is to 'coil' a turban around the head; the notion of coiling is preserved in all the other senses of the word.

What actually happens however in space? American astronauts have seen and photographed what happens from their spaceships, especially at a great distance from Earth, e.g. from the Moon. They saw how the Sun permanently lights up (except in the case of an eclipse) the half of the Earth's surface that is facing it, while the other half of the globe is in darkness. The Earth turns on its own axis and the lighting remains the same, so that an area in the form of a half-sphere makes one revolution around the Earth in twenty-four hours while the other half-sphere, that has remained in darkness, makes the same revolution in the same time. This perpetual rotation of night and day is quite clearly described in the Qur'an. It is easy for the human understanding to grasp this notion nowadays because we have the idea of the Sun's (relative) immobility and the Earth's rotation. This process of perpetual coiling, including the interpenetration of one sector by another is expressed in the Qur'an just as if the concept of the Earth's roundness had already been conceived at the time—which was obviously not the case.

Further to the above reflections on the sequence of day and night, one must also mention, with a quotation of some verses from the Qur'an, the idea that there is more than one Orient and one Occident. This is of purely descriptive interest because these phenomena rely on the most commonplace observations. The idea is mentioned here with the aim of reproducing as faithfully as possible all that the Qur'an has to say on this subject.

The following are examples:

—In sura 70 verse 40, the expression 'Lord of Orients and Occidents'.

—In sura 55, verse 17, the expression 'Lord of the two Orients and the two Occidents'.

—In sura 43, verse 38, a reference to the 'distance between the two Orients', an image intended to express the immense size of the distance separating the two points.

Anyone who carefully watches the sunrise and sunset knows that the Sun rises at different point of the Orient and sets at different points of the Occident, according to season. Bearings taken on each of the horizons define the extreme limits that mark the two Orients and Occidents, and between these there are points marked off throughout the year. The phenomenon described here is rather commonplace, but what mainly deserves attention in this chapter are the other topics dealt with, where the description of astronomical phenomena referred to in the Qur'an is in keeping with modern data.

D. EVOLUTION OF THE HEAVENS.

Having called modern concepts on the formation of the Universe to mind, reference was made to the evolution that took place, starting with primary nebula through to the formation of galaxies, stars and (for the solar system) the appearance of planets beginning with the Sun at a certain stage of its evolution. Modern data lead us to believe that in the solar system, and more generally in the Universe itself, this evolution is still continuing.

How can anybody who is aware of these ideas fail to make a comparison with certain statements found in the Qur'an in which the manifestations of divine Omnipotence are referred to.

The Qur'an reminds us several times that: "(God) subjected the sun and the moon: each one runs its course to an appointed term."

This sentence is to be found in sura 13, verse 2; sura 31, verse 29; sura 35, verse 13 and sura 39, verse 5.

In addition to this, the idea of a settled place is associated with the concept of a destination place in sura 36, verse 38: "The Sun runs its course to a settled place. This is the decree of the All Mighty, the Full of Knowledge."

'Settled place' is the translation of the word *mustaqarr* and there can be no doubt that the idea of an exact place is attached to it.

How do these statements fare when compared with data established by modern science?

The Qur'an gives an end to the Sun for its evolution and a destination place. It also provides the Moon with a settled place. To understand the possible meanings of these statements, we must remember what modern knowledge has to say about the evolution of the stars in general and the Sun in particular, and (by extension) the celestial bodies that automatically followed its movement through space, among them the Moon.

The Sun is a star that is roughly 4½ billion years old, according to experts in astrophysics. It is possible to distinguish a stage in its evolution, as one can for all the stars. At present, the Sun is at an early stage, characterized by the transformation of hydrogen atoms into helium atoms. Theoretically, this present stage should last another 5½ billion years according to calculations that allow a total of 10 billion years for the duration of the primary stage in a star of this kind. It has already been shown, in the case of these other stars, that this stage gives way to a second period characterized by the completion of the transformation of hydrogen into helium, with the resulting expansion of its external layers and the cooling of the Sun. In the final stage, its light is greatly diminished and density considerably increased; this is to be observed in the type of star known as a 'white dwarf'.

The above dates are only of interest in as far as they give a rough estimate of the time factor involved, what is worth remembering and is really the main point of the above, is the notion of an evolution. Modern data allow us to predict that, in a few billion years, the conditions prevailing in the solar system will not be the same as they are today. Like other stars whose transformations have been recorded until they reached their final stage, it is possible to predict an end to the Sun.

The second verse quoted above (sura 36, verse 38) referred to the Sun running its course towards a place of its own.

Modern astronomy has been able to locate it exactly and has even given it a name, the Solar Apex: the solar system is indeed evolving in space towards a point situated in the Constellation of Hercules (*alpha lyrae*) whose exact location is firmly established; it is moving at a speed already ascertained at something in the region of 12 miles per second.

All these astronomical data deserve to be mentioned in relation to the two verses from the Qur'an, since it is possible to state that they appear to agree perfectly with modern scientific data.

The Expansion of the Universe.

The expansion of the Universe is the most imposing discovery of modern science. Today it is a firmly established concept and the only debate centres around the way this is taking place.

It was first suggested by the general theory of relativity and is backed up by physics in the examination of the galactic spectrum; the regular movement towards the red section of their spectrum may be explained by the distancing of one galaxy from another. Thus the size of the Universe is probably constantly increasing and this increase will become bigger the further away the galaxies are from us. The speeds at which these celestial bodies are moving may, in the course of this perpetual expansion, go from fractions of the speed of light to speeds faster than this.

The following verse of the Qur'an (sura 51, verse 47) where God is speaking, may perhaps be compared with modern ideas:

"The heaven, We have built it with power. Verily. We are expanding it."

'Heaven' is the translation of the word *samā'* and this is exactly the extra-terrestrial world that is meant.

'We are expanding it' is the translation of the plural present participle *musi'ūna* of the verb *ausa'a* meaning 'to make wider, more spacious, to extend, to expand'.

Some translators who were unable to grasp the meaning of the latter provide translations that appear to me to be mistaken, e.g. "we give generously" (R. Blachère). Others sense the meaning, but are afraid to commit themselves: Hamidullah in his translation of the Qur'an talks of the widening of the heavens and space, but he includes a question mark. Finally, there are those who arm themselves with authorized scientific opinion in their commentaries and give the meaning stated here. This is true in the case of the *Muntakab*, a book of commentaries edited by the Supreme Council for Islamic Affairs, Cairo. It refers to the expansion of the Universe in totally unambiguous terms.

E. THE CONQUEST OF SPACE.

From this point of view, three verses of the Qur'an should command our full attention. One expresses, without any trace of ambiguity, what man should and will achieve in this field. In the other two, God refers for the sake of the unbelievers in Makka to the surprise they would have if they were able to raise themselves up to the Heavens; He alludes to a hypothesis which will not be realized for the latter.

1) The first of these verses is sura 55, verse 33: "O assembly of Jinns and Men, if you can penetrate regions of the heavens and the earth, then penetrate them! You will not penetrate them save with a Power."

The translation given here needs some explanatory comment:

a) The word 'if' expresses in English a condition that is dependant upon a possibility and either an achievable or an unachievable hypothesis. Arabic is a language which is able to introduce a nuance into the condition which is much more explicit. There is one word to express the possibility (*iḏā*), another for the achievable hypothesis (*in*) and a third for the unachievable hypothesis expressed by the word (*lau*). The verse in question has it as an achievable hypothesis expressed by the word (*in*). The Qur'an therefore suggests the material possibility of a concrete realization. This subtle linguistic distinction formally rules out the purely mystic interpretation that some people have (quite wrongly) put on this verse.

b) God is addressing the spirits (*jinn*) and human beings (*ins*), and not essentially allegorical figures.

c) 'To penetrate' is the translation of the verb *nafaḏa* followed by the preposition *min*. According to Kazimirski's dictionary, the phrase means 'to pass right through and come out on the other side of a body' (e.g. an arrow that comes out on the other side). It therefore suggests a deep penetration and emergence at the other end into the regions in question.

d) The Power (*sulṭān*) these men will have to achieve this enterprise would seem to come from the All-Mighty.[1]

There can be no doubt that this verse indicates the possibility men will one day achieve what we today call (perhaps rather improperly) 'the conquest of space'. One must note that the text of the Qur'an predicts not only penetration through the regions of the Heavens, but also the Earth, i.e. the exploration of its depths.

---

1. This verse is followed by an invitation to recognize God's blessings. It forms the subject of the whole of the sura that bears the title 'The Beneficent'.

2) The other two verses are taken from sura 15, (verses 14 and 15). God is speaking of the unbelievers in Makka, as the context of this passage in the sura shows:

"Even if We opened unto them a gate to Heaven and they were to continue ascending therein, they would say: our sight is confused as in drunkenness. Nay, we are people bewitched."

The above expresses astonishment at a remarkable spectacle, different from anything man could imagine.

The conditional sentence is introduced here by the word *lau* which expresses a hypothesis that could never be realized as far as it concerned the people mentioned in these verses.

When talking of the conquest of space therefore, we have two passages in the text of the Qur'an: one of them refers to what will one day become a reality thanks to the powers of intelligence and ingenuity God will give to man, and the other describes an event that the unbelievers in Makka will never witness, hence its character of a condition never to be realized. The event will however be seen by others, as intimated in the first verse quoted above. It describes the human reactions to the unexpected spectacle that travellers in space will see: their confused sight, as in drunkenness, the feeling of being bewitched . . .

This is exactly how astronauts have experienced this remarkable adventure since the first human spaceflight around the world in 1961. It is known in actual fact how once one is above the Earth's atmosphere, the Heavens no longer have the azure appearance we see from Earth, which results from phenomena of absorption of the Sun's light into the layers of the atmosphere. The human observer in space above the Earth's atmosphere sees a black sky and the Earth seems to be surrounded by a halo of bluish colour due to the same phenomena of absorption of light by the Earth's atmosphere. The Moon has no atmosphere, however, and therefore appears in its true colors against the black background of the sky. It is a completely new spectacle therefore that presents itself to men in space, and the photographs of this spectacle are well known to present-day man.

Here again, it is difficult not to be impressed, when comparing the text of the Qur'an to the data of modern science, by statements that simply cannot be ascribed to the thought of a man who lived more than fourteen centuries ago.

V

The Earth

As in the case of the subjects already examined, the verses of the Qur'an dealing with the Earth are dispersed throughout the Book. It is difficult to classify them, and the scheme adopted here is a personal one.

To explain them more clearly, one might begin by singling out a certain number of verses that deal with more than one subject at a time. These verses are largely general in their application and constitute an invitation extended to men to reflect on divine Beneficence by pondering on the examples provided.

Other groups of verses may be singled out which deal with more specific subjects, as follows:

—the water cycle and the seas.
—the Earth's relief.
—the Earth's atmosphere.

A. VERSES CONTAINING GENERAL STATEMENTS

Although these verses provide arguments intended to lead man to meditate on the Beneficence of God towards His creatures, here and there they contain statements that are interesting from the point of view of modern science. They are perhaps especially revealing by virtue of the fact that they do not express the varied beliefs concerning natural phenomena that were current at the time of the Qur'anic Revelation. These beliefs were later to be shown by scientific knowledge to be mistaken.

On the one hand, these verses express simple ideas readily understood by to those people to whom, for geographical reasons, the Qur'an was first directed: the inhabitants of Makka and Madina, the Bedouins of the Arabian Peninsula. On the other hand, they contain reflections of a general nature from which a more cultivated public of any time and place may learn something instructive, once it starts to think about them: this is a mark of the Qur'an's universality.

As there is apparently no classification of such verses in the Qur'an, they are presented here in the numerical order of the suras:

—sura 2, verse 22:

"(God) is the One who made the earth a couch for you and the heavens an edifice, and sent down water from the sky. He brought forth therewith fruits for your sustenance. Do not join equals with God when you know."

—sura 2, verse 164:

"Behold! In the creation of the heavens and the earth,
In the disparity of night and day,
In the ship which runs upon the sea for the profit
    of mankind,
In the water which God sent down from the sky thereby
    reviving the earth after its death,
In the beasts of all kinds He scatters therein,
In the change of the winds and the subjected clouds
    between the sky and earth,
Here are Signs for people who are wise."

—sura 13, verse 3:

"(God) is the One who spread out the earth and set therein mountains standing firm and rivers. For every fruit He placed two of a pair. He covers the day with the night. Verily in this there are Signs for people who reflect."

—sura 15, verses 19 to 21. God is speaking:

"The earth, We spread it out and set thereon mountains standing firm. We caused all kind of things to grow therein in due balance. Therein We have provided you and those you do not supply with means of subsistence and there is not a thing but its stores are with Us. We do not send it down save in appointed measure."

—sura 20, verses 53 and 54:

"(God is) the One Who has made for you the earth like a cradle and inserted roads into it for you. He sent water down from the sky and thereby We brought forth pairs of plants, each separate from the other. Eat! Pasture your cattle! Verily in this are Signs for people endued with intelligence."

—sura 27, verse 61:

"He Who made the earth an abode and set rivers in its interstices and mountains standing firm. He placed a barrier between the two seas. Is there any divinity besides God? Nay, but most people do not know."

Here a reference is made to the general stability of the Earth's crust. It is known that at the early stages of the Earth's existence before its crust cooled down, the latter was unstable. The stability of the Earth's crust is not however strictly uniform, since there are zones where earthquakes intermittently occur. As to the barrier between the two seas, it is an image which signifies that the waters of the great rivers and the waters of the sea do not mix at the level of certain large estuaries.

—sura 67, verse 15:

"(God is) the One Who made the earth docile to you. So walk upon its shoulders! Eat of His sustenance! Unto Him will be the Resurrection."

—sura 79, verses 30-33:

"After that (God) spread the earth out. Therefrom He drew out its water and its pasture. And the mountains He has firmly fixed. Goods for you and for your cattle."

In many such verses, emphasis is laid upon the importance of water and the practical consequences of its presence in the earth's soil, i.e. the fertility of the soil. There can be no doubt that in desert countries, water is the most important element governing man's survival. The reference in the Qur'an however goes beyond this geographical detail. According to scientific knowledge the character the Earth has of a planet that is rich in water is unique to the solar system, and this is exactly what is highlighted in the Qur'an. Without water, the Earth would be a dead planet like the Moon. The Qur'an gives first place to water among the natural phenomena of the Earth that it refers to. The water cycle is described with remarkable accuracy in the Qur'an.

B. THE WATER CYCLE AND THE SEAS.

When the verses of the Qur'an concerning the role of water in man's existence are read in succession today, they all appear to us to express ideas that are quite obvious. The reason for this is simple: in our day and age, we all, to a lesser or greater extent, know about the water cycle in nature.

If however, we consider the various concepts the ancients had on this subject, it becomes clear that the data in the Qur'an do not embody the mythical concepts current at the time of the Revelation which had been developed more according to philosophical speculation than observed phenomena. Although it was empirically possible to acquire on a modest scale, the useful practical knowledge necessary for the improvement of the irrigation, the concepts held on the water cycle in general would hardly be acceptable today.

Thus it would have been easy to imagine that underground water could have come from the infiltration of precipitations in the soil. In ancient times however, this idea, held by Vitruvius Polio Marcus in Rome, 1st century B.C., was cited as an exception. For many centuries therefore (and the Qur'anic Revelation is situated during this period) man held totally inaccurate views on the water cycle.

Two specialists on this subject, G. Gastany and B. Blavoux, in their entry in the Universalis Encyclopedia (*Encyclopedia Universalis*) under the heading *Hydrogeology* (Hydrogéologie), give an edifying history of this problem.

"In the Seventh century B.C., Thales of Miletus held the theory whereby the waters of the oceans, under the effect of winds, were thrust towards the interior of the continents; so the water fell upon the earth and penetrated into the soil. Plato shared these views and thought that the return of the waters to the oceans was via a great abyss, the 'Tartarus'. This theory had many supporters until the Eighteenth century, one of whom was Descartes. Aristotle imagined that the water vapour from the soil condensed in cool mountain caverns and formed underground lakes that fed springs. He was followed by Seneca (1st Century A.D.) and many others, until 1877, among them O. Volger . . . The first clear formulation of the water cycle must be attributed to Bernard

Palissy in 1580: he claimed that underground water came from
rainwater infiltrating into the soil. This theory was confirmed by
E. Mariotte and P. Perrault in the Seventeenth century.

In the following passages from the Qur'an, there is no trace
of the mistaken ideas that were current at the time of Muhammad :
—sura 50, verses 9 to 11:

"We[1] sent down from the sky blessed water whereby We caused
to grow gardens, grains for harvest, tall palm-trees with their
spathes, piled one above the other—sustenance for (Our) servants. Therewith We gave (new) life to a dead land. So will be
the emergence (from the tombs)." *The Rain makes plants grow*
—sura 23, verses 18 and 19:

"We sent down water from the sky in measure and lodged it in
the ground. And We certainly are able to withdraw it. Therewith
for you We gave rise to gardens of palm-trees and vineyards
where for you are abundant fruits and of them you eat."
—sura 15, verse 22: *They dug wells in Abraham's time*

"We sent forth the winds that fecundate. We cause the water
to descend from the sky. We provide you with the water—you
(could) not be the guardians of its reserves."

There are two possible interpretations of this last verse. The
fecundating winds may be taken to be the fertilizers of plants
because they carry pollen. This may, however, be a figurative expression referring by analogy to the role the wind plays in the
process whereby a non-raincarrying cloud is turned into one that
produces a shower of rain. This role is often referred to, as in the
following verses:

—sura 35, verse 9:

"God is the One Who sends forth the winds which raised up
the clouds. We drive them to a dead land. Therewith We revive
the ground after its death. So will be the Resurrection."

It should be noted how the style is descriptive in the first part
of the verse, then passes without transition to a declaration from
God. Such sudden changes in the form of the narration are very
frequent in the Qur'an.

---

1. Whenever the pronoun 'We' appears in the verses of the text quoted
here, it refers to God.

sura 30, verse 48:

"God is the One Who sends forth the winds which raised up e clouds. He spreads them in the sky as He wills and breaks em into fragments. Then thou seest raindrops issuing from thin them. He makes them reach such of His servants as He ills. And they are rejoicing." Observation ?

-sura 7, verse 57:

"(God) is the One Who sends forth the winds like heralds of is Mercy. When they have carried the heavy-laden clouds, We ive them to a dead land. Then We cause water to descend and ereby bring forth fruits of every kind. Thus We will bring forth e dead. Maybe you will remember." Observation ?

-sura 25, verses 48 and 49:

"(God) is the One Who sends forth the winds like heralds of is Mercy. We cause pure water to descend in order to revive dead land with it and to supply with drink the multitude of attle and human beings We have created." Obvious ?

-sura 45, verse 5:

". . . In the provision that God sends down from the sky and iereby He revives the ground after its death and in the change of direction) of winds, there are Signs for people who are wise."

The provision made in this last verse is in the form of the water ent down from the sky, as the context shows. The accent is on he change of the winds that modify the rain cycle.

—sure 13, verse 17:

"(God) sends water down from the sky so that the rivers flow ccording to their measure. The torrent bears away an increasing oam."

—sura 67, verse 30, God commands the Prophet:

"Say: Do you see if your water were to be lost in the ground, vho then can supply you with gushing water?"

—sura 39, verse 21:

"Hast thou not seen that God sent water down from the sky ind led it through sources into the ground? Then He caused sown ields of different colors to grow." Observation

—sura 36, verse 34:

"Therein We placed gardens of palm-trees and vineyards and We caused water springs to gush forth." Observation

The importance of springs and the way they are fed by rain water conducted into them is stressed in the last three verse It is worth pausing to examine this fact and call to mind t predominance in the Middle Ages of views such as those held k Aristotle, according to whom springs were fed by undergroun lakes. In his entry on *Hydrology* (Hydrologie) in the Unive salis Encyclopedia (*Encyclopedia Universalis*) M.R. Réméniéra a teacher at the French National School of Agronomy (Eco nationale du Génie rural, des Eaux et Forêts), describes the mai stages of hydrology and refers to the magnificent irrigatio works of the ancients, particularly in the Middle East. He note however that an empirical outlook ruled over everything, sinc the ideas of the time proceeded from mistaken concepts. He con tinues as follows:

"It was not until the Renaissance (between circa 1400 an 1600) that purely philosophical concepts gave way to researc based on the objective observation of hydrologic phenomen Leonardo da Vinci (1452-1519) rebelled against Aristotle's state ments. Bernard Palissy, in his *Wonderful discourse on the natur of waters and fountains both natural and artificial* (Discour admirable de la nature des eaux et fontaines tant naturelle qu'artificielles (Paris, 1570)) gives a correct interpretation o the water cycle and especially of the way springs are fed b rainwater."

This last statement is surely exactly what is mentioned in vers 21, sura 39 describing the way rainwater is conducted int sources in the ground.

The subject of verse 43, sura 24 is rain and hail:

"Hast thou not seen that God makes the clouds move gently then joins them together, then makes them a heap. And thou seest raindrops issuing from within it. He sends down from th sky mountains of hail, He strikes therewith whom He wills and He turns it away from whom He wills. The flashing of its light ning almost snatches away the sight."

The following passage requires some comment:

—sura 56, verses 68-70:

"Have you observed the water you drink? Do you bring it down from the rainclouds? Or do We? If it were Our will, We could make it salty. Then why are you not thankful?"

This reference to the fact that God could have made fresh ater salty is a way of expressing divine Omnipotence. Another .eans of reminding us of the same Omnipotence is the challenge) man to make rain fall from the clouds. In modern times how-ver, technology has surely made it possible to create rain arti-cially. Can one therefore oppose the statement in the Qur'an to an's ability to produce precipitations?

The answer is no, because it seems clear that one must take ccount of man's limitations in this field. M.A. Facy, an expert at he French Meteorological Office, wrote the following in the Jniversalis Encyclopedia (*Encyclopedia Universalis*) under the eading *Precipitations* (Précipitations) : "It will never be pos-ible to make rain fall from a cloud that does not have the uitable characteristics of a raincloud or one that has not yet eached the appropriate stage of evolution (maturity)". Man can ever therefore hasten the precipitation process by technical neans when the natural conditions for it are not present. If this vere not the case, droughts would never occur in practice—which hey obviously do. To have control over rain and fine weather still remains a dream therefore.

Man cannot wilfully break the established cycle that maintains the circulation of water in nature. This cycle may be outlined as follows, according to modern ideas on hydrology:

The calories obtained from the Sun's rays cause the sea and those parts of the Earth's surface that are covered or soaked in water to evaporate. The water vapour that is given off rises into the atmosphere and, by condensation, forms into clouds. The winds then intervene and move the clouds thus formed over varying distances. The clouds can then either disperse without producing rain, or combine their mass with others to create even greater condensation, or they can fragment and produce rain at some stages in their evolution. When rain reaches the sea (70% of the Earth's surface is covered by seas), the cycle is soon repeated. When rain falls on the land, it may be absorbed by vegetation and thus aid the latter's growth; the vegetation in its turn gives off water and thus returns some water to the atmo-sphere. The rest, to a lesser or greater extent, infiltrates into the soil, whence it is either conducted through channels into the sea,

or comes back to the Earth's surface network through sprin
or resurgences.

When one compares the modern data of hydrology to what
ˏcontained in the numerous verses of the Qur'an quoted in th
paragraph, one has to admit that there is a remarkable degrɛ
of agreement between them.

The Seas.

Whereas the above verses from the Qur'an have provided mɛ
terial for comparison between modern knowledge about the watɛ
cycle in nature, this is not the case for the seas. There is not
single statement in the Qur'an dealing with the seas which couᴵ
be used for comparison with scientific data *per se*. This does nc
diminish the necessity of pointing out however that none of th
statements in the Qur'an on the seas refers to the beliefs, myth
or superstitions prevalent at the time of its Revelation.

A certain number of verses deal with the seas and navigation
As subjects for reflection, they provide indications of divinɛ
Omnipotence that arise from the facts of common observation
The following verses are examples of this:

—sura 14, verse 32:

"(God) has made the ship subject to you, so that it runs upoᴵ
the sea at His Command."

—sura 16, verse 14:

"(God) is the One Who subjected the sea, so that you eat fresᴴ
meat from it and you extract from it ornaments which you wear
Thou seest the ships plowing the waves, so that you seek of His
Bounty. Maybe, you will be thankful."

—sura 31, verse 31:

"Hast thou seen that the ship runs upon the sea by the Gracɛ
of God, in order to show you His signs. Verily in this are Signs
for all who are persevering and grateful."

—sura 55, verse 24:

"His are the ships erected upon the sea like tokens."

—sura 36, verse 41-44:

"A sign for them is that We bore their offspring in the loaded
Ark. We have created for them similar (vessels) on which they
ride. If We will, We drown them and there is no help and they

will not be saved unless by Mercy from Us and as a gratification for a time."

The reference here is quite clearly to the vessel bearing man upon the sea, just as, long ago, Noah and the other occupants of the vessel were carried in the Ark that enabled them to reach dry land.

Another observed fact concerning the sea stands out, because of its unusual nature, from the verses of the Qur'an devoted to it: three verses refer to certain characteristics shared by great rivers when they flow out into the ocean.

The phenomenon is well known and often seen whereby the immediate mixing of salty seawater and fresh riverwater does not occur. The Qur'an refers to this in the case of what is thought to be the estuary of the Tigris and Euphrates where they unite to form what one might call a 'sea' over 100 miles long, the Shatt Al Arab. At the inner parts of the gulf, the effect of the tides is to produce the welcome phenomenon of the reflux of fresh water to the interior of the dry land, thus ensuring adequate irrigation. To understand the text correctly, one has to know that the English word 'sea' conveys the general meaning of the Arabic word *bahr* which designates a large mass of water and is equally used for both the sea and the great rivers: the Nile, Tigris and Euphrates for example.

The following are the three verses that describe this phenomenon:

—sura 25, verse 53:

"(God) is the One Who has let free the two seas, one is agreeable and sweet, the other salty and bitter. He placed a barrier between them, a partition that it is forbidden to pass."

—sura 35, verse 12:

They mix

"The two seas are not alike. The water of one is agreeable, sweet, pleasant to drink. The other salty and bitter. You eat fresh meat from it and you extract from it ornaments which you wear."

—sura 55, verses 19, 20 and 22:

"He has loosed the two seas. They meet together. Between them there is a barrier which they do not transgress. Out of them come pearls and coral."

In addition to the description of the main fact, these verses refer to what may be obtained from fresh water and seawater:

fish, personal adornment, i.e. coral and pearls. With regard to the phenomenon whereby the river water does not mix with seawater at the estuary, one must understand that this is not peculiar to the Tigris and Euphrates; they are not mentioned by name in the text, but it is thought to refer to them. Rivers with a very large outflow, such as the Mississippi and the Yangtze, have the same peculiarity: the mixing of their fresh water with the salty water of the sea does not often occur until very far out at sea.

But they mix

C. THE EARTH'S RELIEF.

The constitution of the Earth is highly complex. Today, it is possible to imagine it very roughly as being formed of a deep layer, at very high temperature, and especially of a central area where rocks are still in fusion, and of a surface layer, the Earth's crust which is solid and cold. The crust is very thin; its thickness is estimated in units of miles or units of ten miles at the most. The Earth's radius is however slightly over 3,750 miles, so that its crust does not represent (on average) one hundredth of the of the sphere's radius. It is upon this skin, as it were, that all geological phenomena have taken place. At the origin of these phenomena are folds that were to form the mountain ranges; their formation is called 'orogenesis' in geology: the process is of considerable importance because with the development of a relief that was to constitute a mountain, the Earth's crust was driven in proportionately far down: this process ensures a foundation in the layer that underlies it.

The history of the distribution of the sea and land on the surface of the globe has only recently been established and is still very incomplete, even for the most recent and best known periods. It is likely that the oceans appeared and formed the hydrosphere circa half a billion years ago. The continents were probably a single mass at the end of the primary era, then subsequently broke apart. Some continents or parts of continents have moreover emerged through the formation of mountains in maritime zones (e.g. the North Atlantic continent and part of Europe).

According to modern ideas, the dominating factor in the formation of the land that emerged was the development of mountain ranges. The evolution of the land, from the primary to the quaternary era, is classed according to 'orogenic phases' that are themselves grouped into 'cycles' of the same name since the formation of all mountains reliefs had repercussions on the balance between the sea and the continents. It made some parts of the land disappear and others emerge, and for hundreds of millions of years it has altered the surface distribution of the continents and oceans: the former at present only occupying three tenths of the surface of this planet.

In this way it is possible to give a very rough outline of the transformations that have taken place over the last hundreds of millions of years.

When referring to the Earth's relief, the Qur'an only describes, as it were, the formation of the mountains. Seen from the present point of view, there is indeed little one can say about the verses that only express God's Beneficence to man with regard to the Earth's formation, as in the following verses:

—sura 71, verses 19 and 20:
"For you God made the earth a carpet so that you travel along its roads and the paths of valleys."

—sura 51, verse 48:
"The earth, We have spread it out. How excellently We did that."

The carpet which has been spread out is the Earth's crust, a solidified shell on which we can live, since the globe's sub-strata are very hot, fluid and hostile to any form of life.

The statements in the Qur'an referring to the mountains and the references to their stability subsequent to the phenomenon of the folds are very important.

—sura 88, verses 19 & 20. The context invites unbelievers to consider certain natural phenomena, among them:
". . . the mountains, how they have been pitched (like a tent). The Earth how it was made even."

The following verses give details about the way in which the mountains were anchored in the ground:

—sura 78, verses 6 & 7:
"Have We not made the earth an expanse and the mountains stakes."

The stakes referred to are the ones used to anchor a tent in the ground (*autād*, plural of *watad*).

Modern geologists describe the folds in the Earth as giving foundations to the mountains, and their dimensions go roughly one mile to roughly 10 miles. The stability of the Earth's crust results from the phenomenon of these folds.

So it is not surprising to find reflections on the mountains in certain passages of the Qur'an, such as the following:

—sura 79, verse 32:

"And the mountains (God) has fixed them firmly."

—sura 31, verse 10:

"(God) has cast into the ground (mountains) standing firm, so that it does not shake with you."

The same phrase is repeated in sura 16, verse 15; and the same idea is expressed with hardly any change in sura 21, verse 31:

"We have placed in the ground (mountains) standing firm so that it does not shake with them."

These verses express the idea that the way the mountains are laid out ensures stability and is in complete agreement with geological data.

D. THE EARTH'S ATMOSPHERE.

In addition to certain statements specifically relating to the sky, examined in the preceding chapter, the Qur'an contains several passages dealing with the phenomena that occur in the atmosphere. As for the comparison between them and the data of modern science, it is to be noted here, as elsewhere, that there is absolutely no contradiction between today's modern scientific knowledge and the phenomena described.

Altitude.

A familiar feeling of discomfort experienced at high altitude, which increases the higher one climbs, is expressed in verse 125, sura 6:

"Those whom God wills to guide, He opens their breast to Islam. Those whom He wills lose their way, He makes their breast narrow and constricted, as if they were climbing in the sky."

Some commentators have claimed that the notion of discomfort at high altitude was unknown to the Arabs of Muhammad's time. It appears that this was not true at all: the existence on the Arabian Peninsula of peaks rising over two miles high makes it extremely implausible that they should not have known of the difficulty of breathing at high altitude.[1] Others have seen in this verse a prediction of the conquest of space, an opinion that appears to require categorical denial, at least for this passage.

Electricity in the Atmosphere.

Electricity in the atmosphere and the consequences of this, i.e. lightning and hail, are referred to in the following verses:

—sura 13, verses 12-13:

"(God) is the One Who shows you the lightning, with fear and covetousness. He raised up the heavy clouds. The thunder glorifies His Praise and so do the angels for awe. He sends the thunder-bolt and strikes with them who He wills while they are disputing about God. He is All Mighty in His Power."

—sura 24, verse 43 (already quoted in this chapter):

"Hast thou not seen that God makes the clouds move gently, then joins them together, then makes them a heap. And thou seest raindrops issuing from within it. He sends down from the sky mountains of hail, He strikes therewith whom He wills and He turns it away from whom He wills. The flashing of its lightning almost snatches away the sight."

In these two verses there is the expression of an obvious correlation between the formation of heavy rainclouds or clouds containing hail and the occurrence of lightning: the former, the subject of covetousness on account of the benefit it represents and the latter, the subject of fear, because when it falls, it is at the will of the All-Mighty. The connection between the two phenomena is verified by present-day knowledge of electricity in the atmosphere.

---

1. 1. The city of Sanaa, the capital of the Yemen, was inhabited in Muhammad's time. It lies at an altitude of nearly 7,900 feet above sea level.

Shadows.

The phenomenon of shadows and the fact that they move is very simply explained today. It forms the subject of the following observations:

—sura 16, verse 81:

"Out of the things He created, God has given you shade . . ."

—sura 16, verse 48:

"Have (the Unbelievers) not observed that for all the things God created, how their shadow shifts right and left, prostating themselves to God while they are full of humility."

—sura 25, verses 45 and 46:

"Hast thou not seen how thy Lord has spread the shade. If He willed, He could have made it stationary. Moreover We made the sun its guide and We withdraw it towards Us easily."

Apart from the phrases dealing with the humility before God of all the things He created, including their shadow, and the fact that God can take back all manifestations of His Power, as He wills, the text of the Qur'an refers to the relationship between the Sun and the shadows. One must bear in mind at this point the fact that, in Muhammad's day, it was believed that the way a shadow moved was governed by the movement of the sun from east to west. This principle was applied in the case of the sundial to measure the time between sunrise and sunset. In this instance, the Qur'an speaks of the phenomenon without referring to the explanation current at the time of the Revelation. It would have been readily accepted for many centuries by those who came after Muhammad. In the end however, it would have been shown to be inaccurate. The Qur'an only talks moreover of the function the sun has as an indicator of shadow. Evidently there is no contradiction between the way the Qur'an describes shadow and what we know of this phenomenon in modern times.

VI

The Animal and Vegetable Kingdoms

Numerous verses describing the origins of life have been assembled in this chapter, along with certain aspects of the vegetable kingdom and general or specific topics relating to the animal kingdom. The grouping of verses scattered throughout the Book affords a general view of the data the Qur'an contains on these subjects.

In the case of the subject of this and the following chapter, the examination of the Qur'anic text has sometimes been particularly delicate on account of certain difficulties inherent in the vocabulary. These have only been overcome through the fact that scientific data which have a bearing on the subject have been taken into consideration. It is particularly so in the case of living beings, i.e. animal, vegetable and human, where a confrontation with the teachings of science is shown to be indispensable in the search for the meaning of certain statements on these topics contained in the Qur'an.

It will become clear that numerous translations of these passages in the Qur'an, made by men of letters, must be deemed inaccurate by the scientist. The same holds true for commentaries made by those who do not possess the scientific knowledge necessary for an understanding of the text.

A. THE ORIGINS OF LIFE.

This question has always preoccupied man, both for himself and for the living things around him. It will be examined here from a general point of view. The case of man, whose appearance on Earth and reproduction processes are the subject of lengthy exposés, will be dealt with in the next chapter.

When the Qur'an describes the origins of life on a very broad basis, it is extremely concise. It does so in a verse that also mentions the process of the formation of the Universe, already quoted and commented on:

—sura 21, verse 30:

"Do not the Unbelievers see that the heavens and the earth were joined together, then We clove them asunder and We got every living thing out of the water. Will they then not believe?"

The notion of 'getting something out of something' does not give rise to any doubts. The phrase can equally mean that every living thing was made of water (as its essential component) or that every living thing originated in water. The two possible meanings are strictly in accordance with scientific data. Life is in fact of aquatic origin and water is the major component of all living cells. Without water, life is not possible. When the possibility of life on another planet is discussed, the first question is always: does it contain a sufficient quantity of water to support life?

Modern data lead us to think that the oldest living being must have belonged to the vegetable kingdom: algae have been found that date from the pre-Cambrian period, i.e. the time of the oldest known lands. Organisms belonging to the animal kingdom probably appeared slightly later: they too came from the sea.

What has been translated here by 'water' is the word mā' which means both water in the sky and water in the sea, plus any kind of liquid. In the first meaning, water is the element necessary to all vegetable life:

—sura 20, verse 53.

"(God is the One Who) sent water down from the sky and thereby We brought forth pairs of plants each separate from the other."

This is the first reference to the notion of a pair in the vegetable kingdom. We shall return to this later.

In the second meaning, a liquid without any further indication of what kind, the word is used in its indeterminate form to designate what is at the basis of the formation of all animal life:

—sura 24, verse 45:

"God created every animal from water."

We shall see further on how this word may also be applied to seminal fluid[1].

Whether it deals therefore with the origins of life in general, or the element that gives birth to plants in the soil, or the seed of animals, all the statements contained in the Qur'an on the origin of life are strictly in accordance with modern scientific data. None of the myths on the origins of life that abounded at the time the Qur'an appeared are mentioned in the text.

B. THE VEGETABLE KINGDOM.

It is not possible to quote in their entirety all the numerous passages in the Qur'an in which divine Beneficence is referred to concerning the salutary effect of the rain which makes vegetation grow. Here are just three verses on this subject:

—sura 16, verses 10 and 11:

"(God) is the One Who sends water down from the sky. For you this is a drink and out of it (grow) shrubs in which you let (cattle) graze freely. Therewith for you He makes sown fields, olives, palm-trees, vineyards and all kinds of fruit grow."

—sura 6, verse 99:

"(God) is the One Who sent water down from the sky. Therewith We brought forth plants of all kinds and from them the verdure and We brought forth from it the clustered grains, and from the palm-tree its spathes with bunches of dates (hanging) low, the gardens of grapes, olives and pomegranates similar and different. Look at their fruit, when they bear it, and their ripening. Verily, in that there are signs for people who believe."

—sura 50, verses 9-11:

"We sent down from the sky blessed water whereby We caused to grow gardens, grains for harvest, tall palm-trees with their spathes, piled one above the other—sustenance for (Our) servants. Therewith We give (new) life to a dead land. So will be the emergence (from the tombs)."

---

1. It is secreted by the reproductive glands and contains spermatozoons.

The Qur'an adds to these general data others that refer to more specialized subjects:

Balance in the Vegetable Kingdom

—sura 15, verse 19:
"The earth . . . We caused all kinds of things to grow therein in due balance."

The Different Qualities of Various Foods

—sura 13, verse 4:
"On the earth are adjacent parts; vineyards, sown fields, palm-trees, similar and not similar, watered with the same water. We make some of them more excellent than others to eat and verily in this are signs for wise people."

It is interesting to note the existence of these verses because they show the sober quality of the terms used, and the absence of any description that might highlight the beliefs of the times, rather than fundamental truths. What particularly attracts our attention however, are the statements in the Qur'an concerning reproduction in the vegetable kingdom.

Reproduction in the Vegetable Kingdom

One must bear in mind that there are two methods of reproduction in the vegetable kingdom: one sexual, the other asexual. It is only the first which in fact deserves the term 'reproduction', because this defines a biological process whose purpose is the appearance of a new individual identical to the one that gave it birth.

Asexual reproduction is quite simply multiplication. It is the result of the fragmentation of an organism which has separated from the main plant and developed in such a way as to resemble the plant from which it came. It is considered by Guilliermond and Mangenot to be a 'special case of growth'. A very simple example of this is the cutting: a cutting taken from a plant is placed in suitably watered soil and regenerated by the growth of new roots. Some plants have organs specially designed for this, while others give off spores that behave like seeds, as it were,

it should be remembered that seeds are the results of a process
of sexual reproduction).

Sexual reproduction in the vegetable kingdom is carried out
by the coupling of the male and female parts of the generic formations united on a same plant or located on separate plants.
This is the only form that is mentioned in the Qur'an.

—sura 20, verse 53:

"(God is the One Who) sent water down from the sky and
thereby We brought forth pairs of plants each separate from the
other."

'One of a pair' is the translation of *zauj* (plural *azwāj*) whose
original meaning is: 'that which, in the company of another,
forms a pair'; the word is used just as readily for a married
couple as for a pair of shoes.

—sura 22, verse 5:

"Thou seest the grounds lifeless. When We send down water
thereon it shakes and grows and puts forth every magnificent
pair (of plants)."

—sura 31, verse 10:

"We caused to grow (on the earth) every noble pair (of
plants)."

—sura 13, verse 3:

"Of all fruits (God) placed (on the earth) two of a pair."

We know that fruit is the end-product of the reproduction
process of superior plants which have the most highly developed
and complex organization. The stage preceding fruit is the flower,
which has male and female organs (stamens and ovules). The
latter, once pollen has been carried to them, bear fruit which
in turn matures and frees it seeds. All fruit therefore implies
the existence of male and female organs. This is the meaning
of the verse in the Qur'an.

It must be noted that for certain species, fruit can come from
non-fertilized flowers (parthenocarpic fruit), e.g. bananas, certain types of pineapple, fig, orange, and vine. They can nevertheless also come from plants that have definite sexual characteristics.

The culmination of the reproductive process comes with the
germination of the seed once its outside casing is opened (sometimes it is compacted into a fruit-stone). This opening allows

roots to emerge which draw from the soil all that is necessary
for the plant's slowed-down life as a seed while it grows and
produces a new plant.

A verse in the Qur'an refers to this process of germination:
—sura 6, verse 95:

"Verily, God splits the grain and the fruit-stone."

The Qur'an often restates the existence of these components of
a pair in the vegetable kingdom and brings the notion of a
couple into a more general context, without set limits:
—sura 36, verse 36:

"Glory be to Him Who created the components of couples of
every kind: of what the ground caused to grow, of themselves
(human beings) and of what you do not know."

One could form many hypotheses concerning the meaning of
the 'things men did not know' in Muhammad's day. Today we
can distinguish structures or coupled functions for them, going
from the infinitesimally small to the infinitely large, in the living as well as the non-living world. The point is to remember
these clearly expressed ideas and note, once again, that they
are in perfect agreement with modern science.

C. THE ANIMAL KINGDOM

There are several questions in the Qur'an concerning the animal kingdom which are the subject of comments that call for a
confrontation with modern scientific knowledge. Here again,
however, one would gain an incomplete view of all that the
Qur'an contains on this subject if one were to leave out a passage
such as the extract which follows. In this passage, the creation
of certain elements in the animal kingdom is described with the
purpose of making man reflect upon the divine Beneficence extended to him. It is quoted basically to provide an example of
the way in which the Qur'an describes the harmonious adapta-
tion of Creation to man's needs; it relates in particular the case
of those people who live in a rural setting, since there is nothing
that could be examined from a different point of view.
—sura 16, verses 5 to 8:

"(God) created cattle for you and (you find) in them warmth,
useful services and food, sense of beauty when you bring them

ome and when you take them to pasture. They bear your heavy
ads to lands you could not reach except with great personal
fort. Verily, your Lord is Compassionate and Merciful; (He
reated) horses, mules and donkeys for you to ride and for orna-
ent. And He created what you do not know."

Alongside these general remarks, the Qur'an sets out certain
ata on highly diversified subjects:

–reproduction in the animal kingdom.
–references to the existence of animal communities.
–statements concerning bees, spiders and birds.
–remarks on the source of constituents of animal milk.

Reproduction in the Animal Kingdom.

This is very summarily dealt with in verses 45 and 46, sura
3:

"(God) fashioned the two of a pair, the male and the female,
rom a small quantity of liquid when it is poured out."

The 'pair' is the same expression that we have already en-
ountered in the verses which deal with reproduction in the
egetable kingdom. Here, the sexes are given. The detail which
s absolutely remarkable is the precision with which it is stated
hat a small quantity of liquid is required for reproduction. The
ord itself signifying 'sperm' is used. The relevance of this re-
nark will be commented upon in the next chapter.

References to the Existence of Animal Communities.

–sura 6, Verse 38

"There is no animal on earth, no bird which flies on wings, that
(does not belong to) communities like you. We have not neglected
anything in the Book (of Decrees). Then to their Lord they will
e gathered."

There are several points in this verse which require comment.
Firstly, it would seem that there is a description of what happens
o animals after their death: Islam does not apparently, have any
loctrine on this point. Then there is predestination in general[1]

---

1. We saw in the Introduction to the third part of this book what one was
   expected to believe about predestination in its application to man
   himself.

which would seem to be mentioned here. It could be conceived a
absolute predestination or relative, i.e. limited to structures an
a functional organization that condition modes of behaviour
the animal acts upon various exterior impulses in terms of a pa
ticular conditioning.

Blachère states that an older commentator, such as Raz
thought that this verse only referred to instinctive action
whereby animals worship God. Sheik Si Boubakeur Hamza, i
the commentary to his translation of the Koran, speaks of "th
instinct which, according to Divine Wisdom, pushes all beings t
group together, so that they demand that the work of each men
ber serve the whole group."

Animal behaviour has been closely investigated in recent de
cades, with the result that genuine animal communities hav
been shown to exist. Of course, for a long time now the results o
a group or community's work have been examined and this ha
led to the acceptance of a community organization. It has onl
been recently however, that the mechanisms which preside ove
this kind of organization have been discovered for certain species
The most studied and best known case is undoubtedly that of bees
to whose behaviour the name von Frisch is linked. Von Frisch
Lorenz and Tinbergen received the 1973 Nobel Prize for thei
work in this field.

3. Statements Concerning Bees, Spiders and Birds.

When specialists on the nervous system wish to provide strik
ing examples of the prodigious organization directing anima
behaviour, possibly the animals referred to most frequently are
bees, spiders and birds (especially migratory birds). Whatever
the case, there is no doubt that these three groups constitute a
model of highly evolved organization.

The fact that the text of the Qur'an refers to this exemplary
trio in the animal kingdom is in absolute keeping with the excep
tionally interesting character that each of these animals has from
a scientific point of view.

Bees

In the Qur'an, bees are the subject of the longest commentary

–Sura 16, verses 68 and 69:[1]

"Thy Lord inspired the bees: Choose your dwelling in the hills,
1 the trees and in what (man) built. Eat of all fruit and follow
he ways of your Lord in humility. From within their bodies
omes a liquor of different colours where is a remedy for men."

It is difficult to know what exactly is meant by the order to
ollow the ways of the Lord in humility, unless it is to be seen
a general terms. All that may be said, with regard to the knowl-
dge that has been gained of their behaviour, is that here—as in
ach of the three animal cases mentioned as examples in the
2ur'an—there is a remarkable nervous organization supporting
heir behaviour. It is known that the pattern of a bee's dance is
means of communication to other bees; in this way, bees are
ble to convey to their own species the direction and distance of
owers from which nectar is to be gathered. The famous experi-
1ent performed by von Frisch has shown the meaning of this
nsect's movement which is intented to transmit information be-
ween worker bees.

piders

Spiders are mentioned in the Qur'an to stress the flimsiness of
heir dwelling which is the most fragile of all. They have a
efuge that is as precarious, according to the Qur'an, as the
welling of those who have chosen masters other than God.

–sura 29, verse 41:

"Those who choose masters other than God are like the spider
vhen it takes for itself a dwelling. Verily, the flimsiest dwelling
s the dwelling of the spider. If they but knew."

A spider's web is indeed constituted of silken threads secreted
y the animal's glands and their calibre is infinitely fine. Its fra-
;ility cannot be imitated by man. Naturalists are intrigued by
he extraordinary pattern of work recorded by the animal's ner-
ous cells, which allows it to produce a geometrically perfect web.

---

1. One might note in passing, that this last verse is the only one in the
   Qur'an that refers to the possibility of a remedy for man. Honey can
   indeed be useful for certain diseases. Nowhere else in the Qur'an is a
   reference made to any remedial arts, contrary to what may have been
   said about this subject.

Birds

Birds are frequently mentioned in the Qur'an. They appear
episodes in the life of Abraham, Joseph, David, Solomon ar
Jesus. These references do not however have any bearing on t
subject in hand.

The verse concerning the existence of animal communities
the ground and bird communities in the sky has been note
above:

—sura 6 verse 38:

"There is no animal on the earth, no bird which flies on wing
that (does not belong to) communities like you. We have n
neglected anything in the Book (of Decrees). Then to their Lor
they will be gathered."

Two other verses highlight the birds' strict submission to God
Power:

—sura 16, verse 79:

"Do they not look at the birds subjected in the atmosphere
the sky? None can hold them up (in His Power) except God."

—sura 67, verse 19:

"Have they not looked at the birds above them spreading the
wings out and folding them? None can hold them up (in hi
Power) except the Beneficent."

The translation of one single word in each of these verses is
very delicate matter. The translation given here expresses th
idea that God holds the birds up in His Power. The Arabic ver
in question is amsaka, whose original meaning is 'to put one'
hand on, seize, hold, hold someone back'.

An illuminating comparison can be made between these verse
which stress the extremely close dependence of the birds' be
havior on divine order, to modern data showing the degree o
perfection attained by certain species of bird with regard to th
programming of their movements. It is only the existence of
migratory programme in the genetic code of birds that can ac
count for the extremely long and complicated journeys whic
very young birds, without any prior experience and without an
guide, are able to accomplish. This is in addition to their abilit
to return to their departure point on a prescribed date. Professo
Hamburger in his book, Power and Fragility (La Puissance et la

'ragilité)[1], gives as an example the well-known case of the
mutton-bird' that lives in the Pacific, with its journey of over
5,500 miles in the shape of the figure 8[2]. It must be acknowledged that the highly complicated instructions for a journey of
this kind simply have to be contained in the bird's nervous
cells. They are most definitely programmed, but who is the
programmer?

. The Source of the Constituents of Animal Milk.

This is defined in the Qur'an in strict accordance with the data
of modern knowledge (sura 16, verse 66). The translation and interpretation of this verse given here is my own because even
modern translations habitually give it a meaning which is, in my
opinion, hardly acceptable. Here are two examples:

—R. Blachère's translation:[3]
"Verily, in your cattle there is a lesson for you! We give you a
pure milk to drink, excellent for its drinkers; (it comes) from
what, in their bellies, is between digested food and blood."

—Professor Hamidullah's translation:[4]
"Verily, there is food for thought in your cattle. From what is
in their bellies, among their excrement and blood, We make you
drink pure milk, easy for drinkers to imbibe."

If these texts were shown to a physiologist, he would reply that
they were extremely obscure, the reason being that there hardly
appears to be much agreement between them and modern notions,
even on a very elementary level. These translations are the work
of highly eminent Arabists. It is a well known fact however, that
a translator, even an expert, is liable to make mistakes in the
translation of scientific statements, unless he happens to be a
specialist in the discipline in question.

The most valid translation seems to me to be the following:
"Verily, in cattle there is a lesson for you. We give you to
drink of what is inside their bodies, coming from a conjunction

---

1. Pub. Flammarion, 1972, Paris.
2. It makes this journey over a period of six months, and comes back to
   its departure point with a maximum delay of one week.
3. Pub. G. P. Maisonneuve et Larose, 1966, Paris,
4. Pub. Club Français du Livre, 1971, Paris.

between the contents of the intestine and the blood, a milk pure and pleasant for those who drink it." (sura 16, verse 66)

This interpretation is very close to the one given in the *Muntakab, 1973*, edited by the Supreme Council for Islamic Affairs, Cairo, which relies for its support on modern physiology. **?**

From the point of view of its vocabulary, the proposed translation may be justified as follows:

I have translated 'inside their bodies' and not, as R. Blachère and Professor Hamidullah have done, 'inside their bellies'. This is because the word *baṭn* also means 'middle', 'interior of something', as well as 'belly'. The word does not here have a meaning that is anatomically precise. 'Inside their bodies' seems to concur perfectly with the context.

The notion of a 'primary origin' of the constituents of milk is expressed by the word *min* (in English 'from') and the idea of a conjunction by the word *baini*. The latter not only signifies 'among' but also 'between' in the other translations quoted. It is however also used to express the idea that two things or two people are brought together.

From a scientific point of view, physiological notions must be called upon to grasp the meaning of this verse.

The substances that ensure the general nutrition of the body come from chemical transformations which occur along the length of the digestive tract. These substances come from the contents of the intestine. On arrival in the intestine at the appropriate stage of chemical transformation, they pass through its wall and towards the systemic circulation. This passage is effected in two ways: either directly, by what are called the 'lymphatic vessels', or indirectly, by the portal circulation. This conducts them first to the liver, where they undergo alterations, and from here they then emerge to join the systemic circulation. In this way everything passes through the bloodstream.

The constituents of milk are secreted by the mammary glands. These are nourished, as it were, by the product of food digestion brought to them via the bloodstream. Blood therefore plays the role of collector and conductor of what has been extracted from food, and it brings nutrition to the mammary glands, the producers of milk, as it does to any other organ.

Here the initial process which sets everything else in motion is the bringing together of the contents of the intestine and blood at the level of the intestinal wall itself. This very precise concept is the result of the discoveries made in the chemistry and physiology of the digestive system. It was totally unknown at the time of the Prophet Muhammad and has been understood only in recent times. The discovery of the circulation of the blood, was made by Harvey roughly ten centuries after the Qur'anic Revelation.

I consider that the existence in the Qur'an of the verse referring to these concepts can have no human explanation on account of the period in which they were formulated.

"The Life is in the Blood" Bible

VII

Human Reproduction

From the moment ancient human writings enter into detail (however slight) on the subject of reproduction, they inevitably make statements that are inaccurate. In the Middle Ages—and even in more recent time—reproduction was surrounded by all sorts of myths and superstitions. How could it have been otherwise, considering the fact that to understand its complex mechanisms, man first had to possess a knowledge of anatomy, the discovery of the microscope had to be made, and the so-called basic sciences had to be founded which were to nurture physiology, embryology, obstetrics, etc.

The situation is quite different in the Qur'an. The Book mentions precise mechanisms in many places and describes clearly-defined stages in reproduction, without providing a single statement marred by inaccuracy. Everything in the Qur'an is explained in simple terms which are easily understandable to man and in strict accordance with what was to be discovered much later on.

Human reproduction is referred to in several dozen verses of the Qur'an, in various contexts. It is explained through statements which deal with one or more specific points. They must be assembled to give a general idea of the verses as a whole, and here, as for the other subjects already examined, the commentary is in this way made easier.

REMINDER OF CERTAIN BASIC CONCEPTS.

It is imperative to recall certain basic concepts which were unknown at the time of the Qur'anic Revelation and the centuries that followed.

Human reproduction is effected by a series of processes which we share in common with mammals. The starting point is the fertilization of an ovule which has detached itself from the ovary. It takes place in the Fallopian tubes half-way through the menstrual cycle. The fertilizing agent is the male sperm, or more exactly, the spermatozoon, a single fertilizing cell being all that is needed. To ensure fertilization therefore, an infinitely small quantity of spermatic liquid containing a large number of spermatozoons (tens of millions at a time) is required. This liquid is produced by the testicles and temporarily stored in a system of reservoirs and canals that finally lead into the urinary tract; other glands are situated along the latter which contribute their own additional secretions to the sperm itself.

The implantation of the egg fertilized by this process takes place at a precise spot in the female reproductive system: it descends into the uterus via a Fallopian tube and lodges in the body of the uterus where it soon literally implants itself by insertion into the thickness of the mucosa and of the muscle, once the placenta has been formed and with the aid of the latter. If the implantation of the fertilized egg takes place, for example, in the Fallopian tubes instead of in the uterus, pregnancy will be interrupted.

Once the embryo begins to be observable to the naked eye, it looks like a small mass of flesh at the centre of which the appearance of a human being is at first indistinguishable. It grows there in progressive stages which are very well known today; they lead to the bone structure, the muscles, the nervous system, the circulation, and the viscerae, etc.

These notions will serve as the terms of reference against which the statements in the Qur'an on reproduction are to be compared.

HUMAN REPRODUCTION IN THE QUR'AN.

It is not easy to gain an idea of what the Qur'an contains on this subject. The first difficulty arises from the fact already mentioned, i.e. that the statements dealing with this subject are scattered throughout the Book. This is not however a major difficulty. What is more likely to mislead the inquiring reader is, once again, the problem of vocabulary.

In fact there are still many translations and commentaries in circulation today that can give a completely false idea of the Qur'anic Revelation on this subject to the scientist who reads them. The majority of translations describe, for example, man's formation from a 'blood clot' or an 'adhesion'. A statement of this kind is totally unacceptable to scientists specializing in this field. In the paragraph dealing with the implantation of the egg in the maternal uterus, we shall see the reasons why distinguished Arabists who lack a scientific background have made such blunders.

This observation implies how great the importance of an association between linguistic and scientific knowledge is when it comes to grasping the meaning of Qur'anic statements on reproduction.

The Qur'an sets out by stressing the successive transformations the embryo undergoes before reaching its destination in the maternal uterus.

—sura 82, verses 6 to 8:

"O Man! Who deceives you about your Lord the Noble, Who created you and fashioned you in due proportion and gave you any form He willed."

—sura 71, verse 14:

"(God) fashioned you in (different) stages."

Along with this very general observation, the text of the Qur'an draws attention to several points concerning reproduction which might be listed as follows:

1) fertilization is performed by only a very small volume of liquid.
2) the constituents of the fertilizing liquid.
3) the implantation of the fertilized egg.
4) the evolution of the embryo.

1. Fertilization is Performed by Only a Very Small Volume of Liquid.

The Qur'an repeats this concept eleven times using the following expression :

—sura 16, verse 4:

. "(God) fashioned man from a small quantity (of sperm)."

The Arabic word *nutfa* has been translated by the words 'small quantity (of sperm)' because we do not have the terms that are strictly appropriate. This word comes from a verb signifying 'to dribble, to trickle'; it is used to describe what remains at the bottom of a bucket that has been emptied out. It therefore indicates a very small quantity of liquid. Here it is sperm because the word is associated in another verse with the word sperm.

—sura 75, verse 37:

"Was (man) not a small quantity of sperm which has been poured out?"

Here the Arabic word *manī* signifies sperm.

Another verse indicates that the small quantity in question is put in a 'firmly established lodging' (*qarār*) which obviously means the genital organs.

—sura 23, verse 13. God is speaking:

"Then We placed (man) as a small quantity (of sperm) in a safe lodging firmly established."

It must be added that the adjective which in this text refers to the 'firmly established lodging' *makīn* is, I think, hardly translatable. It expresses the idea of a firmly established and respected place. However this may be, it refers to the spot where man grows in the maternal organism. It is important to stress the concept of a very small quantity of liquid needed in the fertilization process, which is strictly in agreement with what we know on this subject today.

2. *The Constituents of the Fertilizing Liquid.*

The Qur'an describes the liquid enabling fertilization to take place in terms which it is interesting to examine:

a) 'sperm', as has been stated precisely (sura 75, verse 37)

b) 'a liquid poured out': "Man was fashioned from a liquid poured out" (sura 86, verse 6)

c) 'a despised liquid' (sura 32, verse 8 and sura 77, verse 20)

The adjective 'despised' (*mahīn*) would, it seems, be interpreted not so much on account of the nature of the liquid itself, as more the fact that it is emitted through the outlet of the urinary tract, using the channels that are employed for passing urine.

d) 'Mixtures' or 'mingled liquids' (amšāj): "Verily, we fashioned man from a small quantity of mingled liquids" (sura 76, verse 2)

Many commentators, like professor Hamidullah, consider these liquids to be the male and female agents. The same view was shared by older commentators, who could not have had any idea of the physiology of fertilization, especially its biological conditions in the case of the woman. They thought that the word simply meant the unification of the two elements.

Modern authors however, like the commentator of the *Muntakab* edited by the Supreme Council for Islamic Affairs, Cairo, have corrected this view and note here that the 'small quantity of sperm' is made up of various component parts. The commentator in the *Muntakab* does not go into detail, but in my opinion it is a very judicious observation.

What are the components parts of sperm?

Spermatic liquid is formed by various secretions which come from the following glands:

a) the testicles: the secretion of the male genital gland contains spermatozoons, which are elongated cells with a long flagellum; they are bathed in a sero-fluid liquid.

b) the seminal vesicles: these organs are reservoirs of spermatozoons and are placed near the prostate gland; they also secrete their own liquid but it does not contain any fertilizing agents.

c) the prostate gland: this secretes a liquid which gives the sperm its creamy texture and characteristic odour.

d) the glands annexed to the urinary tract: Cooper's or Méry's glands secrete a stringy liquid and Littré's glands give off mucous.

These are the origins of the 'mingled liquids' which the Qur'an would appear to refer to.

There is, however, more to be said on this subject. When the Qur'an talks of a fertilizing liquid composed of different components, it also informs us that man's progeny will be maintained by something which may be extracted from this liquid. This is the meaning of verse 8, sura 32:

"(God) made his progeny from the quintessence of a despised liquid."

The Arabic word, translated here by the word 'quintessence', is *sulāla*. It signifies 'something which is extracted, the issue of something else, the best part of a thing'. In whatever way it is translated, it refers to a part of a whole.

Fertilization of the egg and reproduction are produced by a cell that is very elongated: its dimensions are measured in ten-thousandths of a millimetre. In normal conditions[1], only one single cell among several tens of millions produced by a man will actually penetrate the ovule; a large number of them are left behind and never complete the journey which leads from the vagina to the ovule, passing through the uterus and Fallopian tubes. It is therefore an infinitesimally small part of the extract from a liquid whose composition is highly complex which actually fulfills its function.

In consequence, it is difficult not to be struck by the agreement between the text of the Qur'an and the scientific knowledge we possess today of these phenomena.

3. The Implantation of the Egg in the Female Genital Organs.

Once the egg has been fertilized in the Fallopian tube it descends to lodge inside the uterus; this is called the 'implantation of the egg'. The Qur'an names the lodging of the fertilized egg womb:

—sura 22, verse 5:

"We cause whom We[2] will to rest in the womb for an appointed term."

---

1. It is estimated that in one cubic centimetre of sperm there are 25 million spermatozoons with, under normal conditions, an ejaculation of several cubic centimetres.

2. God is speaking

The implantation of the egg in the uterus (womb) is the result of the development of villosities, veritable elongations of the egg, which, like roots in the soil, draw nourishment from the thickness of the uterus necessary to the egg's growth. These formations make the egg literally cling to the uterus. This is a discovery of modern times.

The act of clinging is described five different times in the Qur'an. Firstly in verses 1 and 2 of sura 96:

"Read, in the name of thy Lord Who fashioned,

Who fashioned man from something which clings."

'Something which clings' is the translation of the word 'alaq. It is the original meaning of the word. A meaning derived from it, 'blood clot', often figures in translation; it is a mistake against which one should guard: man has never passed through the stage of being a 'blood clot'. The same is true for another translation of this term, 'adhesion' which is equally inappropriate. The original sense of 'something which clings' corresponds exactly to today's firmly established reality.

This concept is recalled in four other verses which describe successive transformations from the small quantity of sperm through to the end:

—sura 22, verse 5:

"We have fashioned you from . . . something which clings."

—sura 23, verse 14:

"We have fashioned the small quantity (of sperm) into something which clings."

—sura 40, verse 67:

"(God) fashioned you from a small quantity (of sperm), from something which clings."

—sura 75, verse 37-38:

"Was (man) not a small quantity of sperm which has been poured out? After that he was something which clings; then God fashioned him in due proportion."

The organ which harbours the pregnancy is qualified in the Qur'an by a word which, as we have seen, is still used in Arabic to signify the uterus. In some suras, it is called a 'lodging firmly

tablished' (sura 23, verse 13, quoted above and sura 77, verse
)[1].

Evolution of the Embryo inside the Uterus.

The Qur'anic description of certain stages in the development
the embryo corresponds exactly to what we today know about
, and the Qur'an does not contain a single statement that is open
criticism from modern science.

After 'the thing which clings' (an expression which is well-
unded, as we have seen) the Qur'an informs us that the embryo
sses through the stage of 'chewed flesh', then osseous tissue
pears and is clad in flesh (defined by a different word from the
eceding which signifies 'intact flesh').

-sura 23, verse 14:

"We fashioned the thing which clings into a chewed lump of
sh and We fashioned the chewed flesh into bones and We
othed the bones with intact flesh."

'Chewed flesh' is the translation of the word *mudga;* 'intact
sh' is *lahm.* This distinction needs to be stressed. The embryo
initially a small mass. At a certain stage in its development, it
oks to the naked eye like chewed flesh. The bone structure de-
lops inside this mass in what is called the mesenchyma. The

. In another verse (sura 6, verse 98) a place of sojourn is mentioned. It
is expressed in a term very similar to the preceding one and would also
seem to signify the maternal uterus. Personally, I believe this to be
the meaning of the verse, but a detailed interpretation would involve
much lengthier explanation which is beyond the scope of this book.
   Another verse which requires extremely delicate interpretation is the
following:
—sura 39, verse 6:
   "(God) fashions you inside the bodies of your mothers, formation
after formation, in three (veils of) darkness." (*zulumāt*)
   Modern intrepreters of the Qur'an see in this verse the three anatomical layers that protect the infant during gestation: the abdominal
wall, the uterus itself, and the surroundings of the foetus (placenta,
embryonic membranes, amniotic fluid).
   I am obliged to quote this verse for the sake of completeness; the
terpretation given here does not seem to me to be disputable from an
anatomical point of view but is this what the text of the Qur'an really
means?

bones that are formed are covered in muscle; the word *laḥm* a
plies to them.

It is known how certain parts appear to be completely out
proportion during embryonic development with what is later
become the individual, while others remain in proportion.

This is surely the meaning of the word *mukallaq* which sigr
fies 'shaped in proportion' as used in verse 5, sura 22 to descri
this phenomenon.

"We fashioned . . . into something which clings . . . into a lun
of flesh in proportion and out of proportion."

The Qur'an also describes the appearance of the senses and t
viscerae:

—sura 32, verse 9:

"(God) appointed for you the sense of hearing, sight and t
viscerae."

It refers to the formation of the sexual organs:

—sura 53, verses 45-46:

"(God) fashioned the two of a pair, the male and the femal
from a small quantity (of sperm) when it is poured out."

The formation of the sexual organs is described in two su
of the Qur'an: *originally?*

—sura 35, verse 11:

"God created you from dust then from a sperm-drop, then I
made you pairs (the male and female)."

—sura 75, verse 39:

"And, (God) made of him a pair, the male and female."

As has already been noted, all statements in the Qur'an mu
be compared with today's firmly established concepts: the agre
ment between them is very clear. It is however very importar
to compare them with the general beliefs on this subject tha
were held at the time of the Qur'anic Revelation in order t
realize just how far people were in those days from havin
views on these problems similar to those expressed here in th
Qur'an. There can be no doubt that they would have been unab
to interpret the Revelation in the way we can today because w
are helped by the data modern knowledge affords us. It was, i
fact, only during the Nineteenth century that people had a sligh
ly clearer view of this question.

Throughout the Middle Ages, the most diversified doctrines
originated in unfounded myths and speculations: they persisted
or several centuries after this period. The most fundamental
tage in the history of embryology was Harvey's statement
1651) that "all life initially comes from an egg". At this time
owever, when nascent science had nevertheless benefited greatly
for the subject in hand) from the invention of the microscope,
eople were still talking about the respective roles of the egg
nd the spermatozoon. Buffon, the great naturalist, was one of
hose in favor of the egg theory, but Bonnet supported the theory
f the seeds being 'packed together': the ovaries of Eve, the
mother of the human race, were supposed to have contained the
eeds of all human beings, packed together one inside the other.
This hypothesis came into favor in the Eighteenth century.

More than a thousand years before our time, at a period when
whimsical doctrines still prevailed, men had a knowledge of the
Qur'an. The statements it contains express in simple terms truths
f primordial importance which man has taken centuries to
discover.

THE QUR'AN AND SEX EDUCATION.

Our epoch believes that it has made manifold discoveries in all
possible fields. It is thought that great innovations have been
made in the field of sex education, and the knowledge of the facts
of life which has been opened up to young people is regarded as
an achievement of the modern world. Previous centuries were
noted for their deliberate obscurity on this point and many people
say that religion—without stating which religion—is the cause
of it.

The information set out above is proof however that fourteen
centuries ago theoretical questions (as it were) on human reproduction were brought to man's attention. This was done as far as
was possible, taking into account the fact that the anatomical
and physiological data needed for further explanations were
lacking. One should also remember that, to be understood, it was
necessary to use simple language suited to the level of comprehension of those who listened to the Preaching.

Practical considerations have not been silently ignored. Ther are many details in the Qur'an on the practical side of life i general, and the way man should behave in the many situation of his existence. His sex life is no exception.

Two verses in the Qur'an deal with sexual relations them selves. They are described in terms which unite the need fo precision with that of decency. When translations and explana tory commentaries are consulted however, one is struck by the divergences between them. I have pondered for a long time o the translation of such verses, and am indebted to Doctor A. K Giraud, Former Professor at the Faculty of Medicine, Beirut, fo the following:

—sura 86, verse 6 and 7:

"(Man) was fashioned from a liquid poured out. It issued (as a result) of the conjunction of the sexual area of the man and the sexual area of the woman."

The sexual area of the man is indicated in the text of the Qur'an by the world *sulb* (singular). The sexual areas of the woman are designated in the Qur'an by the word *tarā'ib* (plural).

This is the translation which appears to be most satisfactory. It is different from the one that is often given by English and French translators, i.e. "(Man) has been created by a liquid poured out which issues from between the vertebral column and the bones of the breast." This would seem more to be an inter-pretation than a translation. It is hardly comprehensible.

The behavior of a man in his intimate relationships with his wife is stated explicitly.

There is the order concerning the menstruation period con-tained in verses 222 and 223, sura 2; God gives the following command to the Prophet:

—sura 2, verses 222 and 223:

"They (the Believers) question thee concerning menstruation. Say: This is an evil. Keep away from women during menstrua-tion and do not approach them until they are clean. When they have purified themselves, go to them, as God ordered it to you.

"Verily, God loves the repentants and loves those who purified themselves.

"Your wives are a tilth. Go to your tilth as you will. Do (some
ood act) for your souls beforehand."

The beginning of this passage is very clear in meaning: it
rmally forbids a man to have sexual contact with a woman who
as her period. The second part describes the process of tilling
hich the sower performs before sowing the seed which is to
erminate and produce a new plant. Through this image there-
re, stress is indirectly laid on the importance of bearing in
ind the final purpose of sexual contact, i.e. reproduction. The
anslation of the final phrase is by R. Blachère: it contains an
rder which seems to refer to the preliminaries before sexual
ntact.

The orders given here are of a very general kind. The prob-
m of contraception has been raised with regard to these verses:
either here, nor anywhere else, is reference made to this subject.

Nor is provoked abortion referred to. The numerous passages
uoted above on the successive transformations of the embryo
ake it quite clear, however, that man is considered to be con-
tituted as of the stage described by the existence of 'something
hich clings'. This being so, the absolute respect of the indi-
idual human being, which is referred to so often in the Qur'an,
rings with it a total condemnation of provoked abortion. This
ttitude is today shared by all monotheistic religions.

Sexual relations are permitted at night during the Fast in the
onth of Ramadan. The verse concerning Ramadan is as follows:
—sura 2, verse 187:

"Permitted to you, on the night of the fast, is to break chastity
ith your wives. They are a garment for you and you are a gar-
nent for them. So hold intercourse with them and seek what God
as ordained for you."

In contrast to this, no exception to the rule is made for pil-
rims in Makka during the celebration days of the Pilgrimage.
—sura 2, verse 197:

"For whom undertakes (the duty of) the Pilgrimage in its
ime, no wooing and no license."

This prohibition is formal, as is the fact that other activities
re forbidden, e.g. hunting, fighting, etc.

Menstruation is again mentioned in the Qur'an in connection
ith divorce. The Book contains the following verse:

—sura 65, verse 4:

"For your wives who despair of menstruation, if you doubt about them, their period of waiting will be three months. For those who never have their monthly periods and those who are pregnant their period will be until they lay down their burden."

The waiting period referred to here is the time between the announcement of the divorce and the time it comes into effect. Those women of whom it is said 'they despair of menstruation' have reached the menopause. A precautionary period of three months is envisaged for them. Once this period is completed, divorced women who have reached the menopause may remarry.

For those who have not yet menstruated, the pregnancy period has to be awaited. For pregnant women, divorce only comes into effect once the child is born.

All these laws are in perfect agreement with physiological data. One can, furthermore, find in the Qur'an the same judicious legal provision in the texts dealing with widowhood.

Thus, the theoretical statements dealing with reproduction, and the practical instructions on the sex life of couples, do not contradict and cannot be placed in opposition to the data we have from modern knowledge, nor with anything that can be logically derived from it.

Qur'anic and Biblical Narrations

General Outlines

A large number of subjects dealt with in the Bible are also found in the Qur'an. Firstly, there are narrations referring to the Prophets; Noah, Abraham, Joseph, Elias, Jonah, Job and Moses; the Kings of Israel; Saul, David, Solomon—to name just some of the main narrations they share in common. There then follow more specific accounts of great events in the course of which the supernatural has intervened, e.g. the Creation of the Earth and Heavens, the Creation of Man, the Flood, the Exodus. Finally, there is all that has to do with Jesus and His mother Mary as far as it concerns the New Testament.

What reflections do the subjects dealt with in the two Scriptures provoke when viewed in the light of our modern knowledge of them from extra-Scriptural sources?

Parallel: Qur'an/Gospel and Modern Knowledge.

With regard to the parallel of Qur'an/Gospels, one must first note that none of the subjects referred to in the Gospels, which

211

were criticized from a scientific point of view (see Part Two of this book), is quoted in the Qur'an.

Jesus is referred to many times in the Qur'an, e.g. Mary's annunciation of the nativity to his father, the annunciation of the miraculous nativity to Mary, Jesus's stature as a Prophet of the highest order, His role as a Messiah, the Revelation He directs to Man which confirms and modifies the Torah, His preachings, His disciples and apostles, the miracles, His Ascension to God, His role in the Last Judgment, etc.

Suras 3 and 19 of the Qur'an (the second of which bears Mary's name) devote long passages to Jesus's family. They describe His mother Mary's nativity, her youth and the annunciation of her miraculous motherhood. Jesus is always called 'Son of Mary'. His ancestry is exclusively given with regard to His mother's side, which is quite logical since Jesus had no biological father. Here the Qur'an differs from Matthew's and Luke's Gospels: as we have already seen, they give the paternal genealogies of Jesus which are, moreover, different from each other.

why?

In the Qur'an, Jesus is placed according to His maternal genealogy in the line of Noah, Abraham, and Mary's father (Ìmrān in the Qur'an):

—sura 3, verses 33 and 34:

"God chose Adam, Noah, the family of Abraham and the family of Ìmrān above all His creatures, as descendants one from another."

So Jesus is descended from Noah and Abraham on His mother Mary's side, and from her father Ìmrān. The errors made in the naming of the 'ancestors of Jesus' found in the Gospels are not present in the Qur'an, nor are the impossibilities in the genealogies contained in the Old Testament of Abraham's ancestry, both of which were examined in the first and second parts of this book.

Once again, this fact must be noted if one is to be objective, and yet again its great importance appears very clearly in the face of the unfounded statements which are made claiming that Muhammad, the author of the Qur'an, largely copied the Bible. One wonders in that case who or what reason compelled him to avoid copying the passages the Bible contains on Jesus's ancestry, and to insert at this point in the Qur'an the corrections that put his text above any criticism from modern knowledge. The Gospels and Old Testament texts are quite the opposite; from this point of view they are totally unacceptable.

Parallel: Qur'an/Old Testament and Modern Knowledge.

In the case of the Old Testament, certain aspects of this parallel have already been dealt with. The Creation of the world, for example, was the subject of a critical study made in the Old Testament section of this book. The same subject was examined with regard to the Qur'anic Revelation. Comparisons were made and there is no need to cover this ground again.

It seems that historical knowledge is too vague and archaeological data too scarce for parallels to be established in the light of modern knowledge on problems concerning the Kings of Israel, who form the subject of narrations in both the Qur'an and the Bible.

Whether or not one can tackle the problem of the Prophets in the light of modern data depends on the extent to which the events described have left traces which may or may not have come down to us.

There are however two subjects dealt with in both the Qur'an and the Bible which should command our attention and which need to be examined in the light of modern knowledge. They are as follows:

—the Flood,
—the Exodus.

—The first because it has not left traces in the history of civilization which support the Biblical narration, whereas modern data do not permit us to criticize the narration contained in the Qur'an.

—The second because the Biblical and Qur'anic narrations evidently complement each other in their broad outlines, and modern data seem to provide both of them with remarkable historical support.

> what about all the flood Histories in the civilizations from all over the globe Australia, Messapotamia. Also if a world wide Flood occurred what evidence would one expect? Eh. Millions of dead creatures buried in silt laid down by water over the world, What do we find? Exactly that

The Flood

*The Biblical Narration of the Flood and the Criticism
Leveled at It—A Reminder.*

The examination of the Old Testament description of the Flood
in the first part of this book led to the following observations:

There is not just one description of the Flood, but two, written
at different times;

—the Yahvist version which dates from the Ninth century B.C.

—the Sacerdotal version dating from the Sixth century B.C., so
called because it was the work of priests of the time.

These two narrations are not juxtaposed, but interwoven so
that part of one is fitted inbetween parts of the other, i.e. paragraphs from one source alternate with passage from the other.
The commentary to the translation of Genesis by Father de Vaux,
a professor at the Biblical School of Jerusalem, shows very clearly
how the paragraphs are distributed between the two sources. The
narration begins and ends with a Yahvist passage. There are
ten Yahvist paragraphs altogether and between each one a Sacerdotal passage has been inserted (there are a total of nine Sacerdotal paragraphs). This mosaic of texts is only coherent when
read from a point of view which takes the succession of episodes
into account, since there are blatant contradictions between the
two sources. Father de Vaux describes them as "two accounts of
the Flood, in which the cataclysm is caused by different agents
and lasts different lengths of time, and where Noah receives into
the Ark a different number of animals."

When seen in the light of modern knowledge, the Biblical description of the Flood as a whole is unacceptable for the following reasons:

214

a) The Old Testament ascribes to it the character of a universal cataclysm.

b) Whereas the paragraphs from the Yahvist text do not date the Flood, the Sacerdotal text situates it at a point in time where a cataclysm of this kind could not have occurred. [?]

The following are arguments supporting this opinion:

The Sacerdotal narration states quite precisely that the Flood took place when Noah was 600 years old. According to the genealogies in chapter 5 of Genesis (also taken from the Sacerdotal text and quoted in the first part of this book), we know that Noah is said to have been born 1,056 years after Adam. Consequently, the Flood would have taken place 1,655 years after the creation of Adam. The genealogical table of Abraham moreover, taken from the same text and given in Genesis (11, 10-32), allows us to estimate that Abraham was born 292 years after the Flood. As we know that (according to the Bible) Abraham was alive in roughly 1850 B.C., the Flood would therefore be situated in the Twenty-first or Twenty-second century B.C. This calculation is in strict keeping with the information in old editions of the Bible which figures prominently at the head of the Biblical text. This was at a time when the lack of human knowledge on the subject was such that the chronological data contained in the Bible were accepted without question by its readers—for want of any arguments to the contrary.[1]

How is it possible to conceive today of a universal cataclysm in the Twenty-first or Twenty-second century B.C. which destroyed life on *all* the earth's surface (except for the people and animals in the Ark)? By this time, civilizations had flourished in several parts of the globe, and their vestiges have now come down to posterity. In Egypt at this time, for example, the Intermediate Period followed the end of the Old Kingdom and preceded the beginning of the Middle Kingdom. In view of our

---

1. Now that certain notions concerning the chronology of ancient times have been established, and the imaginary dates given by the authors of the Sacerdotal text of the Old Testament are no longer credible, those dates have quickly been suppressed in Bibles. In the case of those genealogies that have been preserved, modern commentators of books intended for mass publication fail to draw the readers' attention to the errors they contain.

knowledge of the history of this period, it would be absurd to maintain that the Flood had destroyed all civilization at this time.

Thus it may be affirmed from a historical point of view that the narration of the Flood as it is presented in the Bible is in evident contradiction with modern knowledge. The formal proof of man's manipulation of the Scriptures is the existence of the two texts.

The Narration of the Flood Contained in the Qur'an.

The Qur'an gives a general version which is different from that contained in the Bible and does not give rise to any criticisms from a historical point of view.

It does not provide a continuous narration of the Flood. Numerous suras talk of the punishment inflicted upon Noah's people. The most complete account of this is in sura 11, verses 25 to 49. Sura 71, which bears Noah's name, describes above all Noah's preachings, as do verses 105 to 115, sura 26. Before going into the actual course taken by events, we must consider the Flood as described in the Qur'an by relating it to the general context of the punishment God inflicted on communities guilty of gravely infringing His Commandments.

Whereas the Bible describes a universal Flood intended to punish ungodly humanity as a whole, the Qur'an, in contrast, mentions several punishments inflicted on certain specifically defined communities.

This may be seen in verses 35 to 39, sura 25:

"We gave Moses the Scripture and appointed his brother Aaron with him as vizier. We said: Go to the people who have denied Our signs. We destroyed them completely. When the people of Noah denied the Messengers, We drowned them and We made of them a sign for mankind. (We destroyed the tribes) of 'Ād and Tamūd, the companions of Rass and many generations between them. We warned each of them by examples and We annihilated them completely."

Sura 7, verses 59 to 93 contains a reminder of the punishments brought upon Noah's people, the 'Ād, the Tamūd, Lot (Sodom) and Madiān respectively.

Thus the Qur'an presents the cataclysm of the Flood as a punishment specifically intended for Noah's people: this is the first basic difference between the two narrations.

The second fundamental difference is that the Qur'an, in contrast to the Bible, does not date the Flood in time and gives no indication as to the duration of the cataclysm itself.

The causes of the flooding are roughly the same in both narrations. The Sacerdotal description in the Bible (Genesis 7, 11) cites two causes which occurred simultaneously: "On that day all the fountains of the great deep burst forth, and the windows of the heavens were opened." The Qur'an records the following in verses 11 and 12, sura 54:

"We opened the Gates of Heaven with pouring water. And We caused the ground to gush forth springs, so the waters met according to the decree which has been ordained."

The Qur'an is very precise about the contents of the Ark. The order God gave to Noah was faithfully executed and it was to do the following:

—sura 11, verse 40:

"(In the Ark) load a pair of every kind, thy family, save this one against whom the word has already gone forth, and those who believe. But only a few had believed with him."

The person excluded from the family is an outcast son of Noah. We learn (sura 11, verses 45 and 46) how Noah's supplications on this person's behalf to God were unable to make Him alter His decision. Apart from Noah's family (minus the outcast son), the Qur'an refers to the few other passengers on board the Ark who had believed in God.

The Bible does not mention the latter among the occupants of the Ark. In fact, it provides us with three different versions of the Ark's contents:

—according to the Yahvist version, a distinction is made between 'pure' animals and birds, and 'impure' animals (seven[1] pairs, i.e. seven males and seven females, of each 'pure' species, was taken into the Ark and only one pair of each 'impure' species).

---

1. Surely 'seven' here indicates 'many', as it often does in the Semitic languages of the time.

—according to a modified Yahvist verse (Genesis 7, 8) there was only one pair of each species, whether 'pure' or 'impure'.

—according to the Sacerdotal version, there was Noah, his family (with no exceptions) and a pair taken from each species.

The narration in the Qur'an of the flooding itself is contained in sura 11, verses 25 to 49 and in sura 23, verses 23 to 30. The Biblical narrative does not present any important differences.

In the Bible, the place where the Ark comes to rest is in the Ararat Mountains (Genesis 8, 4) and for the Qur'an it is the Jūdī (sura 11, verse 44.) This mountain is said to be the highest of the Ararat range in Armenia, but nothing proves that the names were not changed by man to tally with the two narratives. This is confirmed by R. Blachère: according to him there is a peak in Arabia named Jūdī. The agreement of names may well be artificial.

In conclusion, it is possible to state categorically what major differences exist here between the Biblical and Qur'anic narrations. Some of them escape critical examination because objective data are lacking. When, however, it is possible to check the statements in the Scriptures in the light of the established data, the incompatibility between the Biblical narration—i.e. the information given on its place in time and geographical extent—and the discoveries that have contributed to modern knowledge is all too clear. In contrast to this, the narration contained in the Qur'an is free from anything which might give rise to objective criticism. One might ask if it is possible that, between the time of the Biblical narration and the one contained in the Qur'an, man could have acquired knowledge that shed light on this event. The answer is no, because from the time of the Old Testament to the Qur'an, the only document man possessed on this ancient story was the Bible itself. If human factors are unable to account for the changes in the narrations which affected their meaning with regard to modern knowledge, another explanation has to be accepted, i.e. a Revelation which came after the one contained in the Bible.

The Exodus

With the Exodus from Egypt of Moses and his followers, (the first stage of their move to Canaan), we come to an event of great importance. It is an established historical event which appears in a known context, in spite of occasional allegations one finds which tend to attribute to it a largely legendary character.

In the Old Testament, the Exodus forms the second book of the Pentateuch or Torah, along with a narration of the journey through the wilderness and the alliance (covenant) concluded with God on Mount Sinai. It is natural for the Qur'an to devote a great deal of space to it too: an account of the dealings Moses and his brother Aaron had with the Pharaoh and of the exit from Egypt is found in more than ten suras containing long descriptions, e.g. suras, 7, 10, 20 and 26, along with more abridged versions and even simple reminders. The name of Pharaoh, the main character on the Egyptian side, is repeated (to the best of my knowledge) seventy-four times in the Qur'an in 27 suras.

A study of both the Qur'anic and Biblical narrations is especially interesting here because, in contrast to what has been noted in the case of the Flood (for example), in the main, the two narrations have many points in common. There are certainly divergences, but the Biblical naration has considerable historical value, as we shall see. This is because it helps to identify the Pharaoh, or rather the two pharaohs in question. This hypothesis, which starts with the Bible, is complemented by the information contained in the Qur'an. Modern data are added to these two Scriptural sources and it is thus possible, through a confrontation between the Bible, the Qur'an and today's knowledge, to situate this episode from the Holy Scriptures in a historical context.

THE EXODUS ACCORDING TO THE BIBLE

The Biblical narration begins with a reminder of the Jews' entry into Egypt with Jacob, who joined Joseph there. Later on, according to Exodus 1, 8:

"Now there arose a new king over Egypt, who did not know Joseph."

The period of oppression followed; the Pharaoh ordered the Jews to build the cities of Pithom and Ramesses (to use the names given to them in the Bible) (Exodus I, 11). To avoid a population explosion among the Hebrews, Pharaoh ordered each new-born son to be thrown into the river. Moses was nevertheless preserved by his mother for the first three months of his life before she finally decided to put him in a rush basket on the river's edge. The Pharaoh's daughter discovered him, rescued him and gave him to a nurse, none other than his own mother. This was because Moses's sister had watched to see who would find the baby, had pretended not to recognize him and then recommended to the Princess a nurse who was really the child's mother. He was treated as one of the Pharaoh's sons and given the name 'Moses'.

As a young man, Moses left for a country called Midian where he married and lived for a long time. We read an important detail in Exodus 2, 23:

"In the course of those many days the king of Egypt died."

God ordered Moses to go and find the Pharaoh and lead his brothers out of Egypt (the description of this order is given in the episode of the Burning Bush). Aaron, Moses's brother, helped him in this task. This is why Moses, once he had returned to Egypt, went with his brother to visit the Pharaoh who was the successor of the king under whose reign he had long ago been born.

The Pharaoh refused to allow the Jews in Moses's group to leave Egypt. God revealed Himself to Moses once again and ordered him to repeat his request to Pharaoh. According to the Bible, Moses was eighty years old at this time. Through magic, Moses showed the Pharaoh that he had supernatural powers. This was not enough however. God sent the famous plagues down upon Egypt. The rivers were changed into blood, there

ere invasions of frogs, gnats and swarms of flies, the cattle
ied, boils appeared on men and animals, there was hail and
lagues of locusts, darkness and the death of the first-born.
fevertheless, the Pharaoh still did not allow the Hebrews to
ave. *Yes he did*

They therefore broke out of the city of Rameses, 600,000 of
lem[1] "besides women and children" (Exodus 12, 37). At this
oint Pharaoh "made ready his chariot and took his army with
im, and took six hundred picked charioteers and all the óther
hariots of Egypt with officers over all of them . . . Pharaoh,
ing of Egypt, pursued the people of Israel as they went forth
efiantly." (Exodus 14, 6 and 8). The Egyptians caught up with
Moses's party beside the sea. Moses raised his staff, the sea
arted before him and his followers walked across it without
vetting their feet. "The Egyptians pursued and went in after
hem into the midst of the sea, all Pharaoh's horses, his chariots,
nd his horsemen." (Exodus 14, 23) "The waters returned and
overed the chariots and the horsemen and all the host of Pha-
aoh that had followed them into the sea; not so much as one of
hem remained. But the people of Israel walked on dry ground
hrough the sea, the waters being a wall to them on their right
land and on their left." (Exodus 14, 28-29).

The text of Exodus is quite clear: Pharaoh was at the head
of the pursuers. He perished because the text of Exodus notes
that "not so much as one of them remained." The Bible repeats
this detail moreover in the Psalms: Psalm 106, verse 11 and
Psalm 136 verses 13 and 15 which are an act of thanks to God
"Who divided the sea of Rushes[2] in sunder . . . and made Israel
pass through the midst of it . . . but overthrew Pharaoh and his
host in the sea of Rushes." There can be no doubt therefore, that
according to the Bible, the Pharaoh of the Exodus perished in
the sea. The Bible does not record what became of his body.

THE EXODUS ACCORDING TO THE QUR'AN

In its broad outlines, the narration of the Exodus contained in
the Qur'an is similar to that of the Bible. It has to be reconsti-

1. We shall later see that the figure has been grossly exaggerated.
2. In Hebrew 'yam souf'.

THE BIBLE, THE QUR'AN AND SCIENC

tuted, however, because it is made up of passages disperse throughout the Book.

The Qur'an does not provide a name which enables us to iden tify who the reigning Pharaoh was at the time of Exodus, an more than the Bible does. All that is known is that one of hi counsellors was called *Hāmān*. He is referred to six times in th Qur'an (sura 28, verses 6, 8 and 38, sura 29, verse 39 and sur 40, verses 24 and 36).

The Pharaoh is the Jews' oppressor:

—sura 14, verse 6:

"When Moses said to his people: Remember the favor of Go to you when He delivered you from Pharaoh's folk who impose upon you a dreadful torment, slaughtered your sons and spare your women."

The oppression is recalled in the same terms in verse 141 su a 7. The Qur'an does not however mention the names of th cities built by the Jews in subjection, as does the Bible.

The episode where Moses is left by the riverside is recorded i sura 20 verses 39-40 and sura 28, verses 7 to 13. In the versior contained in the Qur'an, Moses is taken in by Pharaoh's family We find this in verses 8 and 9, sura 28:

"The family of Pharaoh took him up. (It was intended) that (Moses) should be to them an adversary and a cause of sorrow Pharaoh, Hāmān and their hosts were sinners. Pharaoh's wife said: (He will be) a joy to the eye for me and you. Don't kill him. He may be of use to us or we may take him as a son. They did not sense (what was to come)."

Muslim tradition has it that it was Pharaoh's wife Asiya who took care of Moses. In the Qur'an, it was not the Pharaoh's wife who found him, but members of his household.

Moses's youth, his stay in Midian and marriage are described in sura 28, verses 13 to 28.

In particular, the episode of the Burning Bush is found in the first part of sura 20, and in sura 28, verses 30 to 35.

The Qur'an does not describe the ten plagues sent down upon Egypt as a divine chastisement (unlike the long description in the Bible), but simply mentions five plagues very briefly (sura 7, verse 133) : flooding, locusts, lice, frogs, and blood.

The flight from Egypt is described in the Qur'an, but without any of the geographical data given in the Bible, nor the incredible numbers of people mentioned in the latter. It is difficult to imagine how 600,000 men plus their families could have stayed in the desert for a long time, as the Bible would have us believe.

This is how the death of Pharaoh pursuing the Hebrews is described:

—sura 20, verse 78:

"Pharaoh pursued them with his hosts and the sea covered them."

The Jews escaped. Pharaoh perished, but his body was found: a very important detail not mentioned in the Biblical narration.

—sura 10, verses 90 to 92. God is speaking:

"We took the Children of Israel across the sea. Pharaoh with his hosts pursued them in rebellion and hostility till, when the fact of his drowning overtook him, he said: I believe there is no God except the God in whom the Children of Israel believe. I am of those who submit themselves to Him.

"God said: 'What? Now! Thou has rebelled and caused depravity: This day We save thee in thy body so that thou mayest be a sign for those who come after thee.' But verily, many among mankind are heedless of Our signs."

This passage requires two points to be explained:

a) The spirit of rebellion and hostility referred to is to be understood in terms of Moses's attempt to persuade the Pharaoh.

b) The rescue of the Pharaoh refers to his corpse because it is stated quite clearly in verse 98, sura 11, that Pharaoh and his followers have been condemned to damnation:

—sura 11, verse 98

"Pharaoh will go before his people on the Day of Resurrection and will lead them to the fire."

For those facts which can be checked with historical, geographical and archaeological data therefore, it should be noted that the Qur'anic and Biblical narrations differ on the following points:

—the absence in the Qur'an of place names, both of the cities built by the Hebrews in Moses's group, and on the route taken by the Exodus.

—the absence of any reference to the death of a Pharaoh durin
Moses's stay in Midian.

—the absence in the Qur'an of details concerning Moses's ag
when he addressed his request to the Pharaoh.

—the absence in the Qur'an of the numbering of Moses's follov
ers. These figures are openly exaggerated in the Bible to incre
ible proportions (said to have been 600,000 men plus thei
families forming a community of more than two million ir
habitants.)

—the absence of any mention in the Bible of the rescue of th
Pharaoh's body after his death.

For our present purposes, the points to be noted because the
are shared by both narrations are as follows:

—the confirmation contained in the Qur'an of Pharaoh's oppres
sion of the Jews in Moses's group.

—the absence from both narrations of any mention of the Kin
of Egypt's name.

—the confirmation contained in the Qur'an of the Pharaoh'
death during the Exodus.

CONFRONTATION BETWEEN SCRIPTURAL DATA
AND MODERN KNOWLEDGE

The narrations contained in the Bible and the Qur'an on th
time spent by the sons of Israel in Egypt, and the way they left
give rise to data which may constitute matter for a confrontatio
with modern knowledge. In fact, the balance is very uneven be
cause some data pose many problems while others hardly pro
vide subject for discussion.

1. Examination of Certain Details Contained in the Narrations

The Hebrews in Egypt

It is, apparently, quite possible to say (and without running
much risk of being wrong) that the Hebrews remained in Egyp
for 400 or 430 years, according to the Bible (Genesis 15, 13 anc
Exodus 12, 40). In spite of this discrepancy between Genesis anc
Exodus, which is of minor importance, the period may be said tc

ave begun long after Abraham, when Joseph, son of Jacob, moved with his brothers to Egypt. With the exception of the Bible, which gives the data just quoted, and the Qur'an which refers to the move to Egypt, but does not give any indication as to the dates involved, we do not possess any other document which is able to illuminate us on this point.

Present-day commentators, ranging from P. Montet to Daniel-Rops, think that, in all probability, the arrival of Joseph and his brothers coincided with the movement of the Hyksos towards Egypt in the Seventeenth century B.C. and that a Hyksos sovereign probably received them hospitably at Avaris in the Nile Delta.

There can be no doubt that this guess is in obvious contradiction to what is contained in the Bible (Kings I, 6, 1) which puts the Exodus from Egypt at 480 years before the construction of Solomon's Temple (circa 971 B.C.). This estimation would therefore put the Exodus at roughly 1450 B.C. and would consequently situate the entry into Egypt at circa 1880-1850 B.C. This is precisely the time, however, that Abraham is supposed to have lived, and other data contained in the Bible tell us that there were 250 years separating him from Joseph. This passage from Kings I in the Bible is therefore unacceptable from a chronological point of view.[1] We shall see how the theory put forward here has only this objection, taken from Kings I, to be levelled against it. The very obvious inaccuracy of these chronological data effectively deprives this objection of any value.

Aside from the Holy Scriptures, the traces left by the Hebrews of their stay in Egypt are very faint. There are however several hieroglyphic documents which refer to the existence in Egypt of a category of workers called the *'Apiru, Hapiru* or *Habiru*, who have been identified (rightly or wrongly) with the Hebrews. In this category were construction workers, agricultural labourers, harvesters, etc. But where did they come from? It is very difficult to find an answer to this. Father de Vaux has written the following about them:

---

1. We shall return to this subject later, when we call upon Father de Vaux's help in examining this reference in Kings I.

"They are not members of the local population, they do no
identify themselves with a class in society, they do not all share
the same occupation or status."

Under Tuthmosis III, they are referred to in a papyrus as
'workers in the stables'. It is known how Amenophis II, in the Fif
teenth century B.C., brought in 3,600 of these people as prisoners
from Canaan, because, as Father de Vaux notes, they consti
tuted a considerable percentage of the Syrio-Palestinian popu
lation. Under Sethos I, in circa 1300 B.C., the 'Apiru created
considerable disturbances in the Beth-Shean region of Canaan
and under Ramesses II some of them were employed in the
quarries or for transporting piles used in the works of the
Pharaoh (e.g. the Great Pylon of Ramesses Miamon). We know
from the Bible that the Hebrews, under Ramesses II, were to
build the northern capital, the City of Ramesses. In Egyptian
writings the 'Apiru are mentioned once again in the Twelfth
century B.C. and for the last time under Ramesses III.

The 'Apiru are not just mentioned in Egypt however, so did
the term therefore apply solely to the Hebrews? It is perhaps
wise to recall that the word could initially have been used to
signify 'forced labourers', without regard to their origins, and
that it subsequently became an adjective indicating a person's
profession. We might perhaps draw an analogy with the word
'suisse' (Swiss) which has several different meanings in French
It can mean an inhabitant of Switzerland, a mercenary soldier
of the old French monarchy who was of Swiss extraction, a
Vatican guard, or an employee of a Christian church . . .

However, this may be, under Ramesses II, the Hebrews (according to the Bible) or the 'Apiru (according to the hieroglyphic
texts) took part in the great works ordered by the Pharaoh, which
were indeed 'forced labour'. There can be no doubt that Ramesses
II was the Jews' oppressor: the cities of Ramesses and Pithom,
mentioned in Exodus, are situated at the eastern part of the Nile
Delta. Today's Tanis and Qantir, which are roughly 15 miles
apart, are in the same region as these two cities. The northern
capital constructed by Ramesses II was situated there. Ramesses
II is the Pharaoh of the oppression.

Moses was to be born in this environment. The circumstances
pertaining to his rescue from the waters of the river have al-

:ady been outlined above. He has an Egyptian name: P. Montet
as clearly shown in his book *Egypt and the Bible* (L'Egypte et
. Bible)[1] that the names Mesw or Mesy are on the list of per-
ɔnal names in the dictionary of the hieroglyphic language by
anke. *Mūsā* is the transliteration used in the Qur'an.

he Plagues of Egypt

Under this title the Bible refers to ten punishments inflicted by
od, and provides many details concerning each of these
•lagues'. Many have supernatural dimensions or characteristics.
he Qur'an only lists five plagues, which, for the most part, are
ıerely an exaggeration of natural phenomena: flooding, locusts,
ːe, frogs and blood.

The rapid multiplication of locusts and frogs is described in
ıe Bible. It speaks of river water changed to blood which floods
ll the land (sic) ; the Qur'an refers to blood, but without giving
ny complementary details. It is possible to invent all kinds of
.ypotheses on the subject of this reference to blood.

The other plagues described in the Bible (gnats, swarms of
ies, boils, hail, darkness, death of the first-born and of cattle)
.ave various origins,[?] as was the case of the Flood, and are
ɔnstituted by the juxtaposition of passages from many differ-
ıt sources. *? which sources?*

ʰhe Route Taken by the Exodus

No indication of this is given in the Qur'an, whereas the Bible
efers to it in great detail. Father de Vaux and P. Montet have
ɔoth reopened studies into it. The starting-point was probably
he Tanis-Qantir region, but no traces have been found of the
·est of the route taken which could confirm the Biblical narra-
ion; nor is it possible to say at exactly what point the waters
ɔarted to allow the passage of Moses and his followers.

The Miraculous Parting of the Waters

Some commentators have imagined a tide-race, due perhaps to
ıstronomic causes or seismic conditions connected to the distant

---

1. Pub. Delachaux and Niestlé, Neufchatel, 1959.

eruption of a volcano. The Hebrews could have taken advantag
of the receding sea, and the Egyptians, following in hot pursui
could have been wiped out by the returning tide. All this is pur
hypothesis however. *The Bible says that God parted the water*

2. The Point Occupied by the Exodus in the History of the Pharaohs

It is possible to arrive at much more positive evidence in th
case of the point the Exodus occupies in time.

For a very long time Merneptah, the successor to Ramesses I
was held to be the Pharaoh of the Exodus. Maspero, the famou
Egyptologist of the beginning of this century did, after all, writ
in his *Visitor's Guide to the Cairo Museum* (Guide du visiteur d
Musée du Caire), 1900, that Merneptah "was probably, accord
ing to the Alexandrian tradition, the Pharaoh of the Exodus wh
is said to have perished in the Red Sea." I have been unable t
find the documents on which Maspero based this assertion, bu
the eminence of this commentator requires us to attach the great
est importance to what he claims.

Apart from P. Montet, there are very few Egyptologists o
specialists in Biblical exegesis who have researched into th
arguments for or against this hypothesis. In the last few decade
however, there has been a spate of different hypotheses whicl
seem to have as their sole purpose the justification of an agree
ment with one single detail in the Scriptural narrations, althougl
the inventors of these hypotheses do not bother with the other
aspects of the Scriptures. Thus it is possible for a hypothesis to
suddenly appear which seems to agree with one aspect of a nar
ration, although its inventor has not taken the trouble to com
pare it with all the other data contained in the Scriptures (and
consequently not just with the Bible), plus all the data provided
by history, archaeology, etc.

One of the strangest hypotheses yet to come to light is by J.
de Miceli (1960) who claims to have pinpointed the date of the
Exodus to within one day, i.e. the 9th of April, 1495 B.C. He
relies for his information entirely on calculations made from
calendars and claims that Tuthmosis II was reigning in Egypt at
that time, and was therefore the Pharaoh of the Exodus. The

confirmation of the hypothesis is supposed to reside in the fact that lesions of the skin are to be observed on the mummy of Tuthmosis II. This commentator informs us (without explaining why) that they are due to leprosy, and that one of the plagues of Egypt described in the Bible consisted in skin boils. This staggering construction takes no account of the other facts contained in the Biblical narration, especially the Bible's mention of the City of Ramesses which rules out any hypothesis dating the Exodus before a 'Ramesses' had reigned.

As to the skin lesions of Tuthmosis II, these do not swing the argument in favour of the theory which designates this King of Egypt as the Pharaoh of the Exodus. This is because his son, Tuthmosis III, and his grandson Amenophis II also show signs of skin tumors[1], so that some commentators have suggested the hypothesis of a disease which ran in the family. The Tuthmosis II theory is not therefore tenable.

The same is true for Daniel-Rops's theory in his book. *The People of the Bible* (Le Peuple de la Bible)[2]: He ascribes the role of the Pharaoh of the Exodus to Amenophis II. It does not seem to be any better-founded than the preceding hypothesis. Using the pretext that Amenophis II's father (Tuthmosis III) was very nationalistic, Daniel-Rops proclaims Amenophis II the persecutor of the Hebrews, while his step-mother, the famous Queen Hatshepsut, is cast in the role of the person who took Moses in (although we never discover why).

Father de Vaux's theory, that it was Ramesses II, rests on slightly more solid foundations. He expands on them in his book, *The Ancient History of Israel* (Histoire ancienne d'Israël)[3]. Even if his theory does not agree with the Biblical narration on every point, at least it has the advantage of putting forward one very important piece of evidence: the construction of the cities of Ramesses and Pithom built under Ramesses II referred to in the Biblical text. It is not possible therefore to maintain that the Exodus took place *before* the accession of Ramesses II. This is situated in the year 1301 B.C., according to Drioton and Van-

---

1. The skin lesions are clearly visible on the mummies of these Pharaohs preserved in the Egyptian Museum, Cairo.
2. Pub. Desclée de Brouwer, 1970, Paris.
3. Pub. J. Gabalda and Co., 1971, Paris.

dier's chronology, and in 1290 B.C. according to Rowton's. The two other hypotheses outlined above are untenable because of the following imperative fact: Ramesses II is the Pharaoh of the oppression referred to in the Bible.

Father de Vaux considers the Exodus to have taken place during the first half or towards the middle of Ramesses II's reign. Thus his dating of this event is imprecise: he suggests this period to allow Moses and his followers time, as it were, to settle in Canaan, and Ramesses II's successor, Pharaoh Mernaptah who is said to have pacified the frontiers after his father's death, to bring the Children of Israel into line, as depicted on a stele of the Fifth year of his reign.

Two arguments may be levelled at this theory:

a) The Bible shows (Exodus 2, 23) that the King of Egypt died during the period when Moses was in Midian. This King of Egypt is described in the Book of Exodus as the King who made the Hebrews build the cities of Ramesses and Pithom by forced labour. This King was Ramesses II. The Exodus could only have taken place under the latter's successor. Father de Vaux claims however to doubt the Biblical sources of verse 23, chapter 2 of Exodus.

b) What is more astounding is that Father de Vaux, as director of the Biblical School of Jerusalem, does not refer in his theory of the Exodus to two essential passages in the Bible, both of which bear witness to the fact that the King died during the pursuit of the fleeing Hebrews. This detail makes it impossible for the Exodus to have taken place at any other time than at the end of a reign.

It must be repeated that there can be little doubt that the Pharaoh lost his life as a result of it. Chapters 13 and 14 of Exodus are quite specific on this point: "So he made ready his chariot and took his army with him . . ." (Exodus 14,6). (Pharaoh king of Egypt) "pursued the people of Israel as they went forth defiantly" (Exodus 14,8) . . . "The waters returned and covered the chariots and the horsemen and all the host of Pharaoh that had followed them into the sea; not so much as one of them remained." (Exodus 14,28 and 29). In addition to these verses, Psalm 136 confirms Pharaoh's death and refers to Yahweh who "overthrew Pharaoh and his host in the Sea of Rushes" (Psalms 136,15).

Thus, *during Moses's lifetime, one Pharaoh died when Moses was in Midian and another during the Exodus.* There were not one, but two Pharaohs at the time of Moses: one during the oppression and the other during the Exodus from Egypt. The theory of a single Pharaoh (Ramesses II) put forward by Father de Vaux is unsatisfactory because it does not account for everything. The following observations are further arguments against his theory.

3. Rameses II, Pharaoh of the Oppression Merneptah, Pharaoh of the Exodus

P. Montet has very discerningly resumed the original Alexandrian[1] tradition mentioned by Maspero. It is found much later in the Islamic tradition as well as in the classic Christian tradition.[2] This theory is set out in Montet's book *Egypt and the Bible* (L'Egypte et le Bible)[3] and is supported by additional arguments, based in particular on the narrative contained in the Qur'an, to which the famous archaeologist did not refer. Before examining them however, we shall first return to the Bible.

The Book of Exodus contains a reference to the word 'Ramesses' although the Pharaoh's name is not mentioned. In the Bible 'Ramesses' is the name of one of the cities built by the forced labour of the Hebrews. Today we know that these cities form part of the Tanis-Qantir region, in the eastern Nile Delta. In the area where Ramesses II built his northern capital, there were other constructions prior to his, but it was Ramesses II who made it into an important site, as the archeological excavations undertaken in the last few decades have amply shown. To build it, he used the labour of the enslaved Hebrews.

1. There can be no doubt that in the Golden Age of the Ptolemies, historical documents on Antiquity were preserved at Alexandria, only to be destroyed at the time of the Roman conquest; a loss which is keenly felt today.
2. In the Holy Histories of the early 20th century, as in the History by Abbé H. Lesetre, intended for religious instruction, the Exodus is mentioned as having taken place during Merneptah's reign in Egypt.
3. Pub. Delachaux and Niestlé, Neuchatel, 1959.

When one reads the word 'Ramesses' in the Bible today, one is not particularly struck by it: the word has become very common to us since Champollion discovered the key to hieroglyphics 150 years ago, by examining the characters that expressed this very word. We are therefore used to reading and pronouncing it today and know what it means. One has to remember however that the meaning of hieroglyphics had been lost in circa the Third century B.C. and that Ramesses' name had hardly been preserved anywhere except in the Bible and a few books written in Greek and Latin which had deformed it to a lesser or greater extent. It is for this reason that Tacitus in his *Annals* talks of 'Rhamsis'. The Bible had however preserved the name intact: it is referred to four times in the Pentateuch or Torah (Genesis 47,11; Exodus 1,11 and 12,37; Numbers 33,3 and 33,5).

The Hebrew word for 'Ramesses' is written in two ways in the Bible: 'Râ(e)mss' or 'Râeâmss'[1]. In the Greek version of the Bible, called the Septuagint, it is 'Râmessê'. In the Latin version (Vulgate) it is written 'Ramesses'. In the Clementine version of the Bible in French (1st edition, 1621) the word is the same, 'Ramesses'. The French edition was in circulation at the time of Champollion's work in this field. In his *Summary of the Hièroglyphic System of the Ancient Egyptians* (Prècis du système hiéroglyphique des anciens Egyptiens) (2nd edition, 1828, page 276), Champollion alludes to the Biblical spelling of the word.

Thus the Bible had miraculously preserved Ramesses's name in its Hebrew, Greek and Latin versions.[2]

The preceding data alone are enough to establish the following:

a) There can be no question of the Exodus before a 'Ramesses' had come to the throne in Egypt (11 Kings of Egypt had this name).

b) Moses was born during the reign of the Pharaoh who built the cities of Ramesses and Pithom, i.e. Ramesses II.

---

1. The letter 'e' figures as the *ayin* in Hebrew.
2. It is strange to note moreover, that in old editions of the Bible, commentators did not understand the meaning of the word at all. In the French edition of the Clementine Bible, 1621, for example, an interpretation of the word 'Ramesses' is given which makes total nonsense: 'Thunder of Vermin' (sic).

c) When Moses was in Midian, the reigning Pharaoh (i.e. Ramesses II) died. The continuation of Moses's story took place during the reign of Ramesses II's successor, Merneptah.

What is more, the Bible adds other highly important data which help to situate the Exodus in the history of the Pharaohs. It is the statement that Moses was eighty years old when, under God's orders, he tried to persuade Pharaoh to free his brothers: "Now Moses was eighty years old, and Aaron eighty-three years years old, when they spoke to Pharaoh." (Exodus 7,7). Elsewhere however, the Bible tells us (Exodus 2,23) that the Pharaoh reigning at the time of the birth of Moses died when the latter was in Midian, although the Biblical narration continues without mentioning any change in the sovereign's name. These two passages in the Bible imply that the total number of years spanning the reigns of the two Pharaohs ruling at the time when Moses was living in Egypt must have been eighty years at least.

It is known that Ramesses II reigned for 67 years (1301-1235 B.C. according to Drioton and Vandier's chronology, 1290-1224 B.C. according to Rowton). For Merneptah, his successor, the Egyptologists are unable, however, to provide the exact dates of his reign. Nevertheless, it lasted for at least ten years because, as Father deVaux points out, documents bear witness to the tenth year of his reign. Drioton and Vandier give two possibilities for Merneptah: either a ten-year reign, 1234-1224 B.C., or a twenty-year reign 1224-1204 B.C. Egyptologists have no precise indications whatsoever on how Merneptah's reign came to an end: all that can be said is that after his death, Egypt went through a period of serious internal upheavals lasting nearly 25 years.

Even though the chronological data on these reigns are not very precise, there was no other period during the New Kingdom concordant with the Biblical narration when two successive reigns (apart from Ramesses II-Merneptah) amounted to or surpassed eighty years. The Biblical data concerning Moses's age when he undertook the liberation of his brothers can only come from a time during the successive reigns of Ramesses II and

Merneptah[1]. All the evidence points towards the fact that Moses was born at the beginning of Ramesses II's reign, was living in Midian when Ramesses II died after a sixty-seven year reign, and subsequently became the spokesman for the cause of the Hebrews living in Egypt to Merneptah, Ramesses II's son and successor. This episode may have happened in the second half of Merneptah's reign, assuming he reigned twenty years or nearly twenty years. Rowton believes the supposition to be quite feasible. Moses would then have led the Exodus at the end of Merneptah's reign. It could hardly have been otherwise because both the Bible and the Qur'an tell us that Pharaoh perished during the pursuit of the Hebrews leaving the country.

This plan agrees perfectly with the account contained in the Scriptures of Moses's infancy and of the way he was taken into the Pharaoh's family. It is a known fact that Ramesses II was very old when he died: it is said that he was ninety to a hundred years old. According to this theory, he would have been twenty-three to thirty-three years old at the beginning of his reign which lasted sixty-seven years. He could have been married at that age and there is nothing to contradict the discovery of Moses by 'a member of Pharaoh's household' (according to the Qur'an), or the fact that Pharaoh's wife asked him if he would keep the newly-born child she had found on the bank of the Nile. The Bible claims that the child was found by Pharaoh's daughter. In view of Ramesses II's age at the beginning of his reign it would have been perfectly possible for him to have had a daughter old enough to discover the abandoned child. The Qur'anic and Biblical narrations do not contradict each other in any way on this point.

The theory given here is in absolute agreement with the Qur'an and is moreover at odds with only one single statement in the Bible which occurs (as we have seen) in Kings I 6,1 (N.B. this book is not included in the Torah). This passage is the subject of much debate and Father de Vaux rejects the historical data contained in this part of the Old Testament, which dates the Exodus

1. The period spanning the two reigns Sethos I—Ramesses II, which is said to have lasted roughly eighty years, is out of the question: Sethos I's reign—which was too short for this—does not square with the very long stay in Midian which Moses made as an adult and which took place during the reign of the first of the two Pharaohs he was to know.

in relation to the construction of Solomon's temple. The fact that it is subject to doubt makes it impossible to retain it as a conclusive argument against the theory outlined here.

The Problem of the Stele Dating from the Fifth Year of Merneptah's Reign

In the text of the famous stele dating from the fifth year of Merneptah's reign critics think they have found an objection to the theory set out here, in which the pursuit of the Jews constituted the last act of his reign.

The stele is of great interest because it represents the only known document in hieroglyphics which contains the word 'Israel'.[1] The inscription which dates from the first part of Merneptah's reign was discovered in Thebes in the Pharaoh's Funeral Temple. It refers to a series of victories he won over Egypt's neighbouring states, in particular a victory mentioned at the end of the document over a "devastated Israel which has no more seed . . " From this fact it has been held that the existence of the word 'Israel' implied that the Jews must already have settled in Canaan by the fifth year of Merneptah's reign, and that in consequence, the Exodus of the Hebrews from Egypt had already taken place.

This objection does not seem tenable because it implies that there could have been no Jews living in Canaan all the while there were Jews in Egypt—a proposition it is impossible to accept. Father de Vaux however, in spite of the fact that he is a supporter of the theory which makes Ramesses II the Pharaoh of the Exodus, notes[2] the following about the settling of the Jews in Canaan: "In the South, the time when communities related to the Israelites settled in the Kadesh region is unclear and dates from before the Exodus." He therefore allows for the possibility that certain groups may have left Egypt at a time different from that of Moses and his followers. The *'Apiru* or *Habiru* who have sometimes been identified with the Israelites were already in Syria-Palestine long before Ramesses II and the Exodus: we have documentary evidence which proves that Amenophis II

---

1. The word is followed by a generic determinative which leaves no doubt as to the fact that this term signifies a 'human community or group'.
2. In his book *'The Ancient History of Israel'* (Histoire ancienne d'Israel)

brought back 3,600 prisoners to work as forced labourers in Egypt. Others were to be found in Canaan under Sethos I where they caused unrest in the Beth-Shean region: P. Montet reminds us of this in his book *Egypt and the Bible* (L'Egypte et la Bible). It is quite plausible to suppose therefore that Merneptah was obliged to deal severely with these rebellious elements on his borders while inside them were those who were later to rally around Moses to flee the country. The existence of the stele dating from the fifth year of Merneptah's reign does not in any way detract from the present theory.

Moreover, *the fact that the word 'Israel' figures in the history of the Jewish people is totally unconnected with the notion that Moses and his followers settled in Canaan.* The origin of the word is as follows:

According to Genesis (32,29), Israel is the second name given to Jacob, son of Isaac and grandson of Abraham. The commentators of the *Ecumenical Translation of the Bible-Old Testament* (Traduction oecuménique de la Bible-Ancien Testament), 1975, think that its meaning is probably that 'God shows Himself in His Strength'. Since it has been given to a single man, it is not surprising that it was given to a community or group of people in memory of a distinguished ancestor.

The name 'Israel', therefore appeared well before Moses: several hundred years before to be exact. It is not surprising consequently to see it cited in a stele from the reign of the Pharaoh Merneptah. The fact that it is cited does not at all constitute an argument in favour of a theory which dates the Exodus before the fifth year of Merneptah's reign.

What it does do is refer to a group which it calls 'Israel', but Merneptah's stele cannot be alluding to a politically established collectivity because the inscription dates from the end of the Thirteenth century B.C. and the Kingdom of Israel was not formed until the Tenth century B.C. It must therefore refer to a human community of more modest proportions.[1]

---

1. "The name 'Israel' (in the stele) is accompanied by the generic determinative 'people' instead of the determinative 'country', as is the case for the other proper names in the stele" writes Father B. Couroyer, Professor at the Biblical School of Jerusalem, in his commentary to the translation of the Book of Exodus (Pub. Editions du Cerf, Paris, 1968, page 12).

Nowadays, we know that the entry of 'Israel' into history was preceded by a long formatory period of eight or nine centuries. This period was distinguished by the settling of many semi-Nomadic groups, especially the Amorites and the Arameans all over the region. In the same period, Patriarchs began to appear in their communities among whom were Abraham, Isaac and Jacob-Israel. The second name of this last Patriarch was used to designate the original group, the nucleus of a future political entity which was to appear long after Merneptah's reign, since the Kingdom of Israel lasted from 931 or 930 to 721 B.C.

4. The Description Contained in the Holy Scriptures of the Pharaoh's Death During the Exodus.

This event marks a very important point in the narrations contained in the Bible and the Qur'an. It stands forth very clearly in the texts. It is referred to in the Bible, not only in the Pentateuch or Torah, but also in the Psalms: the references have already been given.

It is very strange to find that Christian commentators have completely ignored it. Thus, Father de Vaux maintains the theory that the Exodus from Egypt took place in the first half or the middle of Ramesses II's reign. His theory takes no account of the fact that the Pharaoh perished during the Exodus, a fact which should make all hypotheses place the event at the end of a reign. In his *Ancient History of Israel* (Histoire ancienne d'Israël), the Head of the Biblical School of Jerusalem does not seem to be at all troubled by the contradiction between the theory he maintains and the data contained in the two Books of the Bible: the Torah and Psalms.

In his book, *Egypt and the Bible* (L'Egypte et la Bible), P. Montet places the Exodus during Merneptah's reign, but says nothing about the death of the Pharaoh who was at the head of the army following the fleeing Hebrews.

This highly surprising attitude contrasts with the Jews' outlook: Psalm 136, verse 15 gives thanks to God who "overthrew Pharaoh and his host in the Sea of Rushes" and is often recited in their liturgy. They know of the agreement between this verse and the passage in Exodus (14,28-29): "The waters returned

and covered the chariots and the horsemen and all the host of
Pharaoh that had followed them into the sea; not so much as one
of them remained." There is no shadow of a doubt for them that
the Pharaoh and his troups were wiped out. These same texts are
present in Christian Bibles.

Christian commentators quite deliberately, and in contradic
tion to all the evidence, brush aside the Pharaoh's death. What is
more however, some of them mention the reference made to it in
the Qur'an and encourage their readers to make very strange
comparisons. In the translation of the Bible directed by the Biblical School of Jerusalem[1] we find the following commentary on the
Pharaoh's death by Father Couroyer:

"The Koran refers to this (Pharaoh's death) (sura 10, verses
90-92), and popular tradition has it that the Pharaoh who was
drowned with his army (an event which is not mentioned in the
Holy Text[2]) lives beneath the ocean where he rules over the men
of the sea, i.e. the seals".

It is obvious that the uninformed reader of the Qur'an is bound
to establish a connection between a statement in it which—for the
commentator—contradicts the Biblical text and this absurd
legend which comes from a so-called popular tradition mentioned
in the commentary after the reference to the Qur'an.

The real meaning of the statement in the Qur'an on this has
nothing to do with what this commentator suggests: verses 90 to
92, sura 10 inform us that the Children of Israel crossed the sea
while the Pharaoh and his troops were pursuing them and that
it was only when the Pharaoh was about to be drowned that he
cried: "I believe there is no God except the God in which the
Chilldren of Israel believe. I am of those who submit themselves
to Him." God replied: "What? Now! Thou hast rebelled and
caused depravity. This day We save thee in thy body so that thou
mayest be a Sign for those who will come after thee."

This is all that the sura contains on the Pharaoh's death. There
is no question of the phantasms recorded by the Biblical commentator either here or anywhere else in the Qur'an. The text of the
Qur'an merely states very clearly that the Pharaoh's body will
be saved: that is the important piece of information.

---

1. L'Exode (Exodus), 1968, page 73, Pub. Les Editions du Cerf, Paris.
2. There can be no doubt that this commentator is referring to the Bible.

When the Qur'an was transmitted to man by the Prophet, the bodies of all the Pharaohs who are today considered (rightly or wrongly) to have something to do with the Exodus were in their tombs of the Necropolis of Thebes, on the opposite side of the Nile from Luxor. At the time however, absolutely nothing was known of this fact, and it was not until the end of the Nineteenth century that they were discovered there. As the Qur'an states, the body of the Pharaoh of the Exodus was in fact rescued: whichever of the Pharaohs it was, visitors may see him in the Royal Mummies Room of the Egyptian Museum, Cairo. The truth is therefore very different from the ludicrous legend that Father Couroyer has attached to the Qur'an.

5. *Pharaoh Merneptah's Mummy*

The mummified body of Merneptah, son of Ramesses II and Pharaoh of the Exodus—all the evidence points to this—was discovered by Loret in 1898 at Thebes in the Kings' Valley whence it was transported to Cairo. Elliot Smith removed its wrappings on the 8th of July, 1907: he gives a detailed description of this operation and the examination of the body in his book *The Royal Mummies* (1912). At that time the mummy was in a satisfactory state of preservation, in spite of deterioration in several parts. Since then, the mummy has been on show to visitors at the Cairo Museum, with his head and neck uncovered and the rest of body concealed under a cloth. It is so well hidden indeed, that until very recently, the only general photographs of the mummy that the Museum possessed were those taken by E. Smith in 1912.

In June 1975, the Egyptian high authorities very kindly allowed me to examine the parts of the Pharaoh's body that had been covered until then. They also allowed me to take photographs. When the mummy's present state was compared to the condition it was in over sixty years ago, it was abundantly clear that it had deteriorated and fragments had disappeared. The mummified tissues had suffered greatly, at the hand of man in some places and through the passage of time in others.

This natural deterioration is easily explained by the changes in the conditions of conservation from the time in the late Nineteenth century when it was discovered. Its discovery took place

in the tomb of the Necropolis of Thebes where the mummy had
lain for over three thousand years. Today, the mummy is dis-
played in a simple glass case which does not afford hermetic in-
sulation from the outside, nor does it offer protection from pollution by micro-organisms. The mummy is exposed to fluctuations
in temperature and seasonal changes in humidity: it is very far
from the conditions which enabled it to remain protected from
any source of deterioration for approximately three thousand
years. It has lost the protection afforded by its wrappings and
the advantage of remaining in the closed environment of the
tomb where the temperature was more constant and the air less
humid than it is in Cairo at certain times of the year. Of course,
while it was in the Necropolis itself, the mummy had to with-
stand the visits of grave plunderers (probably very early on) and
rodents: they caused a certain amount of damage, but the conditions were nevertheless (it seems) much more favourable for
it to stand the test of time than they are today.

At my suggestion, special investigations were made during this
examination of the mummy in June 1975. An excellent radio-
graphic study was made by Doctors El Meligy and Ramsiys, and
the examination of the interior of the thorax, through a gap in
the thoracic wall, was carried out by Doctor Mustapha Maniala-
wiy in addition to an investigation of the abdomen. This was the
first example of endoscopy being applied to a mummy. This tech-
nique enabled us to see and photograph some very important
details inside the body. Professor Ceccaldi performed a general
medico-legal study which will be completed by an examination
under the microscope of some small fragments that spontaneously
fell from the mummy's body: this examination will be carried out
by Professor Mignot and Doctor Durigon. I regret to say that definitive pronouncements cannot be made by the time this book
goes to print.[1]

What may already be derived from this examination is the discovery of multiple lesions of the bones with broad lacunae, some
of which may have been mortal—although it is not yet possible to
ascertain whether some of them occurred before or after the
Pharaoh's death. He most probably died either from drowning,
according to the Scriptural narrations, or from very violent

1. November, 1975 for the First French edition.

shocks preceding the moment when he was drowned—or both at once.

The connection of these lesions with the deterioration whose sources have been mentioned above renders the correct preservation of the mummy of the Pharaoh somewhat problematical, unless precautionary and restorative measures are not taken very soon. These measures should ensure that the only concrete evidence which we still possess today concerning the death of the Pharaoh of the Exodus and the rescue of his body, willed by God, does not disappear with the passage of time.

It is always desirable for man to apply himself to the preservation of relics of his history, but here we have something which goes beyond that: it is the material presence of the mummified body of the man who knew Moses, resisted his pleas, pursued him as he took flight, lost his life in the process. His earthly remains were saved by the Will of God from destruction to become a sign to man, as it is written in the Qur'an.[1]

Those who seek among modern data for proof of the veracity of the Holy Scriptures will find a magnificent illustration of the verses of the Qur'an dealing with the Pharaoh's body by visiting the Royal Mummies Room of the Egyptian Museum, Cairo!

---

1. The mummy of Ramesses II, who was another witness to Moses's story, has been the subject of a study comparable to the one carried out on the mummy of Merneptah; the same restoration work is required for it.

Translators' Note:
The results of these medical studies carried out in Cairo, 1975, were read by the author before several French learned societies, including the 'Académie Nationale de Médecine' (National Academy of Medecine), during the first part of 1976. The knowledge of these results led the Egyptian Authorities to take the decision to transport the mummy of Ramesses II to France. Thus it arrived for treatment in Paris on the 26th September 1976.

The Qur'an, Hadíths and Modern Science

The Qur'an does not constitute the sole source of doctrine and legislation in Islam. During Muhammad's life and after his death complementary information of a legislative nature was indeed sought in the study of the words and deeds of the Prophet.

Although writing was used in the transmission of hadith from the very beginning, a lot of this came also from the oral tradition. Those who undertook to assemble them in collections made the kind of enquiries which are always very taxing before recording accounts of past events. They nevertheless had a great regard for accuracy in their arduous task of collecting information. This is illustrated by the fact that for all of the Prophet's sayings, the most venerable collections always bear the names of those responsible for the account, going right back to the person who first collected the information from members of Muhammad's family or his companions.

A very large number of collections of the Prophet's words and deeds thus appeared under the title of Hadiths. The exact meaning of the word is 'utterances', but it is also customary to use it to mean the narration of his deeds.

Some of the collections were made public in the decades following Muhammad's death. Just over two hundred years were to pass before some of the most important collections appeared. The most authentic record of the facts is in the collections of Al Bukhari and Muslim, which date from over two hundred years after

Muhammad and which provide a wider trustworthy account. In recent years, a bilingual Arabic/English edition has been provided by Doctor Muhammed Muhsin Khan, of the Islamic University of Madina.[1] Al Bukhari's work is generally regarded as the most authentic after the Qur'an and was translated into French (1903-1914) by Houdas and Marcais under the title *Les Traditions Islamiques* (Islamic Traditions). The Hadiths are therefore accessible to those who do not speak Arabic. One must, however, be wary of certain translations made by Europeans, including the French translation, because they contain inaccuracies and untruths which are often more of interpretation than of actual translation. Sometimes, they considerably change the real meaning of a hadith, to such an extent indeed that they attribute a sense to it which it does not contain.

As regards their origins, some of the hadiths and Gospels have one point in common which is that neither of them was compiled by an author who was an eyewitness of the events he describes. Nor were they compiled until some time after the events recorded. The hadiths, like the Gospels, have not all been accepted as authentic. Only a small number of them receive the quasi-unanimous approval of specialists in Muslim Tradition so that, except al-Muwatta, Sahih Muslim and Sahih al-Bukhari, one finds in the same book, hadiths presumed to be authentic side by side with ones which are either dubious, ór should be rejected outright.

In contrast to Canonic Gospels which though questioned by some modern scholars but which have never been contested by Christian high authorities, even those hadiths that are most worthy to be considered as authentic have been the subject of criticism. Very early in the history of Islam, masters in Islamic thought exercised a thorough criticism of the hadiths, although the basic book (The Qur'an) remained the book of reference and was not to be questioned.

I thought it of interest to delve into the literature of the hadiths to find out how Muhammad is said to have expressed himself, outside the context of written Revelation, on subjects that were to be explained by scientific progress in following centuries. Al-

---

1. Pub. Sethi Straw Board Mills (Conversion) Ltd and Taleem-ul-Qur'an Trust, Gujranwala, Cantt. Pakistán. 1st edition 1971, for Sahih Al Bukhari.

though Sahih Muslim is also an authentic collection, in this study I have strictly limited myself to the texts of the hadiths which are generally considered to be the most authentic, i.e. those of Al Bukhari. I have always tried to bear in mind the fact that these texts were compiled by men according to data received from a tradition which was partially oral and that they record certain facts with a greater or lesser degree of accuracy, depending on the individual errors made by those who transmitted the narrations. These texts are different from other hadiths which were transmitted by a very large number of people and are unquestionably authentic.[1]

I have compared the findings made during an examination of the hadiths with those already set out in the section on the Qur'an and modern science. The results of this comparison speak for themselves. The difference is in fact quite staggering between the accuracy of the data contained in the Qur'an, when compared with modern scientific knowledge, and the highly questionable character of certain statements in the hadiths on subjects whose tenor is essentially scientific. These are the only hadiths to have been dealt with in this study.

Hadiths which have as their subject the interpretation of certain verses of the Qur'an sometimes lead to commentaries which are hardly acceptable today.

We have already seen the great significance of one verse (sura 36, verse 36) dealing with the Sun which "runs its course to a settled place". Here is the interpretation given of it in a hadith: "At sunset, the sun . . . prostrates itself underneath the Throne, and takes permission to rise again, and it is permitted and then (a time will come when) it will be about to prostrate itself . . . it will ask permission to go on its course . . . it will be ordered to return whence it has come and so it will rise in the West . . ." (Sahih Al Bukhari). The original text (The Book of the Beginning of the Creation, Vol. IV page 283, part 54, chapter IV, number 421) is obscure and difficult to translate. This passage nevertheless contains an allegory which implies the notion of a course the Sun runs in relation to the Earth: science has shown the

---

1. Muslim specialists designate the first by the word *Zannī* and the second by the word *Qat'ī*.

contrary to be the case. The authenticity of this hadith is doubt-ful (*Zannī*).

Another passage from the same work (The Book of the Beginning of the Creation, vol.IV page 283, part 54, chapter 6, number 430) estimates the initial stages in the development of the embryo very strangely in time: a forty-day period for the grouping of the elements which are to constitute the human being, another forty days during which the embryo is represented as 'something which clings', and a third forty-day period when the embryo is designated by the term 'chewed flesh'. Once the angels have intervened to define what this individual's future is to be, a soul is breathed into him. This description of embryonic evolution does not agree with modern data.

Whereas the Qur'an gives absolutely no practical advice on the remedial arts, except for a single comment (sura 16, verse 69) on the possibility of using honey as a therapeutic aid (without indicating the illness involved), the hadiths devote a great deal of space to these subjects. A whole section of Al Bukhari's collection (part 76) is concerned with medicine. In the French translation by Houdas and Marcais it goes from page 62 to 91 of volume 4, and in Doctor Muhammad Muhsin Khan's bilingual Arabic/English edition from page 395 to 452, of volume VII. There can be no doubt that these pages contain some hadiths which are conjectural (*Zannī*), but they are interesting as a whole because they provide an outline of the opinions on various medical subjects that it was possible to hold at the time. One might add to them several hadiths inserted in other parts of Al Bukhari's collection which have a medical tenor.

This is how we come to find statements in them on the harms caused by the Evil Eye, witchcraft and the possibility of exorcism; although a certain restriction is imposed on the paid use of the Qur'an for this purpose. There is a hadith which stresses that certain kinds of date may serve as protection against the effects of magic, and magic may be used against poisonous snakebites.

We should not be surprised however to find that at a time when there were limited possibilities for the scientific use of drugs, people were advised to rely on simple practices; natural treatments such as blood-letting, cupping, and cauterization, head-

THE BIBLE, THE QUR'AN AND SCIENCE

shaving against lice, the use of camel's milk and certain seeds such as black cumin, and plants such as indian Qust. It was also recommended to burn a mat made of palm-tree leaves and put the ash from it into a wound to stop bleeding. In emergencies, all available means that might genuinely be of use had to be employed. It does not seem—a priori—to be a very good idea, however, to suggest that people drink camel's urine.

It is difficult today to subscribe to certain explanations of subjects related to various illnesses. Among them, the following might be mentioned:

—the origins of a fever: there are four statements bearing witness to the fact that "fever is from the heat of hell" (Al Bukhari, The Book of Medicine, vol. VII, chapter 28, page 416).

—the existence of a remedy for every illness: "No disease God created, but He created its treatment" (Ibid. chapter 1, page 395). This concept is illustrated by the Hadith of the Fly: "If a fly falls into the vessel of any of you, let him dip all of it (into the vessel) and then throw it away, for in one of its wings there is a disease and in the other there is healing (antidote for it). i.e. the treatment for that disease" (Ibid. chapter 15-16, pages 452-453, also The Book of the Beginning of Creation part 54, chapters 15 & 16.)

—abortion provoked by the sight of a snake (which can also blind). This is mentioned in The Book of the Beginning of Creation, Vol. IV(chapter 13 and 14, pages 330 & 334).

—haemorrhages between periods. The Book of Menses (Menstrual Periods) Vol. VI, part 6, pages 490 & 495 contains two hadiths on the cause of haemorrhages between periods (chapters 21 & 28). They refer to two women: in the case of the first, there is a description (undetailed) of the symptoms, with a statement that the haemorrhage comes from a blood vessel; in the second, the woman had experienced haemorrhages between periods for seven years, and the same vascular origin is stated. One might suggest hypotheses as to the real causes of the above, but it is not easy to see what arguments could have been produced at the time to support this diagnosis. This could nevertheless have been quite accurate.

—the statement that diseases are not contagious. Al Bukhari's collection of hadiths refers in several places (chapters 19, 25, 30,

31, 53 and 54, Vol. VII, part 76, of the Book of Medicine) to certain special cases, e.g. leprosy (page 408), plague (pages 418 & 422), camel's scabies (page 447), and also provides general statements. The latter are however placed side by side with glaringly contradictory remarks: it is recommended, for example, not to go to areas where there is plague, and to stay away from lepers.

Consequently, it is possible to conclude that certain ḥadiths exist which are scientifically unacceptable. There is a doubt surrounding their authenticity. The purpose of reference to them lies solely in the comparison that they occasion with the verses of the Qur'an mentioned above: these do not contain a single inaccurate statement. This observation clearly has considerable importance.

One must indeed remember that at the Prophet's death, the teachings that were received from this fell into two groups:
—firstly, a large number of Believers knew the Qur'an by heart because, like the Prophet, they had recited it many, many times; transcriptions of the text of the Qur'an already existed moreover, which were made at the time of the Prophet and even before the Hegira[1].
—secondly, the members of his following who were closest to him and the Believers who had witnessed his words and deeds had remembered them and relied on them for support, in addition to the Qur'an, when defining a nascent doctrine and legislation.

In the years that were to follow the Prophet's death, texts were to be compiled which recorded the two groups of teachings he had left. The first gathering of hadiths was performed roughly forty years after the Hegira, but a first collection of Qur'anic texts had been made beforehand under Caliph Abu Bakr, and in particular Caliph Uthman, the second of whom published a definitive text during his Caliphate, i.e. between the twelfth and twenty-fourth years following Muhammad's death.

What must be heavily stressed is the disparity between these two groups of texts, both from a literary point of view and as regards their contents. It would indeed be unthinkable to compare the style of the Qur'an with that of the hadiths. What is more, when the contents of the two texts are compared in the

---

1. The Hegira was in 622, ten years before Muḥammad's death.

light of modern scientific data, one is struck by the oppositions
between them. I hope I have succeeded in showing what follows:
—on the one hand, statements in the Qur'an which often appear
to be commonplace, but which conceal data that science was later
to bring to light.
—on the other hand, certain statements in the hadiths which are
shown to be in absolute agreement with the ideas of their times
but which contain opinions that are deemed scientifically unacceptable today. These occur in an aggregate of statements concerning Islamic doctrine and legislation, whose authenticity is
unquestioningly acknowledged.

Finally, it must be pointed out that Muḥammad's own attitude
was quite different towards the Qur'an from what it was towards
his personal sayings. The Qur'an was proclaimed by him to be a
divine Revelation. Over a period of twenty years, the Prophet
classified its sections with the greatest of care, as we have seen.
The Qur'an represented what had to be written down during his
own lifetime and learned by heart to become part of the liturgy
of prayers. The hadiths are said, in principle, to provide an account of his deeds and personal reflections, but he left it to others
to find an example in them for their own behaviour and to make
them public however they liked: he did not give any instructions.

In view of the fact that only a limited number of hadiths may
be considered to express the Prophet's thoughts with certainty,
the others must contain the thoughts of the men of his time, in
particular with regard to the subjects referred to here. When
these dubious or inauthentic hadiths are compared to the text of
the Qur'an, we can measure the extent to which they differ. This
comparison highlights (as if there were still any need to) the
striking difference between the writings of this period, which
are riddled with scientific inaccurate statements, and the Qur'an,
the Book of Written Revelation, that is free from errors of this
kind.[1]

---

1. The truth of the hadiths, from a religious point of view, is beyond question. When they deal, however, with earthly affairs there is no difference between the Prophet and other humans. One hadith gives an account of an utterance of the Prophet: "Whenever I command you to do
   something related to Religion do obey, and if I command you something
   according to my own opinion (do remember this) I am a human being".

(Continued on Page 249)

General Conclusions

At the end of this study, a fact that stands forth very clearly is that the predominant opinion held in the West on the texts of the Holy Scriptures we possess today is hardly very realistic. We have seen the conditions, times and ways in which the elements constituting the Old Testament, the Gospels and the Qur'an were collected and written down: the circumstances attendant upon the birth of the Scriptures for these three Revelations differed widely in each case, a fact which had extremely important consequences concerning the authenticity of the texts and certain aspects of their contents.

The Old Testament represents a vast number of literary works written over a period of roughly nine hundred years. It forms a highly disparate mosaic whose pieces have, in the course of centuries, been changed by man. Some parts were added to what already existed, so that today it is sometimes very difficult indeed to identify where they came from originally.

Through an account of Jesus's words and deeds, the Gospels were intended to make known to men the teachings he wished to leave them on completion of his earthly mission. Unfortunately, the authors of the Gospels were not eyewitnesses of the data they recorded. They were spokesmen who expressed data that were quite simply the information that had been preserved by the various Judeo-Christian communities on Jesus's public life, passed down by oral traditions or writings which no longer exist today, and which constituted an intermediate stage between the oral tradition and the definitive texts.

(Continued from Page 248)
Al Saraksi in his 'Principles' (*Al Usul*) transmitted this statement as follows: "If I bring something to you on your religion, do act according to it, and if I bring you something related to this world, then you have a better knowledge of your own earthly affairs".

This is the light in which the Judeo-Christian Scriptures should be viewed today, and—to be objective—one should abandon the classic concepts held by experts in exegesis.

The inevitable result of the multiplicity of sources is the existence of contradictions and oppositions: many examples have been given of these. The authors of the Gospels had (when talking of Jesus) the same tendency to magnify certain facts as the poets of French Medieval literature in their narrative poems. The consequence of this was that events were presented from each individual narrator's point of view and the authenticity of the facts reported in many cases proved to be extremely dubious. In view of this, the few statements contained in the Judeo-Christian Scriptures which may have something to do with modern knowledge should always be examined with the circumspection that the questionable nature of their authenticity demands.

Contradictions, improbabilities and incompatibilities with modern scientific data may be easily explained in terms of what has just been said above. Christians are nevertheless very surprised when they realize this, so great have been the continuous and far-reaching efforts made until now by many official commentators to camouflage the very obvious results of modern studies, under cunning dialectical acrobatics orchestrated by apologetic lyricism. A case in point are the genealogies of Jesus given in Matthew and Luke, which were contradictory and scientifically unacceptable. Examples have been provided which reveal this attitude very clearly. John's Gospel has been given special attention because there are very important differences between it and the other three Gospels, especially with regard to the fact that his Gospel does not describe the institution of the Eucharist: this is not generally known.

The Qur'anic Revelation has a history which is fundamentally different from the other two. It spanned a period of some twenty years and, as soon as it was transmitted to Muhammad by Archangel Gabriel, Believers learned it by heart. It was also written down during Muhammad's life. The last recensions of the Qur'an were effected under Caliph Uthman starting some twelve years after the Prophet's death and finishing twenty-four years after it. They had the advantage of being checked by people who already knew the text by heart, for they had learned it at the

ime of the Revelation itself and had subsequently recited it con-
tantly. Since then, we know that the text has been scrupulously
reserved. It does not give rise to any problems of authenticity.

The Qur'an follows on from the two Revelations that preceded
t and is not only free from contradictions in its narrations, the
ign of the various human manipulations to be found in the Gos-
els, but provides a quality all of its own for those who examine
t objectively and in the light of science i.e. its complete agreement with modern scientific data. What is more, statements are
to be found in it (as has been shown) that are connected with
science: and yet it is unthinkable that a man of Muḥammad's
time could have been the author of them. Modern scientific
knowledge therefore allows us to understand certain verses of the
Qur'an which, until now, it has been impossible to interpret.

The comparison of several Biblical and Qur'anic narrations of
the same subject shows the existence of fundamental differences
between statements in the former, which are scientifically unacceptable, and declarations in the latter which are in perfect
agreement with modern data : this was the case of the Creation
and the Flood, for example. An extremely important complement
to the Bible was found in the text of the Qur'an on the subject
of the history of the Exodus, where the two texts were very
much in agreement with archaeological findings, in the dating
of the time of Moses. Besides, there are major differences between the Qur'an and the Bible on the other subjects : they serve
to disprove all that has been maintained—without a scrap of
evidence—concerning the allegation that Muḥammad is supposed
to have copied the Bible to produce the text of the Qur'an.

When a comparative study is made between the statements
connected with science to be found in the collection of hadiths,
which are attributed to Muḥammad but are often of dubious
authenticity (although they reflect the beliefs of the period),
and the data of a similar kind in the Qur'an, the disparity becomes so obvious that any notion of a common origin is ruled out.

In view of the level of knowledge in Muḥammad's day, it is
inconceivable that many of the statements in the Qur'an which
are connected with science could have been the work of a man.
It is, moreover, perfectly legitimate, not only to regard the
Qur'an as the expression of a Revelation, but also to award it a

very special place, on account of the guarantee of authenticity i
provides and the presence in it of scientific statements which
when studied today, appear as a challenge to explanation i
human terms.

TRANSLITERATION OF THE ARABIC INTO LATIN CHARACTERS USED IN THIS BOOK

ء	'	ض	ḍ	
أ	a	ط	ṭ	
ب	b	ظ	ẓ	
ت	t	ع	'	
ث	t̲	غ	ḡ	
ج	j	ف	f	
ح	ḥ	ق	q	
خ	k̲	ك	k	
د	d	ل	l	
ذ	d̲	م	m	
ر	r	ن	n	
ز	z	ه	h	
س	s	و	first letter of the word ... w / otherwise .... u
ش	s̲	ي	y	
ص	ṣ			

ā, ī and ū indicate the elongation of the corresponding Arabic vowel